(continued from front flap)

future activity to strengthen and promote the benefits to society of labor-management participation.

Eight years ago, Studs Terkel's book *Working* revealed the discontent in the American workplace. *Working Together* documents ways in which workers and managers are cooperatively overcoming that alienation.

JOHN SIMMONS (right) is a professor of Labor/Management Relations at the University of Massachusetts at Amherst, and serves as the national coordinator of the Association for Workplace Democracy. A graduate of Harvard and Oxford, Mr. Simmons has worked for the World Bank and is the author of *The Education Dilemma* (1980) and of numerous articles on management and economic development for such periodicals as *The Economist*, *The Atlantic*, and *International Development Review*.

WILLIAM MARES (left) is the author of *The Marine Machine* (1971) and co-author of *Passing Brave* (1973) and *The Golden Ode* (1974). A graduate of Harvard College and the Fletcher School of Law and Diplomacy, Mr. Mares is a free-lance writer who has contributed to the *Christian Science Monitor*, *The Economist*, the Chicago *Sun-Times*, and other periodicals.

Front-of-jacket photograph
by Jerry Cosgrove/Cosgrove Associates
Jacket design by Janet Odgis

WORKING
TOGETHER

John Simmons & William Mares

WORKING
TOGETHER

ALFRED A. KNOPF • NEW YORK • 1983

Bu s.
3 3 1. 0 1 / 2
S 59 w

To our parents and wives
who have nurtured the values
needed to live and work together

84-10249

Contents

Figures & Tables

Preface

When Studs Terkel's book *Working* was published in 1972, both of us were moved by the voices of its men and women. In spite of the differences in the jobs they held, they all seemed to make a powerful plea for a better way to organize work, one that would give them more control over the largest block of waking time in their lives, one that would engage their talents and commitments. A year later, the government study *Work in America* added the quantitative evidence to support fundamental workplace reform.

This book draws upon visits to fifty companies and agencies in the United States and Europe where people are struggling to build a more common economic purpose. Almost invariably, they began that search with the same conviction: "There has to be a better way."

Our collaborative effort is a result of a long friendship and our own experiences at work as, respectively, an economist in international development and a journalist. John Simmons saw that his colleagues at the World Bank were not working as effectively as they could to achieve the organization's objectives, and helped launch a project to increase participation in decision-making. Bill Mares has written about some of the issues of work reform. As a team of enthusiast and skeptic, we logged 50,000 miles on this odyssey to investigate what people were doing. As we crisscrossed the country and visited Europe, the skeptic came to believe that there could be a better way, while the enthusiast came to acknowledge the boulders and washouts on the road toward participation.

Many people, from San Francisco to Stockholm, have been

generous with their time and comments. They range from employees on the shopfloor and in back offices to company presidents. Friends and colleagues provided valuable criticism. Richard Balzer, George Benello, Martin Carnoy, Edward Cohen-Rosenthal, Richard Edwards, Miriam French, Harvey L. Friedman, George G. W. Goodman, Robert H. Guest, Pehr Gyllenhammar, Charles Heckscher, Peter Knight, Michael Maccoby, David Magnani, Lee Ozley, Lauck Parke, Corey Rosen, Adele Smith Simmons, William Foote Whyte, Daniel Yankelovich, and Stanley Young made helpful comments on the draft manuscript. John Beck, Irving Bluestone, Luis Grenados, Delmar L. Landen, Frank Leonard, Rene McPherson, Christopher Meek, Terry Mollner, Robert Schrank, Robert Sherry, Joan Sweeney, and Alfred Warren read draft chapters.

We have made a concerted effort to avoid using gender-specific language. Thus, for general references like "his (a worker's) job," we have sought to substitute non-specific wording.

This book has been a cooperative effort. Without the research, typing, editing, humor, and tireless devil's advocacy of Robert Drago, Christine Hadsel, and Anne Jackson, this would have been a far lesser book. The staff and facilities of the Labor Relations and Research Center, University of Massachusetts at Amherst, were invaluable. Lillian Forguites and Cait Whittle provided fine assistance in the typing. Finally, we would like to thank our editor, Ashbel Green, for his patience and his skilled shepherding of the manuscript.

J.S. & W.M.

Amherst, Massachusetts
Burlington, Vermont
April 1982

[I]

ANATOMY
OF THE PROBLEM

The problems of the workplace are not new. What is new, however, is the understanding that if American organizations do not
deal more effectively with their problems, an increasing number
of them face decline and possible extinction. Who would have
thought in 1970 that the Chrysler Corporation would be on its
knees ten years later, begging for a government subsidy?

The old problem—to which are added a crisis in competitive
standing and high unemployment—is how to do a better job. How
can organizations improve the quality of their products and
services and reduce costs in order to better serve the needs of
society?

Each generation of owners, managers, and academics has
sought viable solutions to this problem. Rarely, however, have
workers participated in the search. At least some management
people have now come to recognize the need for challenging the
basic assumptions underlying their current practices.

In Part I we will provide an overview of problems in the workplace, and review current assumptions about the best way to manage. Our thesis is that a major cause of the current economic
problems with quality and productivity lies in the strong division
between the thinkers and the doers, between managers and the
managed, between owners and non-owners. We will describe
some of the roots of that division of labor, and seventy years of
attempts to moderate its effects.

[1]

There Has to Be
a Better Way

Participation is not a program or a technique; it's an almost mystical philosophy of change for helping people to fulfill themselves.
—RICHARD DANJIN,
United Auto Workers shop committeeman

The worker is the money-maker out there. I feel that the workers and the utility people know more about the operation than I do, so they should be involved in it.
—JOHN WESTELL, superintendent,
Matsushita Industrial Corporation

If employees who are stockholders don't have voting rights, they don't own the company.   —RICHARD BIERNACKI, president,
Fastener Industries

All three persons quoted above are actors in a national effort in which people are gaining more control over their lives at work. This process is called many things: work reform, job redesign, work humanization, employee participation, workplace democracy. The common theme is simply stated: in hundreds of companies, workers, managers, and owners are wrestling with better ways to organize work. Approaches include quality control circles, Scanlon Plans, Quality of Work Life programs, employee stock ownership plans and cooperatives. We generally use the term "participation" to describe the practice of increased employee involvement in both management and ownership of the companies that employ them.

Increased worker and manager participation may run the gamut from group problem-solving to the election of employees to a board of directors. It can improve people's self-esteem and

3

income on the one hand, and the effectiveness and profitability of companies that practice it on the other. In fact, several "Fortune 500" companies such as Procter & Gamble and IBM are resolutely tight-lipped about their participation schemes just because they have proved so profitable. As one manager put it, "We aren't doing this stuff for altruistic reasons."

People who have had experience with workplace democracy do not confuse it with political democracy. The main distinction is that workplace democracy is based on people's direct, face-to-face involvement in the decisions that affect their work, while political democracy usually means voting for someone they have never met to deal with problems several steps removed from their daily concerns. The major similarities between the two types of democracy are that both strive for effective communication and decision-making among different groups in an organization or a society, and that both are based on the principle of fairness.

A growing number of owners, managers, and workers believe that some of the rights of citizenship can and should be extended to the workplace. That is, employees should be treated as stakeholders in their jobs, just as parents and citizens have responsibility for the future of their families and communities.

Here are some of the results:

- Between 1971 and 1979, the Dana Corporation improved its productivity 126 percent in sales per employee (corrected for inflation). Managers at 400 facilities in 23 countries began to draw 24,000 lower-level employees into the decision-making process. The board of directors expanded participation in company ownership to 80 percent of the employees. By 1980, Dana was No. 2 of the Fortune 500, as measured by a five-year average return on equity.

- Two thousand Rath Packing Company employees saved their jobs in Waterloo, Iowa, by purchasing a 60 percent interest in their firm.

- At four General Motors plants, there are no management levels between work teams and the plant manager. Team members elect their leaders and discipline their peers. Absenteeism rates are one-tenth that of the typical General Motors plant.

- The Internal Revenue Service acknowledged that twelve plywood cooperatives in the Pacific Northwest, which have been democratically owned and managed for more than thirty years, were justified in paying 25 percent to 60 percent higher wages than comparable mills owned by Weyerhaeuser and others because of their higher productivity.

- Threatened by mounting losses, Pan American Airlines shareholders elected two employees to the board of directors to improve organizational effectiveness.

- Charles Valentine, who never made more than $125 a week as a warehouse laborer at the Lowe's Companies, a building supply chain, retired with $660,000 through participation in an Employee Stock Ownership Plan.

- The city of Dallas, Texas, saved $114,000 in six months in 1981 by implementing ideas proposed by quality control circles. The cost of initiating the circles was $23,000.

There have been less successful efforts as well:

- General Foods built a new dog-food plant in Topeka, Kansas, designed according to highly touted socio-technical principles and giving workers great discretion in running their own jobs, but reverted to traditional techniques when the experiment posed a threat to corporate management.

- A much-publicized experiment in autonomous work groups at a coal mine in Rushton, Pennsylvania, fell apart because of disagreements over incentives and intra-union jealousy.

- Employee-owners at South Bend Lathe in Indiana went on strike "against themselves" when they disagreed with management.

The purpose of this book is to outline the conditions for successful participation efforts, although we hasten to add that this is not a cookbook for participatory management or a formula for happy, company-song-singing workers. Our two-year study has revealed that many owners, managers, and workers hold firmly to several myths about participation. We have found these myths largely disproved by organizations which are effectively using a participatory philosophy. A partial list of the most common myths follows:

- Participation is no more than "being nice" to the workers.
- People sit around all day in meetings, so there is less time for getting work done.
- Workers don't want a job in which they have to think.
- Efficiency and democracy don't mix.
- It takes too long to make decisions.
- Workers cannot raise enough money to buy a business.
- Participation in either management or ownership is only a new management gimmick to "bust" or avoid unions.
- Workers don't want anything except the "long green."
- Workers cannot balance their short-term interests with the firm's long-term needs.
- Americans are too individualistic to work in groups.

These myths, and other objections to participation, will be addressed by illustrations from private firms and public agencies. At the same time, strong reasons do exist why increased participation is not yet widely practiced in America:

First, genuine reform of the traditional organization of work involves a redistribution of power within an organization. One need not be a psychologist to know that those with power in any context share it only reluctantly.

Second, participation connotes the demystification of management. Acquiring more control over one's life at work entails making decisions about the rules and regulations of the business. For more than sixty years, a wall has existed in most organizations between those who manage and those who are managed. Increased participation breaches that wall to mutual benefit. James F. Lincoln—founder of Lincoln Electric Company, the nation's leading manufacturer of welding equipment—summarized the change when he wrote, "Let every worker manage; let every manager work."[1]

Third, managers have not felt the need to change. There has been no tiger at the gates, no crisis to force them to consider new approaches. Distant shareholders regularly receive their dividend checks, and executives their bonuses.

At present, serious consideration of workplace democracy is being thrust upon companies by better and cheaper foreign products, mismanagement, low morale, high wages, and generally poor economic conditions. We will look at over fifty organizations that have taken steps to alter the relationship among owners, managers, and workers. Some were forced to seek new ways to involve their employees in management or ownership because of a crisis, others were not. We will not try to solve the national unemployment problem. We do not offer solutions to high interest rates, low housing starts, discrimination, or the shape of technology to come. Instead, we focus on the human side of workplace reform through talks with people who are wrestling with new forms of organization, rather than problems of finance, engineering, or marketing—people who are looking for more productive and more fulfilling ways to get a job done.

In the late 1970s, the American economy, though the world's largest, was surely not the healthiest. It was reeling before a second set of massive OPEC-induced oil price boosts. Interest rates appeared to be stabilizing at high levels. Business leaders complained that excessive government regulations and taxation policies were stifling initiative and stunting capital formation. Most of these factors lie outside the scope of our present concerns. But there are at least two notes in the litany of economic difficulties that are clearly germane: the decline in productivity, and the decay of the work ethic.

Though the scores of books that appear yearly on the general subject of the economy point to almost as many "reliable indicators" as likely causes of economic woes, most economists and other observers agree that by one measurable standard, productivity, our system is not working well.

Productivity represents, and is measured in terms of, the amount of goods or services produced by an average person in one hour with the materials and methods available to him or her. Productivity in the United States grew fairly steadily from the end of World War II to 1973, as Figure 1 on page 9 shows. The average productivity increase from 1960 to 1970 was 2.4 percent. The 1970s, however, present a much bleaker picture. The average increase for the decade was 1.3 percent per year, and only 0.8 percent for the last half of the decade. Productivity declined markedly in 1974, and again in 1978, 1979, and 1980. Internationally, this performance placed the United States sixteenth, after England, out of sixteen industrial nations in rate of productivity increase in 1980. The leaders, Sweden, Germany, and Japan, had average productivity increases of five times the American level for the decade of the seventies. These three countries have relied upon, among other things, employee participation for more than twenty years.

Explanations for this decline are numerous but incomplete. Edward Denison of the Brookings Institution, for instance, has listed sixteen possible reasons, including reduced investment in research and development, aging equipment, government regulations and taxation policies, and high energy prices.

Denison concludes that "none of these suggestions individually seems to be able to explain more than a small part of the decline. Perhaps we have experienced a situation where everything went wrong at once."[2]

A closer look at the data reveals a different possibility: it is the productivity of white-collar workers, not blue-, that is the source of the problem. In the three years from 1977 to 1980, blue-collar employment rose 2 percent while white-collar rose 12 percent, representing numerically 600,000 new blue-collar workers and 5,500,000 new white-collar workers. Output of American goods and services rose 7.9 percent, after correction for inflation, over

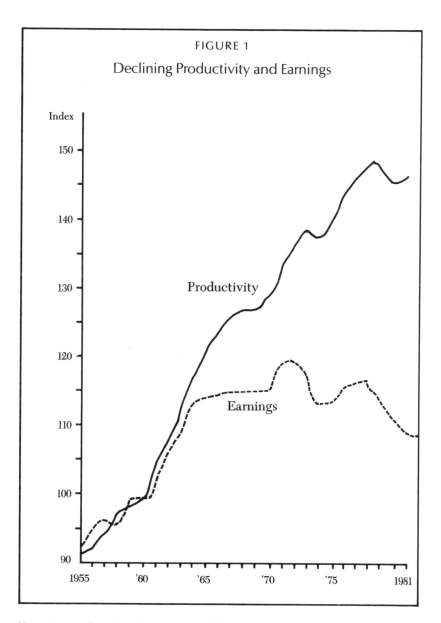

FIGURE 1

Declining Productivity and Earnings

Note: Average Gross Weekly Earnings in 1977 (constant) dollars, indexed to 1960 = 100, for all wage earners in private, non-agricultural sector.
Productivity measured by output per hour of all persons in non-agricultural private sector, indexed to 1960 = 100.
Source: *Economic Report of the President* (Washington, D.C.: U.S. Government Printing Office, February, 1982), pp. 277–8.

the same period. The number of white-collar employees thus rose more rapidly than output, which means that white-collar productivity fell, by 4 percent. There are 20,000,000 more white-collar workers than blue-collar in the United States. Government payrolls are not the problem, since only 13 percent of the rise was for government jobs.[3] Other advanced industrial countries have even higher energy costs than the United States, much greater governmental restrictions on incentives to invest, and a larger social service structure than ours, and yet enjoy steadily rising productivity.

Have either employees or shareholders (or both) been taking more than their fair share? Gross weekly earnings paid to employees, when corrected for inflation, show a steady increase in Figure 1 from 1955 to 1972, paralleling the growth in productivity increase from 1955 to 1972. (Data for 1945 to 1955 are also parallel.) After 1973, however, we find a widening gap between productivity and earnings. Employees have paid a steep price for the productivity problems of the country, with every drop in productivity reflected in an even sharper decline in earnings. By 1981, earnings had fallen to their lowest level since 1961. If the bracket creep that inflation brings to income tax payments is also considered, the real earnings of the average employee had sunk to the level of the mid-1950s.

Have shareholders gained from the employees' loss? Calculations similar to those made for productivity and weekly earnings show that corporate profits before taxes also grew steadily during the fifties and sixties, with profits in 1968 being almost 60 percent higher than in 1960. Profits reached their all-time high in 1978— but then, over the next three years, declined by 36 percent.[4] For the first time since the Great Depression, both owners and employees were becoming worse off together.

Along with their complaints about inadequate investment incentives, many managers blamed their workers for the decline in productivity. Denison noted that the most popular reason given for the decline was that "young people don't work like we did

at their age," but he added, "this was hardly anything new."
Eighty percent of the chief executive officers surveyed by the
Gallup Organization for the U.S. Chamber of Commerce said
that "worker attitude" was the main reason for the decline in
productivity.

Robert Zager of the Work in America Institute has warned,
however, against indulging in glib generalizations on the basis of
the Department of Labor's imperfect productivity index. The
index, he argues,

> [does not] show how productive workers are, only how pro-
> ductively employers use them. Nothing is more common
> than to find workers conscientiously performing unneces-
> sary tasks. . . . To most people, "labor productivity" refers
> to certain characteristics of workers: diligence, skill,
> strength, stamina. True, such attributes have a great impact
> on productivity. A company's index, however, can change
> sharply in either direction simply as a result of a manage-
> ment change.[5]

Through the 1950s and '60s, rising real income and the economy's seemingly unlimited growth gave little ground for questioning about how work was organized. Workers did not expect to find
challenge in their jobs; they took the money and spent it on their
families and leisure. But with the decline in real wages through
inflation, the stultifying quality of many jobs became less acceptable. One survey found that between 1957 and 1978, the percentage of workers who looked on their work as a source of personal
fulfillment fell from 50 percent to 25 percent.[6]

Another survey revealed that 60 percent of the workforce in
1977 said it would prefer another job to the one it held at the
present. This was a rise of 16 percent from 1969.[7]

Managers looked at these results and concluded that the "work
ethic" was dead, but surveys of workers suggest something else.
For instance, 75 percent of the working population said they
would continue to work even if they could live comfortably for the
rest of their lives without working. This was a rise from 67 percent
eight years earlier.[8] The real problem seemed not to be whether

people had lost the desire to work, but whether, as Michael Maccoby and Katherine Terzi wrote, they were "turned off by their jobs."[9]

Surveys of worker attitudes over the past ten years have shown that workers increasingly feel they have insufficient authority to do their jobs properly, insufficient support from supervisors for doing jobs in new ways, and insufficient challenges or rewards to use their skills and intelligence as adults. One result is that workers are often ashamed of their efforts. Twenty-seven percent said they would not buy the products they make.[10]

Another aspect of the "new workforce" is that the number of American workers with high-school diplomas has doubled in the last thirty years. One survey found that a third of the workers felt they had more formal schooling than their jobs required.[11] Workers have a greater awareness of the disparity between how they are treated in the workplace and on the outside. They are more conscious of the distance between the rhetoric of the traditional work ethic they are asked to practice and the servitude in which their specialized job and organizational structure holds them. In short, they are being told to behave like farmers, but feel treated like sharecroppers.

Robert Schrank, an analyst of the work reform movement, suggests an additional reason for workers' lack of attentiveness to their jobs. "In our economy, the central objective is to have a good time. If people enjoy taking days off, if they find that life can be enjoyable, that they don't have to suffer endlessly—when people get that notion in their heads, it's very bad for managers who are, after all, trying to get workers 100 percent interested in their jobs 100 percent of the time. . . . Many of the efforts to resurrect the work ethic are really strivings to reinterest workers in the tasks at hand."[12]

Along with managers' lamentations about the "lazy, turned-off" workers, the business press in the late 1970s began to report that American management techniques and style had serious flaws. When workers suggested that managers could contribute to a rise in productivity by changing their *own* ways, their suggestions were dismissed. But when professors from the Harvard

Business School began to castigate managers for their shortsight-
edness, it was news.

In August 1980, the *Harvard Business Review* published a semi-
nal article by Robert H. Hayes and William J. Abernathy, entitled
"Managing Our Way to Economic Decline." The two Harvard
Business School professors denounced the American manager for
his obsessive concentration on the short-term financial bottom
line. They chided those companies that turned their boards over
to financiers and lawyers with no background in or attachment to
the particular product or methods of production. American
managers had become mesmerized by the "science of management," which permitted managers to slide easily and profitably
between companies, whether they produced potato chips, lawn
furniture, or steel. Furthermore, in many conglomerates the entrepreneurial spirit was crowded out by too many layers of bureaucracy. People at the top dealt not in products but in whole
companies, shifting them around like chess pieces to fit a corporate profit schedule.

Hayes and Abernathy said that the fallacy of the "gunslinger"
as manager is that "there is no need to invent, build or develop
anything yourself. They all assume that given the capital and good
financial management, anything of value can be bought and
any problem can be sold. A sense of commitment—to one's
workers, customers, suppliers, even one's fellow managers—is
an impediment."[13]

Many American managers regard with envy the extraor-
dinarily successful Japanese peacetime economy. They ask, as did
a recent national television special, "If Japan Can, Why Can't
We?" as Japanese goods fill our living rooms and garages. The
Japanese appear to possess a formula for employee "happiness"
and company loyalty which results in a workforce with greater
discipline and higher per-person productivity than that of the
United States.

W. Edwards Deming, statistician and one of the founders of the
movement to improve quality control in Japan, said that the current interest in Japanese production techniques will accomplish
nothing unless "management does its part. And management in

this country has simply fallen down on the job. [Most] management in this country has negative salvage value."[14] He added that only a small portion of quality control and productivity problems are "specific" to the workers; most problems are "common" to the whole operation, which is management's responsibility. Management is also responsible for providing economic security for the workers, so that they will, in turn, be willing to share their knowledge with the company.

In commenting on the profession of management, Robert Reich, former director of policy planning at the Federal Trade Commission, said:

> The professional manager in America exists above the industrial din, away from the dirt, noise, and irrationality of people and products. He plans, organizes, and controls large enterprises in a calm, logical, dispassionate, and decisive manner. He surveys computer printouts, calculates profits and losses, sells and acquires subsidiaries, and imposes systems for monitoring and motivating employees, applying a general body of rules to each special circumstance. . . . And because the professional manager deals in abstractions, he can move from company to company with relative ease, manipulating people and capital as he goes. Without any abiding commitment to the company, he is a master of the quick fix, yielding the sort of short-term profits institutional investors love.[15]

There are signs from both managers and workers that a rigid dichotomy between them is no longer as effective a way to organize the workplace as in the past. In this book, we use the terms "participation" or "workplace democracy" to describe the careful, though often jerky, process of increasing workers' control over their lives at work through increased involvement in decisions that affect their jobs or their stake in a company. Participation is no panacea for the ills of society or the economy, nor does it even assure "happy" workers. What it can do is build more effective organizations. The American society and economy are headed for more, not less, complexity, and that fact alone should induce a consideration of broadened participation.

There are many critics of the notion of participation as even a partial solution to American economic and cultural malaise. Some argue that worker participation is just another form of cooptation, because it enlists workers' help in the perpetuation of a rotten economic system. Giving workers superficial control over their workplace, they maintain, is only a gesture to disguise the fact that the means of production remains in the hands of an ever-decreasing proportion of owners and executives. It is certainly true that, with several exceptions such as the United Auto Workers and the United Steelworkers, the push for more participation has come from management, not from the unions or the workforce in general, and it has primarily come in response to the need for higher productivity and quality.

On the financial side, the main criticism of encouraging participation by workers through stock ownership is that it is no more than a quick fix for firms in need of an influx of cash.

Other critics argue that participation is a ruse to cover inadequate wages, that it is just a way to keep the "natives" distracted while their jobs are exported or automated out of existence. Many unions are naturally suspicious that participation programs will be used as "speed-up" or union-busting devices.

Managers and company owners, for their part, worry that international competition does not permit the luxury of employee participation which could threaten efficiency. They hear pleas for patience and time; they fear that decision-making by consensus is too cumbersome and lengthy. There is also the claim that workers are not capable of handling the complex decisions necessary to keep a business going—that the only thing they want to carry home at night is an empty lunch box, not managerial headaches.

"Give 'em an inch and they'll take a mile," said one Chevrolet executive in a *Harvard Business Review* article in 1971, expressing the common fear that once workers participate in deciding matters that have traditionally been the province of managers, they are bound to want even more control. "Aside," he added,

> from the real costs in reduced effectiveness (partly bal-
> anced, of course, by better motivation, higher output, less
> waste, and so on), the impact of this new participation on
> the process and structure of management, though hard to
> estimate, must be anticipated, because what is really in-
> volved is politics, the conscious sharing of control and
> power. History does not offer many examples of oligarchies
> that have abdicated with grace and goodwill.[16]

The answer, we believe, is that people who act as adults in everyday life—who manage families, serve as PTA presidents, run Little Leagues, and accomplish a wide range of other adult tasks —surely deserve a chance and encouragement to assume similar responsibility in their workplaces. According to a U.S. Chamber of Commerce poll, 84 percent of the workforce wants to participate more than they do at present in decisions that affect their work. They claim that greater participation would encourage them to work harder and do a better job. A Peter Hart Associates poll has shown that 66 percent of the workforce would prefer to work in an employee-owned firm.[17]

The notion that the man or woman on the shopfloor and in the back office can contribute expertise to an entire enterprise may seem obvious. But for the last seventy years, the premise that the workplace should be completely divided between order-givers and order-takers has been generally in force. That belief is due primarily to the work of a brilliant, compulsive engineer named Frederick Winslow Taylor, the father of "scientific management."

[2]

The Plum and the Lash

Who shall rule the workplace? This question was central for almost all observers of the industrializing world in the late nineteenth and early twentieth centuries. Journalists, academics, company presidents, and engineers alike worried about the place of millions of unskilled workers in the new industrial organizations.

The most widely publicized response from America came from Frederick Winslow Taylor, who argued for a cadre of managers, carefully selected for their intelligence, skill, and lasting devotion to a company. Their power would lie not in brute force and hierarchical position but in their "scientifically" determined command of the details and specifications of work itself. Workers, Taylor believed, were interested only in money and were incapable of thinking farther ahead than the next paycheck. Everyone would benefit financially from the division between brain and brawn, thought and action, on the shopfloor.

Breaking jobs down into their smallest possible components became one of the cornerstones of the Taylor-devised assembly line. Adjusting workers to their machines, rather than vice versa, became an accepted practice.

While some of Taylor's ideas seem outdated and crude in the 1980s, no one has had more influence, through his successors, even today. It is worthwhile to take a brief look at Taylor's life and thought.

In the spring of 1909, Frederick Taylor, mechanical engineer, inventor, and creator of the Taylor System of Task Management, gave three lectures to students at the six-month-old Harvard Graduate School of Business Administration. He was well known among engineers for his co-invention of "high-speed steel," his experiments in machining metals, and the numerous patents he had taken out. He had been a manager and business consultant and, for the previous eight years, a tireless promoter of his system of management.

Taylor was asked to speak on his system at Harvard because it promised a partial solution to one of the most hotly debated industrial issues of the day, the "man problem," or how to get more work out of workers. He minced no words in his lectures:

> The management of workmen consists mainly in the application of three elementary ideas:
>   First: Holding a plum for them to climb after.
>   Second: Cracking the whip over them, with an occasional touch of the lash.
>   Third: Working shoulder to shoulder with them, pushing hard in the same direction, and all the while, teaching, guiding and helping them.[1]

The most difficult problem facing all managers, Taylor said, was the inclination of all workers to "soldier," or malinger. There were two types of soldiering: the "natural" form, which comes from the instinct of men to take it easy; and the much more insidious "systematic" form, which grows out of workers' "association with other men, with the deliberate object of keeping their employers ignorant of how fast work can be done."

The ability of workers to soldier, he claimed, "lies in the ignorance of employers and their foremen as to the time in which various kinds of work should be done, and this ignorance is truly profound. If employers and foremen knew exactly how much time their workmen should spend in doing each kind of work, it is perfectly evident that there would be no earthly object for soldiering."[2]

Taylor's solution was "scientifically" to measure and time all components of each job to come up with the "one best way" to get it done. Management would assume the burden of all the thinking, planning, and directing of every job, down to the most minute detail. The worker, for his part, would readily accept this division of labor on the assurance of receiving a 30–100 percent premium over the average pay for his work.

Together, workmen and managers (without the disruptive and unnecessary intercession of trade unions) would create a great "mental revolution." Production would soar and each individual would earn the highest wages and advancement commensurate with his abilities and effort. Never again, Taylor promised, would workers and managers battle over the division of the financial pie, because, apron to apron, they would surely bake an ever-larger one.

Taylor was born into the comfort of Philadelphia's Main Line in 1856. One of his most notable traits was his obsession with measuring everything, from the boundaries of playing fields to the length of his stride while walking. After graduating from Exeter, he did not go on to Harvard, because of poor eyesight. Instead, he signed on for four years as an apprentice pattern-maker and machinist at a small pump manufacturing company owned by a family friend. He later said, "I wanted an opportunity to learn fast, rather than [to earn] wages." He was probably the only machinist in America at that time who, of an evening, would trade his cover-alls for cricket whites.[3]

In 1878, at twenty-two, Taylor took a second manual laborer's job with the Midvale Steel Company, whose president was also a family friend. The twelve years he spent at Midvale represented a crucial period in his life, and coincided with an extraordinary expansion and consolidation in American industry. Existing forms of control over the workforce and the means and processes of production seemed increasingly inadequate. It was a time that marked the entry of engineers into the management of many growing enterprises. As the size and complexity of firms increased, owners and managers came squarely up against the "man problem." The traditional methods of personal influence, example, and coercion by foremen and contractors were losing their effectiveness in the more highly industrialized factories. How were managers to assert and maintain control over thousands of workers as diverse as third-generation iron puddlers and newly arrived European peasants?

In Taylor's experience, the foreman was king of the workplace. He had usually risen the hard way, succeeding because of a combination of technical skills, ambition, and grit. The keys to his kingdom were his knowledge and his ability to get the work done.[4]

Taylor advanced rapidly at Midvale, from common laborer to clerk, machinist, gang boss, foreman, master mechanic, chief draftsman, and chief engineer. Even with twelve-hour workdays, he completed correspondence courses for an engineering degree.

Taylor's elevation to gang boss was the watershed in his life. This first job in management involved a three-year "war" with the workmen over what he considered to be their cozy ways of restricting work to about a third of what the machines were capable of producing. He fought them tooth and nail with transfers, fines, and firings. Most of the strife, he was convinced, came from confusion and conflict about what constituted a fair day's work. He therefore set about measuring work objectively so that both employer and employee would submit willingly to the discipline of numbers instead of using a rule of thumb.

Taylor's solutions remain with us today as "time studies." Once a manager could measure and time the motions of "first-class men" as they worked, there would be irrefutable benchmarks against which to judge the performance of all workers. Further, engineers and managers would eventually absorb all the knowledge and skill needed to determine how the job should be done, instead of relying on the workers.

By 1890, Taylor had formulated a system for measuring individual tasks in the workplace. He left Midvale to promote his managerial skills and theories, and became a consultant to a number of small firms. While he continued to write professional papers for engineering magazines, he also took out a number of patents and proposed improvements in the piece-rate system.

In 1898, he was hired to redesign some machine shops at Bethlehem Iron Company. He claimed his work there provided triumphal evidence for his system. He made a Pennsylvania Dutchman named Noll (Taylor called him Schmidt in his descriptions of the experiments) as famous in industrial mythology as Stakhanov or Rosie the Riveter.

In a yard adjoining the Bethlehem iron works were some 80,000 tons of 92-pound iron "pigs," which had to be moved. Taylor saw this as an excellent way to test his theories of "task management."

The task was simple enough. Each man had to take a pig from the pile, carry it up an inclined plank, and dump it into a waiting railroad car. After watching the men work for a few days, Taylor and his aides concluded that a first-class handler ought to be able to carry 47 tons a day instead of the average 12½ tons.

> Once we were sure that 47 tons was a proper day's work for a first-class pig iron handler, the task which faced us as managers under the modern scientific plan was clearly before us. It was our duty to see that the 80,000 tons of pig iron was loaded onto cars at the rate of 47 tons per man per day in place of the 12½ tons, at which rate the work was then being done. And it was further our duty to see that this work was done without bringing on a strike among the men, without any quarrel with the men, and to see that the men were happier and better contented when loading at the new rate.[5]

To prove this could be done, Taylor "scientifically" selected Schmidt as the test worker. Besides being energetic and strong, the pig-iron handler "shall be so stupid and phlegmatic that he more nearly resembles in his mental make-up the ox than any other type."[6]

The plum was a 60 percent increase in wages, from $1.15 to $1.85 per day. The instructions were: "If you are a high-priced man, you will do exactly as this man tells you, from morning till night. When he tells you to pick up a pig and walk, you pick it up and you walk, and when he tells you to sit down and rest, you sit down. You do that right straight through the day. And what's more, no back talk."[7]

Taylor admitted that

This seems to be rather rough talk. And indeed it would be if applied to an educated mechanic, or even to an intelligent laborer. With a man of the mentally sluggish type of Schmidt, it is appropriate and not unkind, since it is effective in fixing his attention on the high wages which he wants and away from what, if it were called to his attention, he probably would consider impossibly hard work. . . . He practically never failed to work at this pace during the three years that the writer was at Bethlehem. . . . One man after another was picked out and trained to handle the pig iron at the rate of 47 tons per day until all the pig iron was handled at this rate, and the men were receiving 60% more wages than the other workmen around them.[8]

In 1901, Taylor retired with the small fortune he had made from his metal-machining patents, and spent the next fourteen years tirelessly promoting his managerial system. Only two American companies ever implemented the complete Taylor system, but several score used substantial portions of it. Taylor presided over a growing number of assistants, who set up many of the actual time studies, task and bonus systems, and schedules of men and materials in various factories.[9]

As Taylor became known in the business world, he attracted government interest. General William Crozier, head of the Army Ordnance Department, had been concerned about inefficiency in the army's arsenals, and hired Taylor to overhaul the entire system. However, at the Watertown (Massachusetts) arsenal, iron molders walked off their jobs when one of Taylor's aides began to make time studies. Molders at another arsenal, in Rock Island, Illinois, also rebelled at being studied, and protested to their Congressman.

The uproar at Watertown might have been localized and patched up if the Eastern Rate Case had not recently placed Taylor in the national limelight. Arguing for the railroad customers against a fare hike by the Eastern railroads, attorney (later Supreme Court Justice) Louis D. Brandeis asserted that the railroads were so grossly inefficient that if they introduced the techniques of scientific management they could save as much as $1 million a day. It was the first time the term "scientific management" had been used with Taylor's theories in mind. The controversy insured that any new major application or experiment involving Taylor or his methods would attract public attention.

Faced with the protests of the Watertown iron molders, Congress impaneled a full-scale commission to investigate the "Taylor and other systems of shop management," under the chairmanship of Professor Robert F. Hoxie, a University of Chicago economist. After exhaustive hearings, and studies of various places where Taylor's system was used, the commission concluded "that while scientific management is to date the latest word in the sheer mechanics of production and inherently in line with the march of events . . . [and] has conferred great benefits on industry . . . neither organized nor unorganized labor finds in it any adequate protection to its standards of living, and progressive means of industrial education, or any opportunity for industrial democracy by which labor may create for itself a progressively efficient share in efficient management. . . ."[10]

An even more eloquent expression of labor's suspicions came from John Frey, editor of the *International Molders' Union Journal,* and a member of the Hoxie Commission: "The one great asset of the wage worker has been his craftsmanship. . . . The really essential element in it is not manual skill and dexterity, but something stored up in the mind of the worker. This something is partly the intimate knowledge of the character and usage of the tools, materials, and processes of the craft which . . . has enabled the workers to organize and force better terms from the employers. . . . The greatest blow that could be delivered against unionism and the organized workers would be the separation of craft knowledge from craft skill."[11]

Most workers, Frey wrote, were still unaware of the "more insidious, more dangerous" aspects of systems such as Taylor's. "Gathering up all this scattered craft knowledge, systematizing it and concentrating it in the hands of the employer and then doling it out again only in the form of minute instructions, giving to each worker only the knowledge needed for the mechanical perform-ance of a particular, relatively minute task . . . when it is com-pleted, the worker is no longer a craftsman in any sense, but is an animated tool of the management."[12]

Taylor believed that precise definitions of the job were not only management's prerogative, but its sacred duty, if it wanted to achieve maximum productivity. To do this, he advocated the sub-division of labor into its smallest constituent parts. All aspects of planning were to be taken off the shopfloor. Control would be such that jobs would be "idiot-proof." He had an engineer's faith that technology defined the nature of the job, and that human beings were secondary to technology. "In the past, man has been first; in the future the system must be first."[13]

Just as Rudyard Kipling enjoined British imperialists to assume the "white man's burden," so Taylor preached to a managerial constituency that they should shoulder "new burdens, new duties and responsibilities never dreamed of in the past. Managers [must] assume, for instance, the burden of gathering together all of the traditional knowledge which in the past has been possessed by the workmen and then of classifying, tabulating and reducing this knowledge to rules, laws and formulae which are immensely help-ful to the workmen in doing their daily tasks."[14]

It is tempting to dismiss Taylor's one-dimensional view of the workingman and his conviction that bonuses of 30–100 percent would automatically elicit greater effort and productivity. And yet Taylor shaped the attitudes of many American managers for most of this century. One of Taylor's disciples wrote, "Training a worker means merely enabling him to carry out the directions of his work schedule. Once he can do this, his training is over, whatever his age."[15]

By the 1970s, however, many people could no longer identify with their jobs. Their alienation from Taylorist ways of organizing work came to a head. As Gary Bryner, former president of the

United Auto Workers local at Lordstown, Ohio, said, "If you're a worker and you turn in a suggestion that saves somebody's life, you get a twenty-five-dollar savings bond. If you're a worker and you turn in a suggestion that does away with six of your brothers' jobs, you get six thousand dollars—that's the way workers perceive the company; just money-hungry bastards that would do anything to save money. That's how GMAD [General Motors Assembly Division] got its nickname as 'Gotta Make Another Dollar.' "[16]

In 1952, the classic study of auto workers by Professors Charles Walker and Robert Guest, then at Yale University, graphically described the alienation of assembly line workers: "The sense of becoming depersonalized, of becoming anonymous as against remaining one's self, is for those who feel it a psychologically more disturbing result of the work environment than either the boredom or the tension that arise from the repetitive and mechanically paced work."[17]

A telephone operator with New England Bell said, "The biggest feeling I have is that we have less contact with the public. It's always 'get rid of them' philosophy because you're being constantly timed. I just feel that they're trying to make robots out of us as much as they can. Each month you're supposed to be setting new goals, but how high can you go?"[18]

Supervisors were not immune to job alienation either: "All you're doing is checking on people. This goes on all day. The job is boring . . . it's more or less like you have a factory full of robots working the machinery. . . . If it breaks down or something goes wrong, you're there to straighten it out. . . . A man should be treated as a human, not as a million-dollar piece of machinery. People aren't treated as good as an IBM machine."[19] Alienation from the job and from fellow employees was steadily growing at all levels in the American labor force.

For two observers who recognized the economic impact of Taylorism, its human impact was either insignificant or unknown. According to Peter Drucker, teacher and consultant, Taylor's theories "may well be the most powerful as well as the most lasting contribution America has made to Western thought since the Federalist Papers," because Taylor "made the manual worker productive" by dividing planning from doing.[20] Lenin, fresh from the success of the Russian Revolution, saw Taylorism in 1921 as "a combination of the refined brutality of bourgeois exploitation and a number of the greatest scientific achievements in the field on analyzing mechanical motions. We must organize in Russia the study and teaching of the Taylor System and systematically try it out and adapt it to our ends."[21]

In 1979 William Batten, chairman of the New York Stock Exchange, provided a new perspective:

> The way work is organized today is still rooted in the so-called scientific management theories developed by Frederick Taylor back in the early days of this century. Though most companies have long since softened the precisely measured, dehumanizing time-study approach to work efficiency, the basic thrust remains. Generally speaking, management identifies and closely monitors all aspects of the workday, from how each job is to be performed to, in some cases, the exact number of minutes employees may spend at the water-cooler during the workday.
>
> Too often, management seems tacitly to regard the worker as simply a machine that happens to have inconvenient emotional and physical needs instead of particular parts that wear out and have to be replaced. And, too often, a well-intentioned management committee constructs a profile of a "typical" employee, designs standard procedures to be followed by that "typical" employee, inscribes the procedures in an attractive company manual—and settles back, content in its belief that it has adopted a sensitive, "human" approach to all its employees.[22]

Over the past sixty years, a small but growing number of people have begun to challenge Taylor's legitimacy.

[3]

Responses to Taylor

From Watertown to Lordstown

Frederick Winslow Taylor was the most prominent and vociferous observer of the "man problem" in the first two decades of this century. His pronouncements were part of a worldwide debate on how to unite man and machine for the highest efficiency. This problem posed itself on two levels, the practical and the theoretical. On the practical level, companies sought to mold millions of workers into pliant yet responsive cogs in their complex industrial machinery. On the theoretical plane, people asked how the beliefs and practices of political democracy could be squared with the demands of authoritarian management for a uniform workforce which checked its civil rights at the factory gate or office door.

Taylor's "great mental revolution," guided by management, promised economic benefits to all. After World War I, there were a few voices calling for a real revolution, on the Bolshevik model. Between the two extremes was a wide range of recommendations for "industrial democracy." Over the next sixty years, experiments with increased employee participation in management and ownership prospered and waned, never gaining a majority of support among American workers or managers, but ever present.

During World War I, a number of defense plants established joint union-management committees to work on production bottlenecks and speed the war effort. When the war ended, the residue of goodwill between many unionists and some outsiders formed the basis of the amorphous concept of "industrial democracy." The phase encompassed proposals as conventional as profit-sharing, as unusual as worker representation on boards, and as radical as nationalization of basic industries. As one analyst of the period said, "Somehow the industrial democracy advocates hope to enfranchise the wage earner, to construct a web of rights, responsibilities, and interlocking authorities, that would join employers and employees into a common enterprise and, in doing so, finally break down the old troubling divide between them."[1] However, there was no development of a unified constituency for specific programs to realize "industrial democracy," so the discussion remained on the level of "glittering generalizations."[2]

Even though management solidified its control over the workplace and its processes, Taylor's "great mental revolution," which divided thinking from doing, did not occur. Absenteeism, shoddy workmanship, and high turnover plagued factory after factory. It was more difficult than expected to find the one best way to ensure discipline and raise productivity.

One plant that was beset by shoddy workmanship and other problems was a branch of Western Electric (a subsidiary of American Telephone & Telegraph) at Hawthorne, Illinois, which produced a variety of telephone equipment. Dr. Elton Mayo, an industrial psychologist at the Harvard Graduate School of Business Administration, was hired in 1924 to find out why, despite the best efforts of Taylor's time-and-motion experts, worker morale and production remained low.

Mayo began his studies with the conventional Taylor premise that if various adjustments in working conditions were made, management could determine the one best way for doing each particular job, which would result in higher production. The first part of the experiment isolated a number of women in a separate room, where their production of radio relay equipment was continually monitored. Following an initial period of work under existing conditions, the women were put on a group piece rate. After eight weeks, the group was allowed to take two rest periods of five minutes apiece. Subsequent changes included rearrangement of seating and changes in lighting.

The astonishing result was that with each variation production increased. Out of curiosity, the researchers then reversed the variables: turned the lights back down, changed seating positions again, and reduced the break time; *still* production increased.[3]

The conundrum became famous as the Hawthorne Effect: production rose *not* because of mechanical changes or improvements in working conditions but because of the personal attention researchers and managers paid to individual workers. The women were consulted about many elements of the changes and were able to veto those they disapproved of. "The group unquestionably develops a sense of participation in the critical determinations and becomes something of a social unit," Mayo observed.[4]

For the first time in their working lives, the women felt they were treated as adults who had something to contribute. Moreover, Mayo wrote, the chief supervisor "clearly understood from the first that any hint of 'the supervisor' in his methods might be fatal to the interests of the inquiry. . . . Thus he took a personal interest in each girl and her achievement; he showed pride in the record of the group. He helped the group to feel its duty was to set its own conditions of work."[5]

Research at Hawthorne and elsewhere demonstrated that if respect and attention were added to decent wages and pleasant working conditions, workers would be happier and therefore more productive. This work formed the cornerstone for the "Human Relations" school of management, an initial antidote to Taylorism.

Looking back on what changes were actually made in building radio relay equipment, we can see that it was more than simply paying attention to people, which is what most people mean when they talk about the "Hawthorne effect." The women at Western Electric got more control over their work. They helped determine what changes were to be made and could veto those they did not like. They began to work as a group. The supervisor became less of an order-giver and disciplinarian and more of a coach and resource; he helped the group understand its responsibility to establish its working conditions. The changes at Hawthorne did, in a small way, give workers more control, if even temporarily, and thus helped open the door to the reversal of Taylorism.[6]

The Human Relations approach remained in vogue for the next thirty years, as the formation of human relations departments in hundreds of companies attested. It added the patina of human kindness to the prod of Taylorist measurement and control. The school has been criticized by critics on the left and on the right, for quite different reasons. The left dismissed it as an effort to build company loyalty and reduce union sympathies, while Peter Drucker wrote that tying performance to satisfaction was only a "half-truth": "What we need is to replace the externally imposed spur of fear with an internal self-motivation for performance. Responsibility—not satisfaction—is the only thing that will serve."[7]

In 1981, Drucker said that his recommendations had fallen on "deaf management ears for the last thirty-five years." He believed that decisions should be made at all levels of an organization by those closest to the problem.[8]

Union-management cooperation in defense plants did not last long after World War I. Many companies launched vigorous anti-union campaigns under the patriotic banner of "American Plans." As unions reeled before management assaults and watched their numbers dwindle, leaders such as Samuel Gompers convinced his American Federation of Labor to limit itself to "business unionism." Unions would not challenge the basic capitalist system, or seek a share in its management, but instead would work to assure themselves of recognition and a fair share of the economic pie. Gompers's famous demand for "More!" meant more wages, not more control or more participation in management decisions. Management-chefs would write the recipe and supervise the worker-cooks, but both parties would bargain over the respective portions.

From one perspective, the unions made a pact with the devil. From another, one could say that the unions had their hands full just seeking recognition.

Labor, Gompers wrote, did not want to control business:

Collective bargaining in industry does not imply that wage earners shall assume control of industry or responsibility for financial management. . . . Employees shall have the right to organize and to deal with the employer through selected representatives as to wages and working conditions. . . . There is no belief held in the trade unions that its members shall control the plant or usurp the rights of the owners.[9]

Perhaps Gompers wanted to distance his troops from radicals in Europe, and was trying to demonstrate his Americanism to those frightened by the "Red scare"; in any case, there was no political support for greater worker control at that time in the United States.

As management continued with ever-greater job specialization and subdivision, unions had two basic choices. They could either bargain for more control over the job and insist on a role in defining its perimeters, or they could accept the absolute division of power between management and labor and concentrate on improving the workers' material well-being. "The first option," Robert Cole, a University of Michigan sociologist, has noted, "was clearly a radical one, which the unions eventually rejected in the face of management and government power and the lack of worker support. They accepted the more limited second solution whereby collective bargaining came to legitimize the existing extreme division of labor."[10]

In the effort to control job opportunities and definitions, unions began to negotiate for detailed wage schedules tied to particular jobs. Management would have preferred more flexible incentive systems geared to individual effort. In effect, unions and management agreed to two principles consistent with Taylorism: tight and narrow job classification, and the perpetuation of the dichotomy between workers and managers.[11]

Adversarial relations based on wages and working conditions remained largely unchanged for the next fifty years. The collective bargaining process satisfied the rank-and-file's immediate material concerns.[12] "If you want to enrich the job, enrich the paycheck," said William Winpisinger, president of the International

Association of Machinists and Aerospace Workers, in 1976. Many unionists in the 1920s would have said the same thing.

Unlike craft unions, industrial unions had relatively few weapons with which to bargain over control. For them, the strike became almost the only weapon for asserting their rights. Leaders were limited by having to go to the picket line with issues that were readily definable, fit for compression onto a placard. To win a strike, leaders had to fight for the lowest common denominators of wages, benefits, and safe conditions. People were not going to strike for more interesting or satisfying work. There was little effort to influence management procedures except with regard to the hated practice of speedup.[13]

Alongside the prevailing current of adversarial relations between labor and management in this century, there has also existed a quiet stream of cooperation and joint problem-solving. This cooperation has usually followed an external or internal company crisis and usually has not lasted more than a few years. It is important, however, to take notice of this minor tradition, because it shows that labor-management cooperation in making joint decisions was not peculiar to the 1970s.

In 1923, unions and management of the Baltimore & Ohio Railroad set up joint committees to address production problems. The unions had made great gains in membership during World War I, when the lines were under government ownership. With the return to private control, managers adopted "scientific management" techniques and increased the amount of outside contract work. The unions argued that the workers could do the repair work more efficiently than any outside contractor, and B&O president Daniel Willard was persuaded to let them prove it. The unions, fearing for their members' jobs, and the company, fearing for its profit margins, began to develop cooperative ways to improve maintenance.

Starting at the Glenwood repair shop near Pittsburgh, the idea of joint committees spread to the rest of the B&O system, as well as to other carriers. By the end of the decade, there were labor-management committees on railroads that owned a sixth of the total mileage in the U.S.

Cooperation didn't come easily. Suspicions abounded: Many foremen were as convinced as Taylor had been that any letup in control would allow workers to "soldier." Workers were fearful that cooperation would provide a wedge into a new "sweating system." Committees met every two weeks for free-ranging discussions on ways to improve production and working conditions on the shopfloor. They rigorously avoided contractual issues. The idea, in the words of Willard, was to give "every employee an enlightened and enlarged view of his own worth and importance as a part of the great organization known as the Baltimore & Ohio Railroad."[14]

Management committee members were drawn from all supervisory levels; union representatives were almost invariably from the shop committee. This was to assure that the committees would not compete with existing union structures.

Between 1924 and 1928, the Baltimore & Ohio management received 21,585 suggestions from employees, of which 18,237 were adopted. Most related to very modest changes in shopfloor conditions, but implementing them doubtless contributed to an overall improvement in efficiency and morale. Between 1922 and 1939, appeals of grievances by workers dropped by 80 percent, from 2.53 to 0.52 per 100 workers.[15]

Benefits for the unions included improved working conditions, an accelerated and smoother grievance procedure, an increase in union membership and individual pay, stabilization of employment, which lasted at least until the Depression, and access to more complete information concerning the railroad's operations.

There were, however, disagreements over the sharing of productivity gains. Some foremen became defensive when cooperation committees were given the power to go straight to their superiors with suggestions for improvements or changes. At times, members from each side accused the other of taking credit for suggestions not its own. The Depression put great economic pressure on committee efforts, but several railroads were able to maintain some committees even through those dark years.

In 1941, labor historian Sumner Slichter concluded his study of labor-management cooperation on the railroads. He wrote that the most important single factor in their success or failure was the degree of support from top management and union leaders. "There is no substitute for this support. . . . Shop superintendents and master mechanics will not display much interest in the plan if their superiors are not interested in it. If the local management is indifferent or hostile, it is virtually impossible to maintain interest among the union members of the committee. Equally important is the interest of the top leaders of the unions. Unless they give strong support to the plan as a matter of union policy, the interest of the local leaders is likely to lag."[16]

During World War II, there was another round of labor-management cooperation. Responding to the crisis of wartime production demands, the AFL-CIO enthusiastically supported pleas for cooperation from the chairman of the War Production Board, Donald Nelson. By the end of the war, there were some 5,000 committees whose members had buried the hatchet in order to deal with a generally acknowledged crisis.

Committee membership was again voluntary, and activities were distinct from the collective bargaining process. As with the railroad groups, representation from the union side tended to be existing union leaders, in order to dispel fears of competing structures. In a variety of plants, committees sponsored discussions, suggestion boxes, and other ways of eliciting ideas about how to improve production. At R. Hoe & Company, which was converted during the war from making printing presses to manufacturing periscopes, "workers [were] continuously informed of the jobs on hand and the work ahead. Present and future contracts and cutbacks [were] discussed. Correspondence with the War Production Board on contracts and available plant facilities [was] read and discussed at Committee meetings."[17]

The most successful committees were usually in unionized shops. "Without a union," journalist Stuart Chase wrote, "there is no matrix from which to choose the labor members, no discipline to hold them on the job. But the union must be well past the fighting stage, and over into the second stage of smooth collective bargaining. If the workers do not trust the management, and vice versa, the chances for effective cooperation are remote. . . . The appeal to patriotism may override this barrier to a degree, but only in a few cases has it accomplished a real working team."[18]

Chase thought that the effective committee exposed "a great rich mine of human effort. . . . Will that mine shut down when the war ends? Of the managers and workers I talked to, not one thought so. To a man, they believed that something had been discovered too valuable to lay aside."[19]

But at the end of the war, without the glue of patriotism to hold the former combatants together, and no mechanism like the War Production Board to foster their cooperation, workers and managers did fall back into their established, adversarial relationships.

A third example of labor-management cooperation began with a specific crisis: the threat of closure at a small steel company. Joseph Scanlon was an accountant for the LaPointe Steel Company in the late 1930s. The company had such seemingly intractable problems of production and competition that, in desperation, the president asked the workforce for help, promising that if the company survived, all workers would share in the profits. With the help and encouragement of Clinton Golden of the Steelworkers Organizing Committee, Scanlon conducted a series of detailed interviews with rank-and-file workers to find ways to improve production. The suggestions led directly to the saving of the company. Scanlon also devised a way to tie profit-sharing to improved productivity. He worked through the war with the Steelworkers Committee, refining his plan, and continued his research at the Massachusetts Institute of Technology until his death in 1956. By 1980, there were at least 500 active Scanlon Plans across the country modeled after the system he had invented for LaPointe, mostly at manufacturing plants with fewer than 1,000 employees.

Scanlon believed that no one knew more about the running of a steel mill than those on the shopfloor, that there should be a way to tap the mental resources of these experts, then reward them with a share in the monetary gains from their participation. His plan set up a two-tiered participation scheme, with committees composed of labor and management representatives from each department which met regularly to discuss problems and make suggestions for improvements. A screening committee reviewed and (usually) approved suggestions.

Economic gains were shared by using a ratio of dollar sales to total unit labor costs, monitored weekly or monthly. Seventy-five percent of any surplus was returned to all but the most senior managers, proportionate to each person's salary or wage. Since the plan rewarded the group rather than the individual, pressure to produce more or better came from employees and peers, rather than from management's insistence.

The Scanlon Plan is interesting for a number of reasons. In the first place, it was sponsored and developed by a union. Second, the committees did not threaten local union leadership. Frederick Taylor had always said that if the worker followed management's instructions, the resulting "great mental revolution" would bring him significant financial gains. By contrast, Scanlon Plans encouraged a cooperative search by managers and workers for shopfloor improvements with group financial rewards.

Despite their record of productivity improvements, Scanlon Plans did not take American industry by storm. Neither Scanlon himself nor his disciples were willing to market the plans very aggressively, preferring to convince management that they should never be imposed without general rank-and-file approval. The plans require genuinely participative managers open to suggestions, criticism, and possibly bruised egos. They involve much more than checking suggestion boxes and handing out an occasional savings bond award. They seem to work best in small plants or at those with a strong family environment. One possible major reason for their failure to gain wider acceptance may have been management fears of losing control.[20]

In response to increased organizing drives and strike activities in the late 1940s and early 1950s, many companies inserted what came to be known as "management rights clauses" into contracts. Before the middle 1950s, the company's exclusive right to management of the business was largely assumed. But under union pressure on the organizing and wage fronts, many companies inserted clauses to make explicit what had been always implied. Typical phrases were "the determination of what shall be produced and how it shall be produced are vested in the company ..." or "It shall be the exclusive right of the company to determine ... the methods, processes, and means of manufacture."[21] These clauses were born partly of fear that unions wanted more than Gompers's "More," but they were also a safety net for management in grievance proceedings. In effect, they were a legal device to give management the power to run the business as it saw fit.

In their pristine form, management rights clauses are meant to retain any right not specifically granted to the union in a collective bargaining agreement. As such, they are similar to the states' rights clauses in the U.S. Constitution, which reserve to the states powers not specifically granted to the federal government.

An example from the 1978 agreement at the Fairbanks Weighing Division of Colt Industries read: "The management of the business and the direction of the working force including the right to hire, the right to plan, direct and control plant operations, to schedule and assign work to employees, and to maintain the efficiency of employees; to determine the means, methods and processes and schedules of production; to determine the products to be manufactured; to determine whether to make or buy; the location and continuation of its manufacturing operations, and operating departments; to establish and require employees to observe reasonable Company rules and regulations, are the sole rights of the Company.

"The foregoing enumerations of Management's rights shall not be deemed to exclude other rights of Management not specifically set forth, the Company therefore retaining all management rights not otherwise specifically covered by this Agreement."

In many cases, the clauses were ceded in exchange for things the unions wanted more, such as higher wages or benefits. Unions were not interested in making the means, methods, and processes of production a contractual issue.

. . .

One of the most influential postwar books on management used Scanlon Plans as an example of excellent management. Douglas McGregor, the author of *The Human Side of Enterprise*, had known Scanlon at the Massachusetts Institute of Technology.

McGregor praised the Scanlon Plans as an innovative way to share economic gains individually through improvements in group performance. Even more important, he said, they were "a formal method providing an opportunity for every member of the organization to contribute his brains and ingenuity as well as his physical effort to the improvement of organizational effectiveness.

"Even the worker doing repetitive work at the bottom of the hierarchy is potentially more than a pair of hands. He is a human resource. His know-how and ingenuity, properly utilized, may make a far greater difference to the success of the enterprise than any improvement in his physical effort."[22]

McGregor's now-famous "Theory X and Theory Y" represented two sharply contrasting management styles. Theory X was almost pure Taylorism. Its principles were:

1. "The average human being has an inherent dislike of work and will avoid it if he can. . . .
2. "Because of this human characteristic of dislike of work, most people must be coerced, directed, threatened with punishment to get them to put forth adequate effort toward the achievement of organizational objectives. . . .
3. "The average human being prefers to be directed, wishes to avoid responsibility, has relatively little ambition, wants security above all."[23]

McGregor argued that the traditional incentives of more pay and fringe benefits were no longer as effective as they had once been, because workers had relatively few physical and safety needs left to be met.

The second style, Theory Y (which was likely to be found in companies with Scanlon Plans), was suited to fulfilling more sophisticated and intangible worker needs. Its principles were:

1. "The expenditure of physical and mental effort in work is as natural as play or rest. . . .
2. "External control and the threat of punishment are not the only means for bringing about effort toward organizational objectives. Man will exercise self-direction and self-control in the service of objectives to which he is committed.
3. "Commitment to objectives is a function of the rewards associated with their advancement.
4. "The average human being learns, under proper conditions, not only to accept but to seek responsibility.
5. "The capacity to exercise a relatively high degree of imagination, ingenuity, and creativity in the solution of organizational problems is widely, not narrowly, distributed in the population.
6. "Under the conditions of modern industrial life, the intellectual potentialities of the average human being are only partially utilized."[24]

McGregor's exposition of Theories X and Y became a central feature of management folk wisdom. It clarified and popularized the distinction between authoritarian and participatory management. What it did not do, however, was to show in practical terms how a firm, or even an individual manager, could shift in approach from X to Y.

In the 1950s, the psychologist Frederick Herzberg (subsequently a professor at Western Reserve University) conducted a series of interviews with workers and managers to find out what they liked and did not like about their work. He divided the results into "satisfiers" and "dissatisfiers." Among the latter were company administration and policy, supervision, work conditions, and pay. In the former category, he placed achievement recognition, work itself, responsibility, and advancement.

Herzberg believed that the way to motivate workers was to accentuate the positive. Managers should give attention to the "satisfiers," and since satisfaction depended upon intellectual and spiritual challenge, they should focus on those aspects of the job. He said that jobs should be "enriched" through what he called "vertical loading," which involved the following steps:

1. "Removing some controls while retaining account-ability.
2. "Increasing the accountability of individuals for their own work.
3. "Giving a person a complete natural unit of work (mod-ule, division, area . . .).
4. "Granting additional authority to an employee in his activity; job freedom.
5. "Making periodic reports directly available to the worker himself, rather than to the supervisor.
6. "Introducing new and more difficult tasks not previ-ously handled.
7. "Assigning individuals specific or specialized tasks en-abling them to become experts."[25]

Herzberg's theories complemented McGregor's ideal of a be-nevolent management anxious to give as much challenge and support to the individual worker as possible. One form of support was that instead of having tasks constantly subdivided into the smallest, least personal components, workers would be encour-aged to take on more responsibility and challenge, which would appeal to their next higher "level of need."

Herzberg's ideas spread rapidly. They were attractive to managers because of their very limited objective of making work-ers more satisfied as individuals. The aim was to give workers more autonomy on the job, not participation in management. Manage-ment would still decide what was to be "enriched," and how.

Another strategy for workplace reform evolved from the reorgani-zation of work by Welsh coal miners, a procedure studied by Eric Trist at the Tavistock Work Research Institute in England in the 1950s. The miners' idea of autonomous work teams was subse-quently picked up and developed by Einar Thorsrud and his col-leagues at the Work Research Institutes in Norway.

The key element of the Tavistock "socio-technical" system was that there should be a balance between the respective demands of the technological "bones" and the human "flesh" that together make up the working body. The Tavistock theories hold that organizations are most effective when they are based on small work groups that have a high degree of independence and autonomy.

Thorsrud, a psychologist who became one of the world's experts on workplace democracy, was concerned about the destructive effect on people of Taylorist job simplification and subdivision. He agreed with Herzberg's desire for job enrichment, but his commitment to maximum feasible participation, or "true industrial democracy," was far stronger. Once, when he and Herzberg were together on a panel at a seminar, Herzberg condemned participation for setting no limits, to which Thorsrud replied, "You are against participation for the very reasons we are in favor of it . . . one doesn't know where it will stop. We think that's good."[26]

The official Norwegian labor and management organizations, as well as the government, asked Thorsrud and others to conduct a wide-ranging study of industrial democracy with the help of people from Tavistock. Four factories volunteered to use autonomous work groups. The results were expressed in observations that would be fully endorsed fifteen years later by a growing number of American managers and workers:

1. "People need adequate elbow room . . . [and to be] their own bosses and . . . not have their boss breathing down their neck. They have too much elbow room if they do not know what to do next.

2. "People need a chance to learn on the job, and continue learning. People can learn only when they are able to set goals for themselves that are reasonable challenges for them, and get feedback in time to change their behavior.

3. "People should be able to vary their work to avoid boredom and fatigue.

4. "People need conditions where they can get help and respect from their workmates.

5. "People need to be able to gain a sense of their own

work contributing to society. People do not like to make
shoddy products.
6. "People need a desirable future. Dead-end jobs do not
permit personal growth."[27]

Thorsrud and Trist came to the United States in the early 1970s
to lecture and consult on a number of work reform projects. Trist
led a project at a coal mine in Rushton, Pennsylvania, and was an
early adviser to the Jamestown Area Labor-Management Committee. Thorsrud lectured widely and assisted in setting up a project
at Harman International Industries in Bolivar, Tennessee.

A more recent development evolved from post–World War II
research in small-group dynamics. Organizational Development
(O.D.) was more than just a way of combining problem-solving
with personal relationships. The aim of O.D. was "to open up
emotional as well as task-related communications in order to develop mutually trusting, solid teams. The small team becomes the
key functional unit and 'team building' becomes one central activity of O.D. practitioners. They are work-based, task-oriented
teams, and their purpose is to develop feelings of group responsibility. The more advanced teams enlarge individual jobs by
making every individual in the team a planner as well as a
doer."[28]

Organizational Development assumed that if one changed
people's attitudes and skills, the organizational structure would
improve. The method was to let groups of eight to ten people
define the problems and issues. Large organizations would eventually be transformed by the mutual support which would develop
among the smaller groups. Despite its name, this approach had as
its premise the adjustment of people to the organization, not vice
versa. Most O.D. consultants, because they were invariably hired
by large organizations, concentrated on helping the individuals to
adjust to these organizations. The structure of the company was
taken as a given: people had to learn skills of group problem-
solving, listening, and self-discipline to function better within it.

Then, if changes in the structure were ever needed, those skills would be used to effect the changes.

A layman's definition of O.D. from one of the Quality of Work Life (QWL) specialists at General Motors went as follows: "It means working with individuals, groups, total organizations and sets of organizations to help them examine their own behavior and, if they want to, change it."[29]

There was, however, some awareness that the expanding traditional hierarchical pyramid was becoming antiquated and less effective. Communications among people making decisions were made more by phone and memo than face to face.

In the mid- to late 1960s, a number of major U.S. corporations, which had used O.D. techniques with their managers, began to employ them with their hourly workers. These experiments frequently took place in new factories, where a fresh start could be made.

Companies such as Procter & Gamble, General Foods, Cummins Engine, and Texas Instruments also experimented with reduced hierarchies, semi-autonomous work groups, job redesign, and peer selection. The majority of these efforts took place in non-union firms or plants where union skepticism was widespread. When the techniques were first introduced into the unionized General Motors assembly plant at Lordstown, Ohio, rank-and-file members referred derisively to O.D. as "Overtime and Doughnuts," because what they considered to be their real problems at work were not discussed.

The quiet, almost academic experiments in O.D. took place against a background of social and political upheaval in this country. Dissent and alienation filtered into the factories and workplaces along with the arrival of a younger, more affluent, more educated, and less tractable workforce.

Dr. Delmar L. "Dutch" Landen, the head of organizational research and development at General Motors, saw the approaching storm clouds. In 1970, he said, "We are on a collision course. We have built institutions which were very effective in their time, but now there are increasing levels of aspirations and different value systems pressing against these institutions."[30]

. . .

The collision came at Lordstown, Ohio, a Chevrolet Vega plant of General Motors' new assembly division, in February, 1972. The plant was billed as having the most advanced engineering design, made to suit the workers, but the Lordstown strike became one of the most famous walkouts in recent American labor history. The issue was not wages or the right to organize, but the quality of working life itself. The workers were angered at the pace of an assembly line where Vegas moved past at 101 per hour, giving each person 36 seconds to complete his or her appointed task. "You just pray for the line to stop," one worker said. Workers had responded with high absenteeism and sabotage before they went on strike for twenty-two bitter days.

The official General Motors explanation for the Lordstown strike was given by the vice-president for industrial relations, George Morris. He said that there was nothing unusual about the strike; such discontent was to be expected in a major reorganization which had combined two divisions of General Motors, and had nothing to do with boredom or frustration on the assembly line. He offered the confirmation that in the ten other corporation consolidations to form the new Assembly Division nine strikes had occurred. Other GM managers, in contrast to Morris, blamed the workers, and meted out disciplinary actions that in turn fueled more discontent.

In an interview with *Automotive News,* Joseph Godfrey, the head of General Motor's Assembly Division, was asked for his views on assembly-line monotony. "Monotony is not quite the right word," he said. "There is a good deal of misunderstanding about that, but it seems to me that we have our biggest problems when we disturb that 'monotony.' The workers may complain about monotony, but years spent in the factories leads me to believe that they like to do their job automatically. If you interject new things, you spoil the rhythm of the job, and work gets fouled up."[31]

General Motors was not alone in this perception: one year earlier, Henry Ford II had summed up his ideas about what workers sought in their jobs: "The average worker wants a job in which he does not have to put much physical effort. Above all, he wants a job in which he does not have to think."[32]

Outside the auto industry, some corporate executives saw more significance to the strike. The manager of employee relations research at Pittsburgh Plate Glass Industries said, "Lordstown had a big shock effect. Managers are seeing a brand-new challenge. Maybe they only thought of it a few months ago, but now they're really aware."[33]

The media reported the strike widely. At the same time the U.S. Department of Health, Education and Welfare was completing a study of the problem of workplace discontent. One of its conclusions was "What the workers want most, as more than 100 studies in the past 20 years show, is to become masters of their immediate environments and to feel that their work and they, themselves, are important. . . . An increasing number of workers want more autonomy in tackling their tasks, greater opportunity for increasing their skills, rewards that are directly connected to the intrinsic aspects of work and greater participation in the design of work and the formulation of their tasks."[34]

Workers at Lordstown did not want to take over management decisions, but they did want to be treated like human beings. As one worker said, "Some of the machines have written on them 'Treat Me with Respect and I Will Give You Top Quality with Less Effort.' I said we should have that printed on sweatshirts and wear them to work, but we wouldn't be able to keep them on for five minutes; we'd be sent home for disrespect."[35] After twenty-two days the union members returned to their jobs at Lordstown, but the bitterness remained.

Although the iron molders at the Watertown Arsenal reacted swiftly and negatively to the elimination of thought and responsibility from their jobs, their managers and those across the country acquired more and more control over work. The concept of employee participation, however, was kept alive by the experience of the B&O and other railroads in the 1920s, the production efforts of World War II, and the success of Joe Scanlon at the La Pointe Steel Company. At the same time, the organizing drives and strikes of the 1940s and '50s exacerbated the already adversarial relations between labor and management. Academics like McGregor, Herzberg, Trist, and Thorsrud, aided by the Welsh coal miners, began to argue and to demonstrate that participation was a radical alternative to Taylorism. By 1970, a small number of managers began to share Landen's nightmare vision of a coming collision between outmoded organizations and changing employee values. The strike at Lordstown led to a renewed interest in finding a better way of working.

After the oil shortage of 1973 and the subsequent recession, the rumbling of workers' frustrations became part of the much larger crisis of production and competition. Nowhere was the growing competitive pressure, primarily from the Japanese, more acutely felt than in the U.S. automobile industry.

[II]

ILLUSTRATIONS
OF PARTICIPATION

Participation comes in many shapes and sizes. In essence, it happens between individuals or among people within a small group. It can take place at all levels of an organization, from the shopfloor and office to the president's suite.

The five chapters that follow describe the spectrum of changes which have occurred in the last ten years in different private and public organizations. They involve new patterns of behavior, new ways to distribute profits and power, and new concepts of ownership and management. The first three chapters in this section focus on increased participation in decision-making. The last two treat the issues surrounding employee ownership.

[4]

Beyond Adversarial Relations

General Motors

The hand-lettered sign reads: "You are entering the war zone. Quality and productivity are our weapons." Next to it are listed monthly sales figures of various General Motors and Japanese cars.

The "war zone" is the front-knuckle and brake-assembly section in the Chevrolet Gear and Axle plant in Detroit. Overhead, a conveyor painted in the maize and blue of the University of Michigan moves parts to feed the assembly line. These knuckle and brake assemblies go into the new J-car, like the Chevrolet Cavalier, General Motors' brightest hope for competing with Japanese imports. The Gear is one of General Motors' oldest factories. Built fifty-eight years ago, it still stands, while several blocks away its brother from Chrysler, the famous Dodge Main, has been leveled, taking with it 10,000 jobs.

For the first time in the Chevrolet division, General Motors management has built a non-synchronized line—it can be stopped and started by workers. Workers can build a "bank of jobs," completing them at a faster than normal pace, then leave the line for a break.

Each Monday morning a group of employees in the front-knuckle section meets for an hour in the offices next to the assembly line. They form one of twenty employee participation circles that discuss daily production problems. They convene in a small room whose four large windows face the sea of machinery and maze of conveyors of the plant floor. On the walls are blueprints of the plant layout, showing the position of each aisle and machine. The new J-car section of the plant is outlined in yellow; large blue-and-yellow posters on the wall proclaim that the J-car has "world class quality." On a table, like drugs captured in a police raid, rest accusatory defective parts; they either arrived defective or were manufactured with defects at the Gear.

This particular Monday, the meeting starts promptly at 9:30 a.m., when first-line supervisor John Wojtowicz arrives and distributes the agenda. On the wall at the end of the table is the sign "Meetings." The next line says, "Oblige everyone," and under that, "Get everyone to participate." Then there are six categories: Purpose of the Meeting, Brainstorming, Evaluation, Decisions, Action Plan, and Re-evaluation. The agenda includes safety inspection, production review, unscheduled down-time, and the savings bond drive. Time is reserved at the end of the meeting to give each person two minutes for expressing his or her additional thoughts.

The first item is the report of the safety chief, an hourly employee, for that week: he has learned that a worker in another plant lost a thumb and forefinger while assembling a disc brake, and reports that the equipment that caused the accident is not being used at the Gear. Next, the group hears that the Lordstown, Ohio, assembly plant has telexed to say it was returning 1,125 brake assemblies because they were deeply pitted by rust, and unacceptable. They are upset. The members all know they cost $3.75 each to make, a fact workers had never been given before they formed a circle. After considerable discussion, the group theorizes that the assemblies got wet in a leaky boxcar in transit; in other words, that the railroad was responsible. Later, during the two-minute individual remarks, one person suggests that the brake assemblies could have been rained upon during a bad storm, when he saw the roof leak over the line. Without the requirement of the meeting to go around the table for everyone's two minutes at the end, the leaky roof would never have been identified.

On another item, the group agrees that its members are fed up with defects in the casting of heavy-duty knuckles supplied by the General Motors Foundry in Saginaw, Michigan; the group agrees by consensus to send them back.

Still another technical problem is the presence of foreign

materials in the bearing bolts. The group decides to invite the supervisor responsible for them to the next meeting. The facilitator of the meeting, Doug Latkowski, says, "When he comes, I want everyone to put in his two cents so that it is not just one person making the criticism."

By the start of the two-minute comments, only about half of the group has spoken. With some friendly prodding, the facilitator goes around the room and encourages everyone to speak on anything, from the dirt on the floor to the way the meeting is conducted. The meeting runs twenty minutes over its scheduled time. Jacques Pasquier, the plant's Quality of Work Life coordinator, gently tells Latkowski afterward that he should have moved the meeting along more quickly.

This exchange of information had never taken place before Quality of Work Life and the formation of the groups. It is the heart of what *Business Week* has called "The New Industrial Relations." Members of the United Auto Workers and first- and second-level supervisors are the troops in this war zone. Both groups see the need to protect their jobs from the Japanese juggernaut, and to do so they have agreed to forsake adversarial relations between themselves. It has not been easy.

By March 1982, however, there were about 200 employee participation circles at the Gear, composed of union and management members, searching for solutions to daily technical problems. The groups had also begun to take over more and more supervisory functions. Some of management's supposedly sacred prerogatives were being shared with union workers, a state of affairs that would have been inconceivable only two years earlier.

Fundamental changes in labor-management relations at General Motors have not been limited to those at the Gear. In 1981, 74 of the 155 General Motors–UAW bargaining units had some form of Quality of Work Life Labor-Management Committee. In these unionized—as well as in five non-union—plants, rank-and-file workers consulted with management on a variety of issues. Grievances in many plants had dropped 80 to 95 percent. Absenteeism was down 50 percent on the average, and 90 percent in four plants. Some enthusiasts were saying a new day had dawned in labor-management relations in the largest manufacturing corporation in the world. While their optimism about the permanence of the changes may be premature, there is no question that a significant change in the adversarial relationship between the UAW and General Motors has taken place. The corporation has come from a management attitude of "the workers be damned" to F. James MacDonald, president of General Motors, saying that QWL "has to be the way to run a business."[1]

The problems at General Motors that led to a radically different management philosophy are sometimes seen solely as the result of the new breed of workers' resisting the authoritarianism and working conditions of conventional firms. The difficulties at Lordstown seemed to justify this analysis. A closer analysis of Lordstown, however, indicates that workers there were reacting to conditions that management had created: the fastest assembly line in the world, as well as the merging of Fisher Body Division with the assembly operations of the car divisions to form the Assembly Division. In the company that once epitomized the pinnacle of excellence in American management, more than worker attitude was behind the problems that plagued it in the 1960s.

By 1968 even Chevrolet, the brightest jewel in the GM crown, was losing its luster. The company's return on investment had fallen from 55 percent in 1964 to 10 percent only five years later. Its share of the domestic car market had slipped from 32 percent in 1962 to 24 percent in 1968. (A 1 percent decline in market share meant about $100 million less in gross profit.) Ford's Falcon, Mustang, and Econoline van were beating Chevrolet into new markets. Projections for 1970 indicated a major operating loss, something unknown in Chevrolet's entire post-Depression history.

When John Z. DeLorean became general manager of Chevrolet at the age of forty-four, he was told to "turn it around." Because of its high morale and strict authority, Chevrolet had been known as the "Marine Corps of GM." DeLorean says that he found a management group which was "proud, hardworking, and burdened with an almost impossible business system." Management structure had been the same since 1945, when the division was producing one type of car and one type of truck. By 1967 there were 50 basic models for cars and 292 for trucks.

To understand better the nature of Chevrolet's problems, DeLorean set out across the country to meet with local production staff and dealers. He was not prepared for what he found:

- People could no longer communicate effectively across departments. For example, after the sales staff in Detroit had launched a massive advertising campaign to promote a four-cylinder Nova, it was found that the manufacturing people had taken most of the four-cylinder production equipment out of the plants because demand had fallen so low. No one had bothered to see if the cars could still be built. The result was a disaster; the customers couldn't buy the cars that the advertising had sold them.[2]

- Production managers were ignored. "They had either been lost in the maze between lower management and the top, or had not gotten attention because people were too busy trying just to meet production requirements." Incredibly, no one seemed to have time to look over suggestions for improving the business. One plant manager had a half-dozen or so plans for improving the efficiency of an operation, which senior management had never approved. He said, "I can't get anyone to listen to me!"[3]

- Planning was haphazard. When one manager was told that he had not met his budget for three years in a row, the manager shot back, "Well, how the hell can I make budget? Here are my schedules, and you have changed them every three days for longer than I can remember."

- Trust was minimal. Dealers said, "The cars you're sending us are lousy. Why does Ford get better products than we do? You don't keep delivery promises. We don't believe anyone in the company anymore."[4]

- Product quality was slipping compared to the Japanese and Ford. A year-old Chevrolet in the early 1960s had a $250 greater resale value than a comparable Ford. By

1969 the two cars were selling for the same price, and threatening a loss of Chevrolet business to leasing companies, which did not want to lose money on resale.

- Managers were not held responsible for their budgets. Every department was outspending its budget every year. When problems developed, the solution seemed to be to pour in more money.[5]

- Finally, "The management system had grown up to handle one product line, and it was never changed to cope with a diverse business."[6] When marketing studies showed that Chevrolet's declining market share was due to its not offering the customer enough choice, product lines were added. One hundred and seventy-nine different engine combinations for cars and 299 for trucks were offered. John DeLorean said, "We could build one million Chevrolets, and not have two cars exactly alike."[7]

A vast staff organization, DeLorean concluded, was stifling initiative and also muting orders from the top. "One of the biggest and yet simplest problems," DeLorean noted, "was in the manufacturing staff. It was overburdened with layers upon layers of management. Between a plant manager and my office there were no less than five levels of management. A plant manager reported to a city manager of plants, who reported to the general manufacturing manager, who reported to the works manager, who reported to me, the general manager. Consequently the manager of the Chevrolet Gear and Axle plant was only a few miles from my office, but almost light years away via management reporting channels. There were five layers of decision-making between his proposal for the plant and my approval." What had happened to the famed Sloan system of management invented by Alfred P. Sloan, Jr., president from 1923 to 1946 and chairman from 1937 to 1956?

"In theory," said DeLorean, "the Sloan system of business management for GM featured two functions: centralized policymaking and control, and decentralized operations. The latter meant that the operating decisions for the day-to-day running of the business were made at the divisional level. It was here that you smelled the clay in the styling studios; ran the plants where engines were built, body panels stamped out, and cars and trucks assembled; created the advertising campaigns; worked with the dealers; and managed all the physical aspects which took a product from design to production and from there to retail sale."[8]

While the causes of success or failure in business are complex, Sloan wrote in *My Years with General Motors* that the two most important factors for success were motivation and opportunity. He felt that the former was supplied by incentive compensation, the latter by decentralization. Good management also required "decentralization with coordinated control." "From decentralization we get initiative, responsibility, development of personnel, decisions close to the facts, flexibility—in short all the qualities necessary for an organization to adapt to new conditions. From coordination we get efficiencies and economies."[9]

Sloan also found that "I got better results by selling my ideas than by telling people what to do,"[10] and "selling" became one of the principles of the decentralized organization. This required all levels of management to make a good case for what they proposed. Sloan wrote that "group decisions do not always come easily. There is a strong temptation for the leading officers to make decisions themselves without the sometimes onerous process of discussion which involves selling your ideas to others. The group will not always make a better decision than any particular member would make; there is even the possibility of some averaging down. But in General Motors I think the record shows that we have averaged up. . . . We have been able to adapt to the great changes in the automobile market in each of the decades since 1920."[11]

By the time he had retired as chairman in 1956, however, Sloan had already seen increased centralization at GM. The reason he gave for the change was that "new and more complex problems have resulted in a somewhat closer degree of coordination than existed in my time."[12] He made this observation before the Assembly Division was created, causing confusion and strikes at nine out of ten plants. Peter Drucker has stated that that decision marked the end of the Sloan system, and confirmed the return to centralized control.[13]

Sloan believed that "where cooperation among the various parts of the business was stressed, where management moved through persuasion rather than command, and where decision-making was forced to the lowest level at which it could be made intelligently," the company could be run most effectively.[14] By the early 1960s, however, command and centralization had returned to GM.

Until 1958, the company was run by "operations men," imbued with the Sloan philosophy and under Sloan's watchful eye. Then Frederic G. Donner, who had risen through the financial side of the business, was elected chairman and chief executive officer. Donner had never directed a division. His financial focus was deleterious to the corporation because it made him concentrate on short-term profits, in part to satisfy Wall Street stock analysts and institutional investors. Poor quarterly earnings also reduced his own bonus. Coupled with a general lack of sensitivity to the product, Donner's attitude would prove disastrous for the long-term strength of the corporation. The guiding management principle under Donner, who remained chairman until 1967, was, according to DeLorean, "Thou shalt not contradict the boss." Donner "would rarely tolerate views opposed to his."[15]

Executives eager to scramble up the corporate ladder worked hard to learn what the chairman wanted, then fed him exactly that. In meetings at headquarters, even with fourteen or fifteen executives present, only three people would have anything substantial to say. The rest would speak only when spoken to, or would paraphrase what had already been said by one of the three senior executives.[16]

"Those lauding GM's management from the outside in the 1960s could not see the organizational fissures developing as they looked at the bright figures appearing on the corporate cash register."[17] Even the model division, Chevrolet, began to lose money. It is not surprising that with such autocratic and non-communicative leadership, suspicion and mistrust characterized relations between all levels of management as well as those between managers and UAW officials.

In 1968, with the exception of Edward Cole, who was then president, top management at General Motors seemed united against
even a research project on broadened worker participation. When
Cole told Louis Seaton, director of labor relations, to hire University of Michigan sociologist Rensis Likert to apply some of his
organizational development techniques to a GM facility, Seaton
replied, "Like hell I will! These professors aren't going into any
GM plant. If they are interested in participative management, we
are not. We have paid the damnedest wages and benefits to keep
the workers and the unions out of management's prerogatives.
There is no other justification for the high wages. Participation is
a lot of economic crap."[18]

But at Cole's insistence, GM signed a contract with Likert and
the Institute for Social Research. With their assistance, Delmar
Landen and his staff planned a series of tests and experiments at
GM plants in Georgia and Michigan; GM staff did the training to
increase cooperation between labor and management. After eighteen months, the Lakewood, Georgia, assembly plant had gone
through a complete turnaround, and losses were turned into a $5.2
million profit in 1970.

Just as the results from Lakewood were coming in, the vice-
president for personnel and labor relations, Earl Bramblet, had a
heart attack, and his deputies were not considered by senior management for his job. Cole went outside for a replacement, a move
unheard of at General Motors, and hired Stephen H. Fuller, professor of union-management relations at the Harvard Business
School, in November, 1971. Fuller shared Cole's belief in the potential of the Lakewood results, and to allow Fuller to concentrate
on realizing that potential, Cole split off labor relations from his
responsibilities. To be sure that Fuller focused on spreading Lakewood's results, Cole appointed Frank Schotters, the manager of
the Lakewood plant, as Fuller's deputy. Cole had begun to believe
that confrontation was no longer the only approach in dealing
with the UAW.

Richard Terrell, an executive vice-president, had also become
interested in the Lakewood experiment, but he saw the resistance
of management to the ideas. He invited the heads of all GM divi-

sions to the plant for two days to discuss what Lakewood was accomplishing and what they were doing in their own plants for human relations. Each division head was asked to report on his most significant "pioneering people project." It was rather embarrassing: one division manager talked about his division's tuition refund plan, which had existed for twenty-five years. The lack of enthusiasm didn't bother Terrell. He called another meeting three months later for the same managers in Montreal, then another in Cambridge, Massachusetts, at Harvard and at MIT. Each time, there was more pressure on the division heads not to relate the same stale projects. The so-called Terrell Meetings continued for three years, and eventually evolved into annual executive QWL conferences. In effect, they were a less than subtle way to pressure executives to explore increased employee participation, but they never became part of a coordinated effort from headquarters to mandate an interest in the subject at all GM facilities.

In 1973, Alfred Warren replaced Schotters as director of personnel development under Fuller. As Warren began to explore the dimensions of his job, he went to see F. James MacDonald, then head of the Chevrolet Division and later president of the corporation. MacDonald told him that whatever else he did, he had to get rid of the term Organizational Development (O.D.). "It's too academic, and poison." Warren found a better description of his efforts when he discovered a letter of understanding between George Morris and UAW's Irving Bluestone while rereading the 1973 GM-UAW contract. The letter called for establishment of a national joint Quality of Work Life Committee.

Irving Bluestone was at that time vice-president in charge of the General Motors unit of the UAW. Over the years he had become interested in broadening worker participation: "I came to the conclusion that the work structure in industrial life in any industrial nation is pretty much the same. The precept of 'scientific management'—breaking the job down into little pieces, elements of which are performed repetitively—is common throughout the industrial world. This creates an organizational framework in which management is the order-giver and the workers are the order-takers. Order-takers are told what to do, in what sequence, what tools to use, how much time in which to perform their job; and in addition, they have thirty-six shop rules which have to be obeyed. If a worker challenges a supervisor, he is subject to discipline.

"The notion of unionism is to bring into the workplace not only decent standards in the economic life of the workman and his family, and decent working conditions, but to bring some measure of democratic values. The notion of industrial democracy is what unionism is all about. I began talking about the fact that management rights clauses give to management the sole authority to determine the methods, means, and processes of manufacture. They exercise this authority to the hilt. Workers are not involved in any way in making those kinds of determinations.

"I felt this was wrong and not only an abuse of the individual who is a worker and an adult, yet is treated as a child, but also very bad management. I concluded that 'scientific management' was neither scientific nor good management."[19]

Bluestone decided from his experience that there was a direct correlation between an increasing number of grievances and the hierarchical and undemocratic work structure in which people labored. "If a worker is a free citizen in a free society outside the workplace, involved in making decisions within his family and his community, why then should he be deprived of all those rights when he works in the workplace?" He quoted Tarrytown UAW local president Ray Calore: "Management is stupid to hire somebody only from the neck down and never consider the most important part of the body, the brain."[20]

Despite a number of labor-management cooperative programs in such areas as health, safety, and alcoholism, unions remained suspicious of cooperation on management issues. They were as suspicious of management as Seaton had been of unions. "I must say," Bluestone noted, "that for many years . . . I couldn't find any friends in the labor movement who agreed with me."

During the 1970 negotiations with GM, Bluestone suggested that both parties consider establishing a joint committee to explore ways to broaden worker participation in decision-making. The corporation rejected his suggestion out of hand as an intrusion on management prerogatives.

Between the 1970 and 1973 negotiations, Bluestone continued to explore the issue of worker participation. He traveled to Europe, talking to people in Germany and Scandinavia. He also became involved in an unusual experiment in workplace reform at the Harman International Industries plant in Bolivar, Tennessee. He heard about the results at Lakewood and pressed GM for details—without success.

Warren and Landen, who had become director of organizational research and development at GM, began to think of ways to implement the QWL Agreement by setting up experiments in different plants. Landen had come to believe, from both his Lakewood experience and the survey data on employee attitudes and behavior, that GM's authoritarian management style had lost most of its effectiveness with a growing proportion of employees—younger, better-educated workers did not toe the line as their predecessors had. He also discovered that in those companies which involved people in decisions affecting their work, managers were able to reduce alienation, improve the quality of decision-making, and raise productivity. "Landen and I," Warren said, "always looked for plants that were in trouble because they were willing to do anything, so our greatest successes have always been with plants that were on the brink of failure."[21]

In the early 1960s, based on the attitude surveys and interviews his staff had been doing, Landen also realized that the talent and energy of the people throughout the organization were not being effectively used. He had observed the growing alienation among younger workers, especially at the production and clerical levels. In spite of higher pay and more water fountains, absenteeism, turnover, and sabotage were on the rise. Equally important, the survey data showed that the morale of many managers was falling.

Landen began to study work reform efforts in Europe and Japan. He started working with GM plant managers who came to him with their problems. No one at headquarters was interested in what he was doing. It was as if his box on the organization chart were connected to his superiors' by a faded dotted line. He has said it was like working in a closet in the basement. However, he used his autonomy to advantage.

The management style that Landen found to be effective required decentralized decision-making, openness, fairness, trust, and participation. Ironically, he rediscovered Sloan's principles and extended them.

To try to implement the QWL clause, Warren and Landen invited —with the reluctant approval of the vice-president for labor relations—Irving Bluestone and his chief lieutenants to a meeting, and matched them with their opposite numbers from management. During the several previous meetings of the joint committee over the two years since the agreement had been signed, the vice-president for labor relations had told his subordinates that he would do all the talking. Now, for the first time, representatives of union and management at the top level convened in a situation that was not a confrontation. Warren remembered what happened when Bluestone encountered an executive whose plant was on strike. The executive said, "You know, I'd kinda like to talk to you." The strike was settled the next day.

One of the meeting activities was to play experientially based learning games that paired union representatives with managers. Again, Warren recalled, they'd never had such interaction, and were sure it was "silly as hell. But I can still remember that as I was monitoring one group, an executive said to Bluestone, 'Goddam it, looks like we're going to give it to that other team,' and Bluestone said, 'Yeah, and I think we can do it, can't we? You and I know how!' So here were two guys doing to other people what they'd been doing to each other for a long time." While the meeting ended at five, they sat together over drinks until midnight. "They were fascinated with each other. They'd never had the chance to sit down and talk about things in a non-threatening environment before."[22]

One executive who went back to his division particularly excited was George Elges, general manager of Buick. He gathered his subordinates and told them what he had learned. The next day, Buick's personnel director—for the first time in his life—walked across the street to the union hall to sit down and talk to local UAW leaders.

Management's decision to explore employee participation was not a philanthropic one. The years 1972 and 1973 were slow for General Motors; for the first time, the company had had to borrow $600 million on the open market. Ironically, the borrowing occurred shortly after a laudatory article on GM in *Fortune* magazine. Warren says, "I think we recognized that we were paying the highest wages in the country to employees, and yet were getting the least amount of work. This wasn't the fault of the employees. It was our fault, the way we were managing. So we recognized the need to have every man and woman in General Motors giving us all they could give us in terms of know-how, capability, and what to do." GM had come the full circle from Seaton, who wanted to "keep the workers and unions out of management's prerogatives."

When the management problem had reached crisis proportions at GM, Landen was ready with some basic ideas for a solution. Cole, Fuller, Warren, MacDonald, and Terrell had the motivation for finding a better way. Irving Bluestone provided the vision and leadership needed for cooperation.

If there was ever a plant that exemplified shopfloor discontent, it was the GM plant in North Tarrytown, New York. Management ran the facility by the authoritarian book. As one manager said, "We solved problems by using our authority and imposing discipline." The 3,000 workers hated their jobs, hated management, hated the company. The plant manager observed that "it was during this time that the young people in the plant were demanding some kind of change. They didn't want to work in this kind of environment. The union didn't have much control over them, and they certainly were not interested in taking orders from dictatorial management."[23] Accumulated grievances often totaled 2,000 or more. A union shop committeeman said his job was "purely political . . . just fight the company." He was expected to respond to any grievance, regardless of its merit, and "jump up and down and scream."[24]

There were so many "78s" filed—forms on which to report work-standards violations—that committee men couldn't begin to follow up on them. Workers became frustrated with their unions as well as with the company. Conditions were noisy, crowded, and dirty.

In 1971, General Motors headquarters informed the manager at Tarrytown that his plant was in danger of being shut down. He approached the president of Local 664, Ray Calore, to see if they could work together to keep it open. Calore decided to trust the manager, and took the lead in allowing the plant to continue working through a building trades strike during the 1971–72 model changeover. In retrospect, this was the first step in building trust between labor and management.

The next year, the plant dropped its truck body manufacturing line and decided to set up a new layout. The first real change in procedure occurred with a question raised by two supervisors in the hard-trim department. When they were presented with charts, plans, and tables for the new layout, the question came up: "Why not ask the workers themselves? They're experts in their own right. They know as much about trim operations as anyone else."[25]

At first, union leaders were skeptical of management's motives. But plans for the conveyors, benches, and materials storage areas that were sent to the workers for review provoked a flood of constructive ideas and suggestions which so impressed supervisors that many of them were adopted. This was the first time management and the union had worked together to anticipate rather than react to problems. The event was also novel in that it involved the union in planning, an activity normally reserved exclusively for management.

Joint planning was extended to two other departments, and the following year employees were involved in rearranging another area, the chassis department.

Meanwhile, various voluntary union-management groups had developed to discuss welding problems; in the metal-finishing department, workers and foremen came up with different metal-finishing procedures.

In 1974, Local 664 and Tarrytown management decided to launch a formal QWL project. Both sides agreed that to go through the next stage of cooperation they needed an impartial third party to help them to develop problem-solving capacities, so they brought in consultant and former machinist Sidney Rubinstein of Princeton, New Jersey.

Rubinstein began working with two supervisors and thirty-four hourly employees in the windshield area of the soft-trim department. All were volunteers who agreed to meet after work and on Saturdays to learn problem-solving skills. One problem was water leaking into cars around the windshields. In the discussions between workers and managers it was learned that each worker began applying sealant at a different point on the rim of the windshield. One of them, when asked why he applied the sealant the way he did, said that he had heard about the leakage from a dealer. He had investigated and learned that it occurred where the radio antenna wires emerged. He decided to start and end the sealant at the wires, so that the extra adhesive would develop a puddle and prevent leakage. Until this problem-solving meeting, the technique had not been shared with other workers. Within a few months the percentage of bad leaks dropped from 35 percent to 2 percent.

In the midst of this progress, the oil crisis of 1974 struck the economy and forced elimination of the second shift. The employees with seniority on the second shift bumped many of the new, younger workers on the first one, who were most active in the participation programs. This knocked out the pilot programs temporarily, and when they were started up again, in 1975, only twelve of the original participants remained. They managed, however, to keep the idea alive, and within a few months small participation groups in different departments began to reappear. In late

1975, a major step was taken to formalize the program. A joint committee was constituted, led by the plant manager, the production manager, the personnel manager, the union's top officers, and two QWL coordinators. The committee surveyed 600 workers in two departments and found that 95 percent of them wanted to stay in the program.

By 1977, the performance of the Tarrytown plant, as measured by the General Motors Assembly Division performance index, had moved it from sixteenth out of eighteen plants across the country to first place. It was chosen to produce the new General Motors X car, the Chevy Citation, the Buick Skylark, the Pontiac Phoenix, and the Oldsmobile Omega, all on the same line.

That fall, the Tarrytown plant began taking fifty workers per week through three days of paid training on the concept of Quality of Work Life, discussions of the plant, functions of management and the union, and problem-solving skills. The trainers assiduously avoided any considerations of grievances for contractual matters. They discussed products, model changes, layout of the plant, organizational structure, safety matters, efficiency.

The cost to General Motors for the training was $1.6 million. A production manager said, "From a strictly production point of view—efficiency and cost—this experience has been entirely positive. We cannot begin to measure the savings that have taken place because of the hundreds of small problems that were solved on the shopfloor before they grew into big problems."[26] But two improvements could be measured: absenteeism at Tarrytown dropped from over 7 percent to between 2 and 3 percent. In December, 1978, there were only 32 outstanding grievances, down from 2,000. By 1980, Tarrytown had become a mecca for managers of other companies, for government officials, and for journalists, all looking for ways to reduce adversarial relations and improve productivity.

Tarrytown exemplifies one of four successful approaches that have emerged from the GM plants in the 1970s. The objective of all four, according to Landen, was to decentralize responsibility, authority, decision-making, and accountability. (The approaches are charted in Figure 2 below.) The first is that of Tarrytown, which set out, through training and problem-solving, to increase participation in what had previously been management's responsibility. In this approach the structure of the organization was left untouched.

The second approach alters the old management hierarchy. Management and the union initiated a two-tiered committee structure, as well as formation of employee participation circles for those who want to join, and team-building training. The Gear exemplifies this approach.

The third is the collateral organization, which creates a structure parallel to the traditional pyramid organization. Its basic purpose is to expand the capacity for planning. It also helps to overcome the resistance of many supervisors to employee participation circles by moving at least 10 percent of their time into a different structure, which increases their responsibilities and authority. A major reason for creating the parallel organiza-

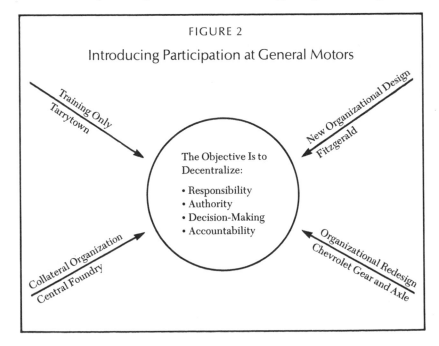

FIGURE 2

Introducing Participation at General Motors

Training Only
Tarrytown

New Organizational Design
Fitzgerald

The Objective Is to
Decentralize:

• Responsibility
• Authority
• Decision-Making
• Accountability

Collateral Organization
Central Foundry

Organizational Redesign
Chevrolet Gear and Axle

tion was the realization that as the rank and file took on more responsibility, there was less for supervisors to do, according to traditional definitions of their jobs.

As Landen explains it, the collateral organization runs "parallel to the traditional structure. Its intent is to get people out of the vertical structure. As you shift responsibilities down, you collapse the organization vertically by putting some of people's time into a collateral system." Such a strategy is being carried out at the Central Foundry in Saginaw, Michigan.

The fourth approach is that being employed at the "greenfields," new plants—like Fitzgerald, Georgia—built since 1972. There, according to Stephen Fuller, "the distinction between labor and management has been eliminated."[27] Managers are "resource people." Employees are carefully screened before hiring. They elect team leaders. There are no pools of additional workers to fill in when people are absent; other team members have to do their jobs. Performance at the "greenfields" is the highest among all GM plants.

In 1976, Ray McGarry became the eighth plant manager of the Gear in ten years. His orders from GM headquarters were simple: make the plant competitive, or shut it down. The forty-two-year-old McGarry was familiar with some techniques of participatory management because he had come from the Chevrolet pressed-metal stamping plant in Parma, Ohio, where some QWL techniques had been tried informally. McGarry's method for making the Gear and its 7,000 employees competitive was to "break the monster into its manageable components, and to use participatory management to accomplish this." He had a vision of the plant as a collection of "small businesses," with all the information needed to run the "businesses" themselves at a profit.

McGarry cut his own staff from thirty-seven to six. These six assumed a variety of planning and control functions. Then he changed the structure by introducing the concept that each of the seven plants at the Gear would become a plant team. (See Figure 3, next page.) Within each plant team were administrative and

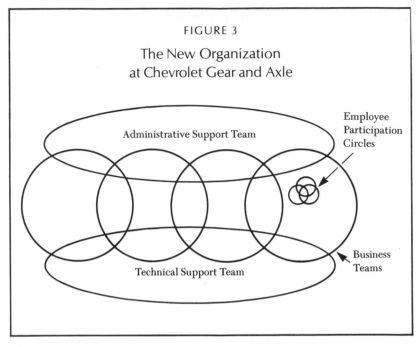

FIGURE 3

The New Organization
at Chevrolet Gear and Axle

Administrative Support Team

Employee
Participation
Circles

Technical Support Team

Business
Teams

technical support teams, plus business teams. The business teams would consist of up to 15 circles and 220 workers.

McGarry's object was a radical shift in the structure of the Gear's organization. He abolished the hierarchical pyramid. He envisioned the administrative and technical team advisers as "resource people" to the self-governing circles built within the business teams. The advisers would coordinate people between business teams and provide help in planning. Group leaders for the circles would be chosen by the employees.

Next, management and labor in a workshop listed their respective goals for the plant: The lists turned out to be quite similar. Everyone wanted better products, less hassle, and greater job security. Then the groups worked on understanding QWL: They sent four union members to another workshop on employee participation circles. They learned statistical methods of judging costs and product quality, and how to make presentations before management.

The process of getting information about QWL down through the Gear was deliberate and slow. At every layer of management or responsibility, there were doubting Thomases. The workers, however, convinced the skeptics when, on their own initiative, they began reaching out for the information they wanted. The work done on the jig grinder, for example, is a final operation. "If the jig grinder doesn't do it right," said Richard Danjin, Gear QWL coordinator and shop committeeman, "you scrap not only that hole it digs but everyone else's work that has gone into the piece before. We've got a jig grinder which everyone has known for fifteen years needs to be replaced or rebuilt. Yet no one ever responded to it."[28]

This problem came up in one of the first meetings of the employee participation circle among the grinders. But the level of sophistication was not high at first. The problem gnawed and gnawed at the circle until after three months the members set to documenting how much money the company was losing by keeping the machine. They went into the costs of materials and electricity, using problem-solving and statistical skills they learned in the group. After reading the circle's documentation, the general superintendent authorized $70,000 for a new grinder.

It is too early to judge how successful the redesign of the Gear will be. There seems to be no slackening of interest from either management or union. John Wojtowicz, a first-line supervisor, says, "I haven't really changed the way I worked since I became a supervisor in 1964. I could always ask someone . . . what should we do on this? We were QWL'ing without realizing it." The most important change is that "the QWL program has given everyone an opportunity to make a contribution. Employees are excited because they were asked to be involved. There is now more trust. They can be honest and not [be blamed] for their honesty.

"We never factored in the people problem before. Sociotechnical design handles the machine and people problems together. Second, everyone in the work area is getting good feedback on his performance. Third, [we get] much more information now: cost data, scheduling information, daily reports on quality control. In fact, we get everything we ask for.

"Fourth, horizontal communications have emerged where none existed before. At the group's request, for example, all the vendors who sell to the group have been in the plant . . . [which] gave the group a chance to stress the importance of the quality of the parts vendors were sending. Vendors met the people who were using [the parts]. The plant superintendent sent members of the circle to the vendors to see the new machines they will be using. When the new equipment comes in, they will work on reassembling it."[29]

Part of a brake shoe assembly, for example, is a spring and a hook. Frequently, either the spring was not properly coiled when it arrived or it would arrive without a hook. People threw the defective part on the floor. A participation circle suggested putting a container at each station for the defective parts, then calling in the vendors to show them their defective work. They developed a new system of lot control to assist in identifying the proper vendor. "Why didn't we do this before?" asked Wojtowicz. "Nobody cared."

John Wojtowicz's enthusiasm is high. "The group has just completed training in problem-solving and leading meetings. They are excited about it. One member of my group had not run again as a district committeeman of the union because of the hassles between the members and management. But he recently told me, 'If this approach takes off, I'm going to run again for committeeman. It would be an easy cake job.' "

Was more money the most important thing to the people in his group? "Money is not the answer to motivation. I have not performed any differently [since I got] my hundred-dollar increase than before. . . . The typical person in this area would like to learn more jobs and be paid more for the knowledge."

Wojtowicz said that several middle managers had mentioned to him that the workers had received a 3 percent increase in real wages, but output of brake assemblies had not increased 3 percent; line speed remained at 500 per hour. "So we talked about that problem. We developed what we called 'a fair day's work' and an 'incentive relief program.' Incentive relief is where you can take a break if you finish your quota. The target we mutually agreed on was four thousand brake assemblies a day. If we ran the line at approximately five hundred sixty per hour, we figured we could reach four thousand and finish at two-fifteen rather than three o'clock. Since nobody else in the world is running a brake line that fast, we have been getting a lot of criticism for doing [it]. But I tell them that it was the men and women on the line who set the rate. This experience has increased the pride of all of us in our work. We want to say that we are working on the fastest-moving brake line in the world and we call it the Amtrak to Toronto. We are not locked into that speed in our contract. The people on the line are controlling it and [it's] tremendous." The new line speed of 560 per hour represented a 12 percent increase in productivity, or four times what management had hoped for.

This experience typifies the union reaction in many General Motors plants. William Horner, a retired UAW official, and now with the Michigan Center for the Quality of Worklife, contends that QWL at GM has enhanced union leadership because it has focused on solving problems, not just processing grievances. "In every place where we've asserted strong leadership [on QWL] we've been re-elected." At the same time, he praised the voluntary nature of the program. "We don't say, 'What's good for me is good for you.' If the individual is happy doing what he's doing, don't screw around with it: leave it alone.

"The whole relationship [between unions and management] is better. We find we've got a hell of a lot more in common than we have in conflict."[30]

A comparable reaction to QWL comes from Richard Danjin: "The old ways simply won't work anymore. We used to get together on Thursday and say, 'Let's all work Saturday and get some overtime.' So we would purposely scrap five hundred axles that would have to be rebuilt on the weekend. You do that now, and you work yourself out of a job, pal. That axle's going to cost twice as much and the Japanese will move in.

"The company is starting to recognize people and . . . [deal] with them on a one-to-one basis. They all sit down and take fifteen minutes to talk about a problem. Ten years ago, that would have been heresy. If you had a problem in the past and went to the foreman, the foreman would just say, 'Screw you—go to work!' "

Danjin says that people don't talk about productivity; they're working at it. "Productivity means that you don't have to build things twice. If I sound like a company man to you, my concern is that these plants be here.

"Management is opening up the books . . . the plant engineer tells the group what it costs to make a casting. They'll tell us what their percentage of profit margin is, and all that. [Chrysler's] not opening up [its] books to Doug Fraser [the president of the UAW], but down here they're telling people what it takes. Maybe in the dark, devious minds of the General Motors Corporation, 'speedup' is what they have in their heads. I don't know. But I do know this. We are getting involved, we are making less scrap, we're getting competitive."

Danjin says that QWL has to be introduced with a combination of "high-minded philosophy and plain old brute force." It takes not so much a carrot and a stick as being sure of the benefits, and having the clout to withstand and overcome jealousy and the threat to the existing power structures of both union and management.

Danjin has teamed up with Jacques Pasquier, QWL coordinator for management. He says that he and Pasquier have been sanctioned "to philosophize QWL into place. His job is to fight off management and mine is to fight the union politicians. We share everything. And we have become literally one person. It's the combination which is so effective. We fight as a team. There's a few of us pairs around GM. We are the cultivators of the process as it grows up out of the ground. We keep the weeds from choking it, put it back up when it rains too hard or someone steps on it."

Jacques Pasquier has been the full-time QWL coordinator at the Gear since 1978. One of the most important results of the program, he said, was the identification of barriers that had slowed the progress of the program. These are some major developments that he described:

- Middle managers were so threatened that McGarry had to evolve an "end run strategy" to get around them. Their basic problem was that "they do not trust their own people, so they find a QWL program based on trust unsettling."

- Some of the superintendents and supervisors "bought into" the program "at the level of language, because they had to." While QWL had become management policy, they did not believe in it.

- Working with the union has been more difficult than expected. "Managers find that they really have to give up ownership in a very important way. When the union has veto power, it is a new situation. Managers are being constantly challenged by workers to learn why things aren't going any faster." They find management holding them back from doing a better job.

- When layoffs are a constant threat, planning and managing a process of organizational change become "particularly difficult."

- Too much publicity, as at Tarrytown, puts a great deal of pressure on a plant to improve performance.[31]

Although managers are reluctant to talk about performance in the participation groups, there have been significant results:

- By March 1982, 52 percent of the Gear's seven thousand employees were in circles, just two years after the first circles had started on the shopfloor.

- After two months of operation a circle in Plant One reduced its scrap cost 50 percent, a savings of $250 a day.

- Controllable absenteeism in the Gear is down from 7 percent to 4.2 percent.

- Grievances are down 85 percent for the Gear.

- The 12 percent increase in productivity on the axle assembly line—the "Amtrak to Toronto"—has been sustained.

- Repairs on the finished product from circles are down 90 percent.

- Management's commitment to the program, already strong, has deepened.

What are the results from the employees' perspective? Tony Kansky, a first-level supervisor for a circle that makes "positraction" gears, gave a questionnaire to the twenty-five people in his group after the project had been going about six months. He said, "The results are very positive." Fourteen of the twenty-five want even more involvement in decisions that affect their jobs. Tony concludes that the circle is a "real breakthrough."

Any member of the union or management, including the plant manager, is at the workers' disposal "to come down to see them to answer questions." Whatever information the groups request, "we give 'em." In the old days the supervisor said, "Do it my way or there's the door." Now we say, 'When you've got a problem, come in and let's talk it over.' "[32]

The people in Kansky's group have begun to act as the big blue-and-white Chevrolet Division poster asks them to—"as if you owned the company."

The development of QWL at GM has not been a smooth, uninterrupted wave that has washed over and cleansed the organization of years of suspicion and antagonism. Nor have the managers and "facilitators" always implemented the program with the patience, balance, and long-range perspective desired by third-party consultants. The surprising thing is not that there have been some failures there, but that there have been so few:

- At Lakewood, Georgia, the first plant where the nascent QWL techniques were tried, there is still no joint UAW-GM QWL committee, because the plant manager tried to impose QWL without involving the local union.

- At a GM Assembly Division plant near Baltimore, a joint labor-management committee was started, but then the plant manager decided that the workforce needed an education in the fundamentals of free enterprise under the capitalist system. The union and management QWL coordinators together brought in an economist who distributed a brochure proving that every worker was a capitalist, and proclaimed how wonderful that was. When UAW headquarters heard about it, Irving Bluestone was enraged; this kind of indoctrination, he said, had nothing to do with QWL. The local union pulled out of the project.

- In Oklahoma City, where a non-union plant was built, management installed a pseudo-QWL project without a joint committee. But the union organizers went to the workers and said this was all very good on the face of it, but it was highly paternalistic because the workers were not involved as full partners.

According to Bluestone, the QWL project in Oklahoma City set worker against worker, and the group leaders became real straw bosses. The United Auto Workers used genuine QWL as an organizing strategy, and the union was voted in. Afterward, Bluestone polled the workers to see if they wanted the pseudo-QWL project continued. It was overwhelmingly defeated. More recently, management and the local union have begun to work out a new program based on co-equal status. "This is not to say that QWL will not be used as an anti-union device," Bluestone said. "The union must simply be cleverer in finding a way to influence the workers to join the union. Instead of allowing management to get the advantage and benefit of these programs, the union ought to do it."[33]

GM management has admitted making mistakes at several plants. Psychologist Howard Carlson, director of QWL research, says that, in the company's enthusiasm, people were sent "into the plants to act as resource people. We called them 'change agents,' which is like putting a button on them and saying, 'I'm here to change you.' Second, we set up a research design which sought to compare management and organizational practices between good and poor operations. With the good plant, however, we had an immediate problem, because its managers asked, 'Why do we need to improve?' and the bad plant rejected the very basis of the definition that got them into the study. Third, we assumed that because we had the support of the president of the corporation, the projects would all flow along smoothly. We assumed too much.

The plants involved, for example, were not given a chance as to whether they would take part in this effort."[34]

The GM and UAW experience provides some lessons about participation. There was no single catalyzing event that launched QWL. There was the alienation at Lordstown and Tarrytown, plus the Lakewood results. Landen had been working for a decade in his closet in the basement. Terrell pushed the managers with his meetings. Perhaps most important was Bluestone, who finally got GM to formalize the opportunity to begin working together.

Carlson argues that one reason for the success of the QWL program has been its very lack of a unified, corporation-wide approach: "I'm sure glad we never had a cohesive strategy." He meant that a project developed by individuals in a specific factory or work site would be far more likely to last. Moreover, its advocates have learned not to peg it to one process or individual. Managers have been told to look hard at the various options, then develop their own programs with the union or alone if there is no union.

Landen says that he is becoming more and more a "structuralist," in that he believes it is critical to build new structures within the organization, as has been done at the Saginaw foundry and the Gear. "If you really want participation, then you have to build a structure where participation can happen. If you want people to accept more responsibility, you don't talk about delegation; you build a product team, and all of a sudden you don't have to delegate anything. If you want better planning, create a parallel organization as at Saginaw."

According to Landen, the GM approach for developing QWL was based on four principles. First, development of mutual trust and respect had to precede everything else. Second, all programs had to be voluntary. Third, GM wanted to create "critical masses and networks of QWL people and programs that are intertwined." Fourth, there has been a change in management's attitudes toward management prerogatives. In the past, GM took the view that management controlled what was happening in the organization, and never sought labor's view. While management still makes final judgments about products and manufacturing processes, hourly employees and union people are much more involved in that decision-making process.[35]

The QWL program remains completely voluntary for the UAW. Either side can withdraw at any time. No ultimate control has changed hands. People are participating in the daily decisions of their working lives, but that participation could end tomorrow.

What appears to have happened at GM is that QWL has become embedded in the organization. As Ted Mills, chairman of the American Center for the Quality of Work Life, has said, "Where QWL works, the ownership of the idea has passed from the organizational development people to the line managers."[36] At GM it has passed to the rank-and-file as well.

"We are promoting an idea," says Howard Carlson, "that management is a body of techniques, knowledge, and philosophy that anyone can tap into and become a manager."

Alfred Warren put the change of management attitude this way: "I think back to an assembly plant. Two people are putting on a bumper. You look at that. You say, what can you do for the quality of their work life? . . . Why not have them talk to salesmen that sell the nuts and bolts, the power guns, and the wrenches? Why not have them talk to the people in our components plant, who make the bumper? Once they begin to do that, they're different people. They now have a dignity. No longer is it just a matter of pay for hands and feet. Now you are paying for somebody to really put his mind to work at it. That's what QWL is all about."[37]

Landen likes to emphasize that QWL at GM is voluntary, but it has come very near to being mandatory for managers. Evaluations for promotion now include the individual manager's QWL initiatives. As Warren says, "We are beginning to evaluate people on their ability to understand [QWL]. We will have to remove some people from their positions because they are unable to understand—just have to say, with great apologies, 'I'm sorry, we just can't have you in this position any longer.' Now, that's a bold move, because we've always backed up our executives, right or wrong."[38] The negative side is that managers may get impatient and feel they must use QWL to compete. GM has always had divisions compete against one another in various ways.

No one at General Motors will discuss the money saved through QWL projects; the standard line is that such considerations are incompatible with the stated purpose of the programs. However, it is unlikely that the corporation would have supported QWL so energetically solely for the sake of the "human" benefits.

One may also find proof that QWL works in the number of local union-management agreements signed prior to national collective bargaining negotiations. In 1973, only six locals settled before the national agreement; in 1976, eight settled; and in 1979, fifty-four settled—forty of which had QWL programs. UAW vice-president Donald Ephlin says there was no question that QWL had an effect on the bargaining, even though union and management specifically agreed to keep contractual matters separate. "When," he said, "people's problems are solved as they occur, and not allowed to fester for up to three years, that is bound to smooth the local bargaining process."[39]

Two events, in late 1981 and early 1982, served to confirm the ever-broadening effect of participation on both management and the union:

In 1981, GM decided to sell its Hyatt roller-bearing plant in Clark, New Jersey, to the plant's eight hundred employees. Faced with a reduced demand for bearings for rear-axle-drive cars, GM found they could produce most of what they needed, and more cheaply, at other plants. The Clark workers hired the Arthur D. Little Company to conduct a feasibility study, which showed that, with some management changes, the plant could achieve a 50 percent increase in productivity. The employees then became seriously interested in buying it. GM offered, and the employees accepted, a favorable price below market value and a three-year contract for bearings. In addition, GM bought $20 million in stock, but without the voting rights attached to the shares or a seat on the board of directors. The employees selected a president, and they now own and manage the plant.

In March 1982, GM and the UAW were forced by competition and the recession to renegotiate their contract six months early.

Union members took cuts in wages and benefits. However, in return, there was a reduction of management prerogatives. For the first time, hourly employees with seniority got job security, profit-sharing, and an end to plant closings, although there was no establishment of employee seats on the GM board. The two sides agreed that both this contract settlement and the favorable terms of the Hyatt sale could be credited at least partly to the greater spirit of cooperation now prevailing in labor-management relations overall. Ray Marshall, Secretary of Labor during the Carter Administration, has commented that "We have all become Japanese in recognizing that we can no longer afford the luxury of business as usual."[40]

QWL and employee ownership will not solve all the company's problems. There is the view that GM is using QWL, stock ownership, and profit-sharing to soften the blow of the immense reduction in jobs that may occur in the next several years. While GM has many other troubles, from high interest rates to foreign competition, participation has made a difference. QWL has succeeded in reviving the interest of many discontented workers in their work and has challenged managers to find a better way.

"Fifteen years ago," says Warren, "I knew that every union officer was a real dyed-in-the-wool son of a bitch. And I'm also sure that those same people I'm talking about knew that I was a first-class bastard. We bred our industrial relations people to conflict. We chose them for their ability to 'fix those bastards.' Now this is slowly changing."[41] GM is moving beyond adversarial relations.

[5]

It Helps to Start with a Crisis

Jamestown, New York

Jamestown is a manufacturing community of 40,000 inhabitants at the extreme western edge of New York State. Local boosters speak of its "centrality," referring to its position midway between Boston and Chicago. Until 1972, its greatest claim to fame was as the birthplace of the crescent wrench and actress Lucille Ball. Since that year, however, Jamestown has become well known for a uniquely American contribution to the worldwide workplace democracy movement: the area labor-management committee.

The Jamestown Area Labor-Management Committee was not a controlled or dispassionate experiment in alternative labor relations. Rather, it was a pragmatic, largely self-help, community-wide response to an economic crisis. Through a network of in-plant committees and training and educational projects, the JALMC has demonstrated one way out of the descending economic spiral of labor unrest, declining productivity, and capital flight that has plagued so much of the Northeast.

"Labor management," as Jamestown likes to call its broad though by no means universal spirit of cooperation, is now, in the words of one unionist, "up there with apple pie and motherhood." "Labor management" is far more than a technique for improved union-management relations. By helping to keep factories alive and saving over 1,300 jobs, cutting the local unemployment from 10 percent to 4 percent, and working out partnerships between classrooms and the shopfloor, the JALMC has probably helped save the entire financial base of the community—and has done it without huge federal grants or innovative economic practices.

. . .

Jamestown was founded in 1806 along the banks of the Chataquoin River, which drains Lake Chautauqua. Before the Civil War, its chief industries were tanning, hatting, and lumber. The coming of the Erie Railroad in the 1860's brought significant changes to the community: the town band played "Ain't I Glad to Get Out of the Wilderness" at the arrival of the first train. As the timber industry declined, local capital was converted into a number of furniture-manufacturing enterprises which first employed Yankee stock, but then began to hire the growing number of European immigrants—many of them Swedes—who were settling in the area. Italians followed the Swedes to work in the furniture and textile mills along the Chataquoin. By 1900, there were fifteen factories in Jamestown, making furniture, veneer, plywood, upholstery, mattresses, and woodworking machinery.

The manufacture of wooden furniture gave way to one of the largest concentrations of metal-furniture construction in the country. Other industries included ball bearings, tents, paving bricks, pianos, photographic paper, wrenches, washing machines, stained glass, boilers, boots, and elevator doors. Most of the factories had between 100 and 400 employees each, and were primarily job shops with batch production, not assembly lines or continuous output. Most were run paternalistically by the men who had founded them: it took the National Labor Relations Act of 1935 to open their doors to unions. After World War II, labor unrest in Jamestown increased dramatically until, by the mid-1960s, both labor and management leaders acknowledged that Jamestown had a "bad labor climate." This deteriorating situation accounted in part for a number of factory departures or closings. Jamestown slid into economic decline.

In the late 1960s, efforts began to find a way out of the maze of suspicion and recriminations that had developed. A representative of the Federal Mediation and Conciliation Service brought together management and labor leaders to consider establishing a labor-management committee along the lines of one established in Toledo, Ohio, in 1946. The Toledo committee's stated purpose had been "The peaceful settlement of labor and management disagreements to remove the impact of industrial strife on the welfare of the community and its citizens." But it did not prove possible to reproduce in late-sixties Jamestown the good-will that had prevailed in wartime Toledo. Labor and management knew that their problems went deeper than the negotiation process—and they already had the Mediation Service to handle that.

A catalyst was added to the tentative discussions between labor and management in 1969 with the election of a new mayor, 29-year-old Stanley Lundine, who had campaigned on a platform of economic renewal. Lundine had roots on both sides of the labor-management fence. One of his first innovations as mayor was to create the post of city ombudsman. To fill the post, he chose Sam Nalbone, a well-known and popular business agent for the machinists union.

Lundine set out to recruit new industry for Jamestown, but his smokestack-chasing trips revealed to him Jamestown's reputation for a poor labor climate. "It was as if we had B.O. or something," he said. "I had thought, with some degree of naïveté, that we could just go out and lure industry into the area, that all we needed was an industrial development program. But then I decided that redevelopment in the conventional sense was just not enough for us."[1]

Lundine and Nalbone met privately with some local labor and management leaders. "We knew that Art Metal [metal furniture] might fold," Nalbone said. "At one time they were the biggest employer here, with fifteen hundred workers. They kept going downhill, even though they built a new building and the company changed hands."[2]

Nalbone's fears were soon realized. Within a year of having constructed a million-square-foot building, the Art Metal Company closed its gates, and seven hundred people were put out of work. This crisis gave Lundine the momentum he needed. He met separately with union and management representatives of a number of factories, and after several months persuaded them to sit down in the same room.

Each side accused the other of causing Jamestown's decline.

Management blamed it on workers' low productivity and featherbedding. Labor damned local businesses for trying to keep out new industry and maintain an artificially low level of wages. But they did agree to meet again under Lundine's stewardship. As the decibel level decreased, the sense of having a common enemy grew, and Lundine was able to get the parties to form a voluntary labor-management committee.

In a path-breaking step, they made a labor and a management leader respectively co-chairmen, with the mayor, ombudsman, and a FMCS official in ex-officio positions. This encouraged the parties to stick together even though membership remained voluntary. As co-chairmen they chose Joseph Mason, a business agent for the International Association of Machinists and Aerospace Workers (District No. 65), and Skip Yahn, plant manager of the American Sterilizer Company (AMSCO) plant. Group discussions soon moved beyond the complaint stage to a consideration of alternative strategies for local economic development, which had previously been left to the business leaders alone.

One choice for the community was to try to slow the decline of manufacturing while converting the economy to a post-industrial model with emphasis on high technology and recreation. A second possibility was to use conventional tax incentives to attract new manufacturing firms. Both of these plans implied rejection of some of the existing companies and their labor forces, and both would require fundamental change in the social and economic structure of the community. The third plan, which was called a "renewal," stressed assistance for local industrial development, the improvement of labor relations, and a search for innovative forms of manpower development and ways to improve productivity through cooperative effort.[3] The committee chose the third route.

One of the committee's ground rules was the deliberate avoidance of any matter covered by collective bargaining, because neither party wanted to be accused of undermining that process. This policy of avoidance became particularly important in the subsequent establishment of in-plant committees.[4]

The committee had to work fast. Even as the Art Metal building stood empty, another local firm, Chautauqua Hardware, announced an imminent closing, which would idle another three hundred workers. Lundine and the committee strove to keep the plant open until new investors could be found. In return for accepting a lower than usual cost-of-living adjustment of 4 percent, the machinists local at the hardware company received Jamestown's first "productivity bonuses." The plant stayed open.

This early success was vital in establishing the committee's credibility in Jamestown's boardrooms and union halls. In the next eighteen months, the JALMC was instrumental in staving off five other threatened plant shutdowns, preserving over 1,300 jobs. Three of the five went from conglomerate to local ownership, and in one plant (Jamestown Metal Products) the employees themselves bought the firm.

A major accomplishment during 1970 (the first full year of the JALMC) was the achievement of a strike-free record. As Lundine said, "It was a most frustrating year. But looking back on it, it unified us." Even as the committee "saved" the first few plants, some members recognized that crisis management could not be a long-term strategy, and the committee agreed to search for funding to hire outside help. Lundine spent an entire year looking for assistance, finally raising enough money, through the Economic Development Agency and local contributions, to pay for salaries. Professor James McDonnell, a labor historian at Buffalo State University, was hired as full-time coordinator. Shortly thereafter the committee also received a small grant from the National Commission on Productivity to bring in a consultant, Dr. Eric Trist, of the Wharton School of the University of Pennsylvania.

Trist, a founder of the Tavistock Work Research Institute in London, was a world-renowned figure in the Quality of Work Life movement. He had developed an interest in participative work redesign and self-managing work teams by studying what the Welsh coal miners had done in the 1950s. The Jamestown effort appealed to him as a way of combining organizational change and productivity improvement at the plant level with community industrial renewal. His vision was the development of a community-based Quality of Work Life center where people from various plants would gather to share information, thereby creating a sort of multiplier effect.[5] Trist was accompanied by two graduate students, John Eldred and Robert Keidel.

People in Jamestown had had little experience with third parties other than federal mediators. At first, the language of behavioral science and organizational development was too remote from their experience. But McDonnell had come from a collective-bargaining background, and he (along with another labor coordinator, James Schmatz) was a master at "understanding two opposing sides, cutting through the verbiage and getting the heat out of the discussion."[6]

With the committee's encouragement, the researchers carried out an analysis of the needs of ten furniture companies in the area. They concluded that there were two major problems facing the industry: (a) an aging workforce, with no mechanism for recruiting and training new workers; and (b) the predominance of small job shops which cramped innovation and slowed response to new markets.

The first element of Trist's strategy to deal with these problems was to establish labor-management committees in individual plants. "It was quite a novel idea for many of us," observed one manager.

One of the first in-plant committees was at the Falconer Glass Company. Its goal was to involve every worker in the production process, to make the enterprise grow and thus benefit both management and labor; the question was, how to do it. Falconer was plagued by excessive breakage of its fragile product, so the workers agreed to implement the president's idea of sharing gains from any reduction of at least 15 percent in breakage losses. Once in effect, the agreement added 5 to 6 percent to the average worker's wages.

The development of in-plant committees did not advance rapidly. Accumulated layers of suspicion, mistrust, and enmity were not to be dissolved in a couple of meetings. The committees had to concur on three levels: that the discussion itself was beneficial;

that cooperation to help the company was worthwhile; and that the monetary payoff was sufficient and equitable.

In 1975, the JALMC received more federal and local funding to send third parties into plants to help management and labor establish joint priorities. Researchers and consultants from Cornell University, under the guidance of Professor William Foote Whyte, took over the roles of outside observers and consultants which had been filled heretofore by Trist and his Wharton colleagues. There was, however, no continuity between the successive groups of consultants. "What was actually encountered was, and continues to be, a pattern of non-linear change, of start-ups and set-backs, of debilitating intrusions from the business environment of the firms and of constant political variances generated by changes in management and union roles."[7]

One of the areas that nevertheless showed significant progress was joint job-costing. It had been particularly difficult for job shops to arrive at correct estimates. For example, in mid-1975, the American Sterilizer Company had sent its plant managers a list of twenty-five items that it was currently buying from outside, and asked them to bid on their production. The company promised that if any plant could meet the outside prices and quality, it would switch to buying in-house. The Jamestown plant manager had no staff to do the study, but at John Eldred's suggestion he submitted the proposal to the labor-management committee, which responded eagerly to the challenge. Calling on the experience of engineers, supervisors, and, especially, hourly workers, a task force came up with a product that could be manufactured at 15 percent below what the company had been paying, and earned the Jamestown plant a three-year contract at $1.5 million a year. Although the plant did not hire additional people for the new production line, management estimated it saved about seventy-five jobs that were otherwise slated to go.

At Hope's Windows, which made custom windows for schools, churches, and public buildings, the estimating department had compiled a dismal record, winning only one bid in ten. The company was even losing money on its successful contracts because the bids were too low. The plant manager had once sent some specifications to another window company, which returned a bid of half that made by his own estimating department. The exasperated manager turned the problem over to Robert Keidel and the labor-management committee. In a matter of months, Hope's success with the bid rate rose to 50 percent. As William Whyte and Christopher Meek, a member of the JALMC staff, noted, "This was not simply because workers revealed to management what they already knew about the jobs. The workers came to understand the elements of costs, and developed cost-saving ideas that would not have occurred to them before. This involvement led them to realize the importance of cost efficiency in protecting jobs. Earlier, when work was slack, workers tended to slow down to avoid being laid off."[8]

Once in-plant committees had been established, the second element of Trist's overall strategy came into play: to make sure that the mechanical skills and talents so necessary to the economic health of the furniture and metalworking industries were passed on to the next generation. Many workers in Jamestown had fought the Taylorization of their jobs by holding on to their knowledge as tightly as they could. They did not volunteer information because it often seemed that improvements led to the replacement of their fellow workers. The committee realized that no amount of capital investment could take the place of the knowledge that would be lost when the older workers retired.

Under its president, Roger Seager, Jamestown Community College had developed an innovative program of teaching "reachout" courses designed to release teachers part-time to address the needs of the community. A brokerage system had been created for short-term skills development in a number of factories. A useful and innovative aspect of the system was the syllabi for training apprentices through the pairing of teacher and skilled worker.

Ten furniture firms faced an immediate crisis: in their combined workforces, there were only three people who could sharpen the blades of the complicated cutting machines on which the industry depended. Two of the three were already in semi-retirement; the third was in his late fifties. Seager offered nursing teacher Elizabeth Black the chance to find a way to pass on their vital skills. For several months, she spent time every day with these veterans, who together had over a hundred years experience. They had never been asked for their opinions or help before. Their suspicions melted in the face of her ignorance mixed with enthusiasm. She helped overcome their nervousness about teaching others, and urged them to concentrate on what they knew better than anyone else—their own craft. The program was a resounding success, and was extended to cover many skills in other factories.

By 1980, over 40 percent of the workforce in the woodworking industry had gone through training to keep the community pool of talent and experience alive. Some larger manufacturing firms, such as the Jamestown Metal Manufacturing Corporation, established their own intramural training programs.

While their interest in labor-management cooperation had been steadily growing, Jamestown officials had not neglected the search for new industry; and in 1974 they were successful: Cummins Engine, the giant manufacturer of diesel engines, announced it would take over the empty Art Metal building and employ up to 1,500 people by the mid-1980s. Cummins has a tradition of innovative and participatory management, and its officials made it clear that Jamestown's revolution in labor-management relations had played a significant part in its decision to settle there. Concurrently, two major local manufacturers, the Blackstone Corporation and Crawford Furniture, announced major expansions.

One of the most successful examples of labor-management cooperation in Jamestown involved the redesign of Carborundum's Monofax plant. This plant (now a division of Standard Oil of Ohio) made crucibles for the glass-manufacturing industry. In the early 1970s, the company was plagued by wildcat strikes because of its changeover to continuous shifts. A new plant manager, Reid Whitworth, observed the development of the JALMC and suggested that Carborundum form one of the first in-plant committees.

In 1974, the company decided that in order to maintain its position in the industry, the plant had to undergo a major renovation, and John Eldred suggested that the labor-management groups form a subcommittee to gather suggestions on how this might be done. While management contracted with a German engineering firm to design the renovations, the subcommittee worked on its own list of suggestions from both hourly and salaried employees. The consulting firm dismissed the subcommittee's efforts as amateurish, and submitted an estimate of $9.1 million for the renovation.

This was far too high for Carborundum officials. As the plant engineer said, "It gave what they thought we wanted, but not what we needed. . . . It was an engineer's dream and a production man's nightmare."[9]

Management turned to the subcommittee and asked its members, two managers and two union men, to develop their own proposal. They in turn solicited suggestions from all of the plant's three hundred employees as to how their respective work areas might be improved. As one member of the subcommittee said matter-of-factly, "It made sense. I mean, who the hell knows better than the guy who works there what's good for him and the company?"

The subcommittee came up with 172 concrete suggestions on everything from placement of equipment to work flow. Over half of these were incorporated into an alternative plan that was turned over to local and division managers for refined cost studies.

The company approved the plan, which reduced the total cost of redesigning the plant by $3.5 million. Local plant managers said that without such a solution, the company would have eventually had to close the plant and idle its three hundred workers. In the words of Robert Franco, the union president, "Corporate management has finally accepted the fact that people on the labor end of work, people who have worked for a living with their hands or bodies, do have a certain amount of intelligence."[10]

Unfortunately, this example of creative labor-management cooperation had an unhappy and embittering consequence. Fifteen Carborundum workers lost their jobs, because the new design permitted the company to assign some workers to two machines instead of one. The union members of the committee were furious, and Franco said he felt betrayed. Management, however, asserted it had never promised that no jobs would be lost; in fact, said the management committee members, they had told the union at the outset that a number of jobs would be eliminated, although they acknowledged that "We didn't do a good job of communicating." Both sides went to some pains "not to blacken this labor-management" (as Franco called the in-plant committee) by blaming it for the loss of the fifteen jobs.

Even so, the Carborundum committee ceased for a time to meet. It took more than a year before the union members would sit down again with management, and then only after attrition in the workforce had led to the rehiring of all the laid-off workers.

The JALMC staff had learned its lesson: without institutionalization of the committee network, individual committees were too vulnerable to shocks. From 1979 on, emphasis was placed on the need for a continuing structure to establish and sustain participation. Christopher Meek took the lead in strengthening the structure of the in-plant committees. He insisted that the two sides jointly write a charter, a statement of philosophy, and a set of rules and procedures, which would take up the slack when a crisis passed and inertia set in. Each committee was to organize "action research teams"—task forces assigned to work on specific problems of production or other issues. Meek and the JALMC staff found that without strong guidelines, cooperation could not be sustained by good feeling alone.

Meek then helped put the new structure into practice at companies in Corry, a small town about twenty-five miles south of Jamestown, across the Pennsylvania border. The largest employer there, Hon Industries, made various kinds of office furniture. Caught in a declining market, the company had had three different owners between 1968 and 1972. The new management tried to improve the labor climate, but even so, there was a long and bitter strike in 1975, with broken windows, tires slashed, and the president hanged in effigy. "We more or less hit bottom," said one union man.

At about this time, the office furniture industry started to change its manufacturing process, but Hon Industries did not move with it. "Our competitors," said Jack Holcomb, a brake operator in the Hon machine shop, "had been installing new equipment which could double and even triple production, while we built a million-dollar office building." Then foreign imports began to take their toll. Management's way to lower costs was to cut piece rates and the incentive plan. "Everybody was trying to hurry, to get more work done. With that, of course, accidents began to skyrocket, and people were going around without any fingers. Scrap rates climbed. The only one in town that was happy about the whole deal was the local scrap dealer. He was riding around in his Lincoln Continental with our profits in his pockets."

In an effort to get outside help, William Dean, a brake operator, and president of the union local, went to the district business agent for the machinists union, Joseph Mason, who was also co-chairman of the JALMC. Mason told Dean about the committee and suggested how to set up its own in-plant version.

The two sides still needed third-party aid to get started. The JALMC coordinators went to Corry several times over the next six months, meeting both sides separately, helping to build trust. Mason said later, "It was an exciting and interesting arrangement, because we went from seeing total and complete adversaries to hearing 'well, maybe he's not so bad'; from talking about the growth that we as individuals wanted, to finding out what labor and management could achieve in cooperation."[11]

Hon manager William Sample said that by themselves, neither labor nor management could see the forest for the trees. "We had a third party sitting there and he said, 'I've listened all day to this. I didn't say anything but I didn't hear you people say anything either. So could you try it again?' And what we found was that when we did it again, we talked through the problems in different terms, and were able to resolve them."

Under Meek's guidance, the Hon partners established their own labor-management steering committee, which was chaired during alternate months by a labor or management representative. Its principal duty was to define areas of concern and assign a subcommittee or task force to investigate them. In four years, the committee formed over twenty specific subcommittees to look at such issues and problems as parking, job evaluation, suggestion systems, and the introduction of a gains-sharing system called Improshare.

Similar to a Scanlon Plan, Improshare set standards against which variations in plant-wide labor productivity could be measured. Gains (but not losses) were split fifty-fifty between the company and the employees. The plan was administered by a committee with members from both sides: the plant manager, the computer department manager, the comptroller (and sometimes the president), and three union members. During Improshare's first three years, productivity increased 11 percent, 22 percent, and 30 percent. As one labor member of the committee said of the system, "I think the secret of our Improshare is not how hard you work, but how smart you work. An idea can be the best thing in the world or the worst thing. Years back, I've heard foremen say, 'It won't work,' and walk away. There was only one way and that was the foreman's way. It's not that way anymore. You give them an idea and if you don't get results, you go to the committee and ask why."[12]

Supervisors were particularly defensive about cooperative problem-solving at first. They had never had to face an employee challenging them with the words "I think we ought to do it this way because it is better."[13]

Jack Holcomb, one of the workers on the committee, gave an example of the way it worked. "I wanted the machine gauges to stay on our machines. For years, people had stolen them from one machine to put them on another. It was a mess and I complained and complained without result.

"Then I got on this committee, and said I wanted those gauges color-coded so they will stay. Finally I got them, and now we haven't lost a gauge since then. Our set-up time has dropped because of this and everything has been great."

Neither Improshare nor the other labor-management committees have evolved without complications. Some hourly workers and even some managers suspected the committee was "cutting deals" behind their backs. Sample said, "Communications are the key to all your undertakings in labor-management. That's why you shouldn't get discouraged if in the first ninety days, things just don't turn all rosy.

"We have all kinds of communications channels at Corry-Jamestown: one-way communications meetings with employees to maybe talk about a new product line or a major customer we've acquired; two-way meetings at the supervisory level, factory manager level, and president's level. There are some employees who aren't going to talk to anybody except the president, no matter what you do. As long as the communications flow and you get the problems identified, you don't care where it comes from."

Some of the major tangible results of Corry-Jamestown's new-found cooperation have been that

- Casual absenteeism has dropped to about 1.5 percent.
- Grievances have been halved.
- The labor-management committee has received over 400 suggestions for consideration.
- Productivity in the first quarter of 1980 rose 26%.

At Corry, Improshare provided some "paycheck enrichment," but the new form of labor-management relations also offered intangible rewards. William Dean said, "I think the most important benefit we have derived from the labor-management, and I think I can speak for a hundred percent of our members, is the fact that now, when you go to work in the morning, you can go in with a smile on your face. That's a very small thing, but it's more important to a lot of people than money. It's something you can take home every night and feel good about.

"You might say I'm a confirmed believer in labor-management. It's the one way that we can survive in this world of foreign competition, rising fuel prices, and so on. This company, when they hire a man, uses the whole man, not just his body, but his brains, too, because most of us come equipped with a brain. The biggest share of people out in the factory want to work for you completely, except for the ten percent that you'll always have and

if they weren't working for Corry-Jamestown, they'd be on relief
and we'd have to take care of them anyway.

"Most workers don't want to be just a number; they want to
have input into their jobs, and we firmly believe that they are the
best people to turn to if you have a problem."[14]

In spite of their success, fewer than fifteen out of more than 100
manufacturing plants in the Jamestown area have had active labor-management committees at any one time. Larry Carter, a
teacher at Jamestown Community College, thought that many
company managers were still hidebound and lost interest if they
didn't realize quick results. "It takes years of relentless pushing to
get some changes. Management knows they should ask for more
participation from workers in decision-making. But it goes against
their values."[15]

Charles Linquist, vice-president for sales at the Webber Knapp
Furniture Company, said that since 1949 his company had sponsored a profit-sharing scheme, in which all employees shared 15
percent of the gross profits. "We involve all our people in management planning, such as product design. We have staff gripe sessions with foremen and key operators every two weeks."

Linquist did not think the JALMC had had a wide impact on
the community. Perhaps labor-management relations had improved at some plants—but then his own had never lost a day to
labor unrest.[16]

One reason for the small number of committees is that cooperation is hard work, and it takes a long time. It is full of ups and
downs. Many committees depend heavily upon the personal trust
that develops between a particular labor leader and a manager.
Part of the initial success depends on the joint recognition of a
crisis, and a willingness to risk losing face by searching for a compromise with the "enemy." Such willingness and self-confidence
are not universal in Jamestown, or anywhere else.

At Jamestown, longtime adversaries realized they had to work
together in order to survive. Individual companies—and, by ex-

tension, the entire community—were threatened by continued battles between management and unions. Over time, labor, management, and advisors worked out the details of cooperation on a plant-by-plant basis. At the same time, they worked together in community-wide activities such as the skills-development program.

All programs were voluntary, and specifically avoided the collective bargaining process. In effect, the three parties built an organization whose driving force was cooperation, not confrontation. No one group ever had veto power over another.

The development of the JALMC was helped by a number of factors. A large number of companies were locally owned, so management had stronger ties to the community than if the companies had been part of conglomerates. Strong unions meant a strong balance of power; labor and management considered themselves equals. There was local political support to back any effort to improve the business climate in the area. By one measure, success has been indisputable: in the 1950s there were 70 different strikes in Jamestown; in the 1960s, 43, and in the 1970s, only 25.[17]

Since the JALMC was started, there have been more than a score of other area labor-management committees established in such communities as Evansville, Indiana; Muskegon, Michigan; St. Louis, Missouri; and Cumberland, Maryland. The largest is in Buffalo, New York, with some 50 committees and 17 companies involved.

[6]

Crow and Cormorant

Japanese Management
in the United States

In 1911, a small volume was published in Tokyo under the title *The Secret of Saving Lost Motion.* Written by an American engineer, the book described ways of scientifically analyzing work and breaking it down into its smallest components for maximum efficiency. The author exhorted his readers to use his new time-and-motion study methods to improve worker productivity. He recommended that all control over work be handled in a management-run planning department. Under management's benevolent guidance, the individual worker would achieve his highest output and be paid a premium wage for it. The essence of "saving lost motion" would be found in "Science, not rule of thumb. Harmony, not discord. Cooperation, not individualism. Maximum output in place of restricted output."[1]

Frederick Taylor's book was an instant success among Japanese businessmen and government officials. Over 1.5 million copies were sold. Employers gave them away free to their employees. A Labor-Management Cooperation Society was established, with a special department called the Industrial Efficiency Institute. Before the end of the decade, there were widespread government-sponsored experiments in navy arsenals, national railroad repair yards, and textile factories. In the railroad industry, intensive, open discussion between labor and management work teams resulted in extraordinary improvements in repair times for train equipment.

There were, of course, deviations from Taylor's preachings, in particular from his exhortation to use time-and-motion studies to arrive at a "scientific" basis for wages. The Japanese preferred to pursue an entirely different direction and to use the recommended measurements to define "correct" job procedures rather than to subdivide work or reorganize managerial tasks.

In the fall of 1980, sixty-nine years after the publication of Taylor's book, the Japan Productivity Center formed the Association to Rescue the United States. The purpose of the group, which soon changed its name to the more tactful Association to Encourage the United States, was to improve the quality and quantity of American manufacturing and to help the United States economy back on its feet. The JPC planned courses, seminars, and films on Japanese production techniques, especially quality control circles as they might be used in the United States.

Masaichiro Muto, managing director of the JPC, said that Japanese managers consider the most important element of productivity to be the rigorous application of quality control, where workers advise management on how to improve products. "American managers tend to be too authoritarian," one Japanese businessman told a newspaper reporter. He recalled a visit to the United States in 1958. "You had so many good things. You must polish it up again."[2]

This rescue mission was formed at a time of organizational soul-searching in the United States. Americans have long prided themselves on their industrial, technological, and managerial primacy in the world, but evidence of Japanese superiority in manufacturing had gradually infiltrated the garages, living rooms, and kitchens of American homes. It was at least partly the burgeoning debate over "reindustrialization" and the financial agonies of the Chrysler Corporation that turned many managerial eyes Eastward. By 1981, the Japanese had taken 23 percent of the American auto market and Detroit was crying "Foul!"

Harvard sociologist Ezra Vogel's book *Japan as Number One* became a modest best-seller. People watched television programs such as "If Japan Can Do It, Why Can't We?"—on Japanese-made TV sets. In the summer of 1981 there were two more books on

Japanese management on the *New York Times* best-seller list.[3]
The United Auto Workers, with 200,000 members out of work,
joined with Ford Motor Company officials to plead successfully
with the government for restrictions on Japanese auto imports.

The last thirty years have seen an extraordinary turnaround for
Japanese industry. From prewar days when "Made in Japan" was
synonymous with shoddy, breakable merchandise, Japan has come
to symbolize one of the highest standards of quality in the world.
It currently outproduces the U.S. in cars, the Swiss in watches, the
Germans in cameras, and the Swedes in ships.

The results of Japanese management efforts were impressive,
especially when compared to their American counterparts. The
following table compares all Japanese automobile producers in
1982 with American companies.[4]

Table 1
Comparison of Japan-U.S.A. Performance

Manufacturing/Machine Stamping Operations	*Japan*	*U.S.A.*
Parts stamped per hour	550	325
Manpower per press line	1	7–13
Time needed to change dies	5 mins	5 hrs
Time needed to build a small car	31 hrs	60 hrs
Total workforce for average automobile plant	2,360	4,250

The Ford Motor Company did a special study comparing its
plants with the Japanese and found that in the latter, output per
worker was three times that in its own plants. Comparable plants
took up one-third the space in Japan. Eighty percent of the Toyo-
tas came off the line with no defects, while the Fords averaged 7
defects per car. James Harbour, a management consultant, found
that while the hourly cost difference between the United States
and Japan is about $500 lower per car in Japan, this is offset by the
$500 shipping charges. Even then, the comparable Japanese car is
$1500 cheaper, thanks to more efficient manufacturing methods,
which are the result of Japanese management expertise.[5]

While one group of Americans petitioned Congress for trade restrictions on Japanese goods, businessmen searched for the "secrets" of Japanese productivity and quality control. Newspaper and television reporters piped back visions of uniformed factory workers singing company songs, running between work stations, cheering the different shifts on to greater production, working ten to twelve hours a day. These images formed an obvious contrast to articles about massive recalls and worker discontent in the United States.

The American businessmen found "secrets" aplenty: an ethnic and cultural unity, an enormous capacity for hard work, "group-directed quest for knowledge,"[6] protected markets, new plants built since World War II, extraordinary capacity for emulation, close relationship between government and business, lifelong employment (albeit for less than a third of the labor force), and dedicated, involved employees.

The most prominent manifestations of Japanese industrial strength on the shopfloor are the teams of workers called quality control circles. There are now over 100,000 of them in Japan. They are study groups of usually eight to twelve workers, led by a foreman or senior employee. They meet regularly to address and solve job-related problems of quality control and, at the same time, to develop internal leadership, reinforce worker morale and motivation, and encourage a group spirit that translates into a strong sense of teamwork on the shopfloor.

The basis for quality control circles, ironically, grew out of ideas brought to Japan after World War II by an American statistician, W. Edwards Deming. Deming defined quality control in a traditional manner: "The control of quality through the application of statistical principles and techniques in all states of production directed toward the economic manufacture of a product that is maximally useful and has a market."[7]

In 1950, Deming was invited by the Japanese Union of Scientists and Engineers to give a series of lectures on statistical quality control. He encouraged his listeners to use statistics to distinguish between problems common to the whole operation and those specific to the individual worker. The former were those common to all machines, such as the purchase of poor thread for a weaving machine. "Special" causes were those related to a specific operator or machine. The use of statistics would help place "responsibility squarely where it belongs (at the local operator, at the foreman or at the door of higher management). . . ."[8]

Deming became a national hero to the Japanese. An annual Deming Prize for quality control was established as a sort of Pulitzer Prize for industry. It remains today a prestigious award for which competition is fierce.

Dr. Joseph Juran, of Columbia University, another quality control expert, went to Japan in 1954 and gave lectures that added a new twist to the subject. He said that quality control should be the special province not of a small number of engineers operating in their bunker of observation and correction but of the entire company. From top down and from bottom up, every person in the company had a right and a duty to raise the quality of the product. Working in joint study groups, each member of the organization should receive training in statistical quality control. Instead of needing platoons of inspectors to watch as workers labor along the production line, the workers themselves would be their own inspectors. This was a reversal of the "extreme division of labor" that characterized Taylor's recommendations.[9]

The idea of quality control circles was the particular contribution of Ichiro Ishikawa, of the Japanese Union of Scientists and Engineers. He started with the premise that neither the worker nor the manager knows the "correct" solution to a problem, so the worker becomes genuinely involved in a cooperative problem-solving process. By contrast, most other motivation schemes, such as Taylor's, assume that the worker really knows what is going on, but won't tell out of malice, suspicion, or lethargy. To obtain his cooperation, it is necessary to cuddle, bribe, or threaten the worker, or treat him or her as anything but a full partner.

Quality control, as developed and practiced in Japan, stands Taylorism on its head. Instead of having the engineer pull all the strings from the planning department, the Japanese push control and responsibility down onto the shopfloor, into the hands of those who are closest to the production process—the workers and their supervisors—and make them a team with a common goal.

According to Keiski Yawata, general manager of Nippon Electric Company, Ltd. (international division), "The American quality control philosophy is one of detection and the Japanese philosophy is one of prevention. It's not a question of which system is right or wrong. Probably the American way fits the American tradition and culture better."[10]

One telling and depressing comparison was made by Professor Robert Cole, an expert on American and Japanese industrial systems, who estimated that at General Motors manufacturing plants the ratio of inspectors to workers is 1 to 10 and at assembly plants 1 to 7. At the Toyota Auto Company, the ratios are 1 to 25 and 1 to 30, respectively.[11]

As an American superintendent at the Japanese-owned Quasar television manufacturing plant in Franklin Park, Illinois, said, "The Japanese feel that the worker is the money-maker and that really we should do everything we can for him. Under Motorola [the previous owner], they always put quantity, not quality, first. It was 'We didn't make rate today, so we brute-force them through.' "[12]

In Deming's view, it could not be overemphasized that quality control depends on the managers even more than on the workers. One of the strongest criticisms of the American work reform movement is that it has been based on a "two-value" logic: all the programs are geared to getting more out of the worker while managers stay as they are. "Often an American businessman feels that if he needs help, he will be considered unqualified for the job, and he must not let that happen. It is precisely the opposite in Japan."[13]

Deming is leery of the sudden popularity of quality control circles in the United States. "I'm afraid that transplanting and shortcut attempts to copy the Japanese are just not going to work. Transplanting circles may be of some benefit, but will not accomplish what has been accomplished in Japan because the group spirit does not exist here—not yet."[14]

There are other conditions for success that are absent here, particularly the lack of guaranteed employment. "Do you think a quality control circle could get people interested in improving the job, working as a group, if they're all going to get dumped in April, or half of them get dumped if business goes down? How are you going to form a circle of people that are recently hired, some off the streets, some that have been there right along, and some who have just gotten canned? There has to be some stability. People have to know they will be on the job years from now. In Japan, [management] is responsible for the employees, for their welfare, *forever.* That requires that you look ahead to stay in business, not just make a quick buck."[15]

American businessmen began to take a serious interest in quality control circles in 1974, when three Lockheed Aircraft engineers returned from Japan awed by the extent of participation there. The concept spread quickly to other corporations, including American Airlines, Northrup, and Hewlett-Packard. A half-dozen consulting firms specializing in quality circles sprang up, promising boosts in productivity and happier workers. One company that installed the quality circles was Westinghouse Electric Corporation. The president of the corporation's Public Systems Company commented, in an advertising supplement in *Business Week* on office productivity, "We are concentrating much of our short-term attention on participative management programs such as quality circles. At the same time, we are seeding technology efforts for both the office and the factory to keep our productivity momentum going for the rest of the decade and beyond. By putting the people programs in place first, we expect to multiply the productivity improvement effectiveness of the technology and capital investments that we will be making in the years ahead."[16]

By the spring of 1981, Harvey Davis, executive director of the International Association of Quality Circles, estimated that over 750 U.S. companies had installed an average of 10 quality circles apiece. Sounding like a convert to a new religion, he said that the idea of participation answered even deeper psychological needs of workers than are usually recognized. "This concept will operate in any industry, manufacturing or service, and in any culture."[17]

Larry Schmaizl, one of ten welders at the Kawasaki motorcycle plant in Lincoln, Nebraska, worked for three months in a sister plant in Kobe, Japan. He said the devotion to the company shown by the workers there was "amazing. They have lots of pride in their work. Everyone takes care of their own mistakes. They will do anything they are told. The job is number one and their families are number two. We are not nearly as dedicated to our job. They don't mind working overtime. They don't even plan their Saturdays because they are so frequently asked to work overtime. . . . If that ever happened in Lincoln, there would be a revolt."[18]

By 1980, Japanese companies had an estimated 200 factories in the U.S. with a total investment of $5 billion. We conducted a series of interviews at three Japanese-owned plants in the United States. Only one of them had introduced quality control circles by 1981, although they all held informal, weekly meetings. Two are well known: Kawasaki and Quasar. The third is a chemical company bought several years ago by the Denka Kagaku Kogyo Corporation, which makes neoprene, a synthetic rubber. We concentrated on talking to the plant managers (all Americans) because we felt they were in the best position to compare American and Japanese leadership styles. They are not local figureheads for their Japanese bosses. They don't serve tea or lead their employees in a company song. But each, in his own way, observed that he probably held his job because his management style and philosophy meshed comfortably with those of his Japanese superiors.

A few miles northwest of the Lincoln, Nebraska, airport, rising out of the cornfields and near some new, lonely-looking housing developments, is a gleaming white factory whose golf-ball-shaped water tower bears a red modernistic letter "K." Beneath that tower work two Japanese and 600 Americans who annually produce about 70,000 motorcycles, snowmobiles, and engine-powered Jet Skis for Kawasaki Motors Corporation. The bread and butter of the plant is the KZ400, a large street bike.

The plant manager, Dennis Butt, has made numerous trips to Japan, but says bluntly, "We don't do it the Japanese way; we do it the American way here."

Butt has the presence and conviction of a preacher, the numerical mind of an engineer, and the bearing of a Marine Corps drill instructor. He spends one or two hours a day—"still not enough" — on the floor, listening and talking to the workers, who are a youthful lot, averaging twenty-six years of age. He thinks the Lincoln plant has a "unique opportunity to pick the best of the Japanese and American systems and combine them."[19]

"My boss knows what it takes in Japan, but here he doesn't know how to keep workers in a positive mood. So he leaves that up to me. He wants two things from me: deliver on the production, and stick to the financial plan. The things he takes for granted are that I will take care of the people and the buildings. He doesn't want any problem with employees. He wants people to feel part of the team. The main thing is you don't become what they call a 'nail,' something that things stick on."

The Kawasaki Corporate Philosophy includes the following paragraph:

> *People Oriented:* The success of Kawasaki depends upon its people; people who are bright, willing to learn, and who respond to dynamic situations. People who are dedicated to teamwork and understanding of each other's individual rights and responsibilities. People who work for the same objectives in a determined atmosphere of success. People with a pride in themselves, their fellow workers, the products produced and the role they play in the society as a producer and economic contributor. . . .[20]

"Once you make a commitment to the people and the product," Butt said, "the improvements are infinite. One of the few Japanese influences we have here is to keep the damned price down and push that labor content down. Don't get rid of people, get more products. If I've got ten people working today and can do it tomorrow with eight, that means I can build more products. One thing that the heavyweights in the U.S. always think is: how can I get rid of some people? That's not the key. That's a decline. You have to think positive. That's not Japanese; that's the way I am, always have been."

Butt runs a very lean organization, with six administrative staff, about 100 non-production personnel, and about 500 workers on the floor. He works most closely with his personnel chief, Robert Summers, a transplanted Ohioan with degrees in economics and business, and previous experience at the Radio Corporation of America. Like Butt, Summers has read widely in Japanese culture and history. He said he wanted to work for Kawasaki because "personnel is prime with Japanese companies and the drive for much of their success comes from the bottom up to the management."[21]

Summers said that the Nebraskan work ethic, and a willingness to put in a hard day's work for a day's pay, was definitely part of Kawasaki's decision to locate the plant in Lincoln. Butt added, "We've got five hundred good, solid Nebraskan kids. They all have good ideas and all want to do a good job. They're all just like I am. By and large, they all grew up in a rural life; they had to get up and do chores before they went to school. They know what living's all about and what being happy's all about.

"We look for good citizens [as employees] first. I don't mean I expect them to shine their shoes every morning or go to church on Sunday. What I mean is people who are making a contribution and feel a responsibility to others. The thing you can't train a person to do is to be a good person. You can train him in anything else, but if he's a snake, you can't beat it out of him."

Even though Butt gave unstinted praise to the Japanese for their "horizontal communications," he had reservations about how well they would work in the United States. "I was brought up as an individual to be responsible for what I do. That's where the creativity comes from in the U.S. and that's why you don't see any in Japan. You don't get individual recognition in Japan. The group gets the recognition. I think I'm creative and imaginative and I'm proud of it. I have maybe fifteen ideas up here and fourteen of them are real dogs, but one of them's a winner. You have to listen to all fifteen to get the good one."

Butt believed that consensus is easier to reach if you concentrate on *what* is right, not *who* is right. "The Japanese are extremely good at that. It's not a personal thing. They set themselves aside. If you and I are knowledgeable about something, yet have different opinions, then obviously one of us is right and one is wrong. And it really doesn't matter who's right and who's wrong. Most Americans get blockheaded. They build a wall in their heads, and even when they are wrong, and they know they are wrong, and have been proven wrong, they'll stand and fight to hold their ground.

"What works best for us is to go out there and talk to people, tell them what we want—that is, good quality and zero defects coming off the line—and let them develop their own strategy. The objective of quality control circles is to improve the quality. That's our objective too, only we don't need a formalized system to do it. With our independent people here, the best system is to just tell them what you want and then get out of their way and let them do it."

In 1974, the Matsushita Electric Industrial Company, Ltd., took over the ailing Quasar television arm of Motorola for $109 million. Some observers thought Matsushita was making a mistake. Quasar had suffered from long-term mismanagement, had lost $3.8 million in 1973, and was headed for more red ink in 1974.

Over the next couple of years, the new parent company closed two satellite factories, decreased the number of employees by more than 50 percent (including a 30 percent cut in management and staff), and put $4 million into new equipment. By 1980, Quasar appeared to be solidly in the black.

The company produces about 600,000 television sets a year. The total workforce in 1980 was 2,500, of which 1,700 were in manufacturing. Only a score of employees were Japanese. Like Kawasaki, the company has not yet introduced quality control circles to the American subsidiary, although there are weekly meetings among small groups of employees.

When Motorola owned the factory, the television defect rate ran 120 to 140 percent, which meant that each set had to be repaired 1.2 to 1.4 times before it left the production line. Today, the defect rate is between 4 percent and 7 percent. Where Motorola had seven inspectors per line, Matsushita has one.

In 1979, Matsushita installed a 24-year Motorola veteran, Richard Kraft, as president. Kraft is a Purdue engineering graduate who chooses his words carefully as he talks under a black-and-white sign similar to ones all over the plant. It reads:

1980 Management Slogan
REACT QUICKLY RESPOND WISELY
The President

"Perhaps one of the reasons why I'm president of the company at this particular time is that my own style is very compatible with the Japanese," Kraft said.

"Many American companies and managers tend to be very autocratic by comparison to the Japanese, who lean over backwards to develop a consensus, to communicate horizontally, to listen to what people have to say. That's been my technique through my life anyway. I believe in selling first one person, then another and another, until everybody is together, and then you go forward as a team.

"If you ask people who work for me now, I think in general they would say they're more informed about what's happening. They feel that they participate more in the discussions and have a better understanding of where we're going, and are more comfortable with the decisions once they're made.

"If you look at the total cycle from the first idea to the final completion of a project, the time it takes to arrive at a decision that gets published is substantially longer. The time for implementation is shorter and the result is better.

"My Japanese compatriots are masters at pulling together the details, organizing them in an understandable way. [In the United States] we talk about a piece here, we pick up a catchword there. We grab it out of the total program and say, 'Well, there's the cure-all. Let's throw in this quality circle and that'll take care of everything.'

"The Japanese, particularly in the early days, said, 'We just don't understand how you do business here. We look at your organization, you have a functional organization. It appears to us that the vertical communication is very, very good.' But, they said, between departments it's terrible. There are virtually walls between departments.

"The Japanese make the moving of a product or a project from one department to another a horizontal move . . . engineering to manufacturing, for example. They make an event out of the hand-over. Everybody knows that it went from this department to that and now we're in a new phase of development. And they know it's a good quality transaction or we wouldn't have let it happen."[22]

Kraft, like Dennis Butt at Kawasaki, says that the Japanese believe that top managers should know their factories inside out. They should be able to explain all phases of production, know the people on the line, and stay in close touch with their first-line supervisors.

"Many American managers, if they walked through the factory, wouldn't be able to tell you beans about what was there. They tell me management is a profession unto itself, that it doesn't make any difference whether you are managing a television factory, a semiconductor factory, textile factory, or whatever. Management's management. It isn't! You have to know the product. You have to know the market. You have to know the customer. You have to be involved."

Quasar's financial turnaround is sometimes cited as being almost miraculous, as if the Japanese had exported a magic fix. Kraft said, however, that its success was primarily due to good, long-term common sense.

"There's no one best answer to everything. It's doing a lot of things right. We pruned our overhead. We put in automatic assembly equipment and an improved computer control system for materials. We put in some additional equipment in our lines to help facilitate some of the heavy work.

"It's the gamut of things that you could read in any management book about how to improve a company. But it's a matter of doing it as a team in a coordinated fashion, with the backing of a company that wants to make it a success and is willing to look at a little longer term and say, 'O.K., you say you can't make a profit for three years, but in three years you can, and here's how you get from here to there.' "

.   .   .

In 1976, Denka Kagaku Kogyo K.K., a large Japanese chemical company, bought a portion of the Petro-Tex Chemical Corporation, in Houston, Texas. Denka already produced neoprene rubber in Japan and wanted to do the same in the United States; it was easier to buy an American company already producing it than to build a new plant.

Out of 380 employees in Texas, Denka has a Japanese president, two Japanese assistants to the president, and three Japanese technical liaisons to the parent company. The rest are Americans.

Marvin Woskow, executive vice-president and the senior American at the company, is a chemist who has worked all his life in the middle of the world's largest petrochemical complex—the Houston-Galveston axis. He said, "At least up to this point, management style is the same as it was under Petro-Tex, especially at the shopfloor or the control-room level. But philosophically I think there's been a difference in attitude that does go down to the shopfloor."[23] Under the new philosophy, managers spent the first eighteen months in "base-building" to develop more harmony between themselves and the workers. He said the parent company wants to have a marriage of the best of both Japanese and American styles of management, and to achieve this they are willing to take some time.

The first base-building attempts were called the Gold Rush Programs. Management, in cooperation with the unions, set a series of targets for production, safety, and housekeeping, asked for and received cooperation from all four unions at Denka, and then posted the guidelines throughout the organization. Each target had a monetary value and if the target was met, all the employees shared in the pool as a sort of gains-sharing plan.

In addition, the company established a joint committee of management and labor, which quickly became known as the PIG (Productivity Improvement Group). For a year, its members worked full time promoting the Gold Rush program by sponsoring dances, safety contests, and slogans, and generally opening lines of communication.

"We attempt to involve as many people as we can," Woskow said, "but it's just a slow process to get everyone nurtured to the idea that they should participate in these activities. For public purposes, I think, there's going to be some knee-jerk suspicion. The union reaction to all this has been more bark than bite. In actual practice, I think the unions have been particularly cooperative. I wouldn't say that union management has been business-oriented, but they have certainly been concerned about the business. They realize that their livelihood is on the line."

In the spring of 1981, Denka decided to institute quality control circles. The need for support from the top, so vital for sustaining American work reform projects, is not even an issue in Japan. "We wanted to move toward a participation system that would allow delegation and problem-solving lower down in the organization. The benefit of being Japanese-owned was that it was an easy job to sell it to management because management was trying to sell it to us."

Woskow was aware of the potential for expecting too much from the quality circles. "Everyone warned us, 'Don't rush into it. Think about the steps.' I think the incidence of failure in the U.S. will be a little higher than in Japan. [QC circles] are the hula hoop of today, so we're all going to join the hula-hoop crowd. Some will fall by the wayside. It's hard for me. I keep pushing to get something going. And the guys who are more familiar with it say, 'Cool it a little bit.' "

Woskow is convinced that rank-and-file workers are more than willing to solve production problems if given the tools and a structure such as quality control circles. "I don't know how we've been able to keep them from doing it for so long. It seems like there is an insatiable desire for information from the workers. I think it's universal. I don't care if you work for General Motors, or Ford, or here, you want to know how things are going, first off with the unit, and secondly with the company as a whole.

"There's a general tendency on the part of most managers not to give out information. They think the workers don't need to know that stuff.

"I tend to overcommunicate. There are people who say to me, 'You talk too much. You shouldn't be giving out this information.' But it's a matter of philosophy. The Japanese, in general, tend to overcommunicate as far as we're concerned, so I feel comfortable."

What is striking about these three American managers is the similarity of their views on Japanese methods of organizing work.

Each of them is obviously competent, thoughtful, and enterprising. Each is a good listener and likes to spend time on the shopfloor. Each acknowledges that he was probably chosen for his present job because his personality and management style are more consensual than authoritarian. All three praise the Japanese for their commitment to the long view, the upward trend line, and the group spirit. At the same time, they feel that the Japanese ideal of complete selflessness is impossible to find or develop in this country because of the force of the individualistic tradition.

Each man placed great emphasis on continuous communication with all employees. For Woscow, it was reflected in his tendency to "overcommunicate." For Kraft, it meant breaking down walls between departments. For Butt, it involved spending time on the floor, where he could get "four hundred ideas a minute" instead of the one which surfaced when he was alone in his office.

These men seemed determined to use the best of both systems, most of which resembled American management techniques used twenty or thirty years ago, but since forgotten. Indeed, Butt observed that his Kawasaki plant in Nebraska was doing nothing more than "implementing Peter Drucker's philosophy to emphasize your strengths and make the weaknesses irrelevant."[24]

Many Japanese firms that have begun operations in the United States have been reluctant to try quality control circles with an American workforce, even though they use them extensively in Japan. This caution stems from uncertainty about whether Americans have the necessary commitment to join and sustain team efforts.[25] Participation through quality control circles obviously works in Japan. Americans should realize, however, that there are strong influences and traditions there that do not exist here: those of the family unit, respect for authority, and group behavior.

Professor Robert Cole does not believe that quality control circles will spread unless American management and labor make a long-term commitment to improve both productivity and the quality of work. "The voluntaristic principle [of QC circles] will have to be maintained more firmly to fit the expectations of American workers; overtime wages must be paid for extra time the workers put in at the work place on QC activities. But these changes are to be expected. Just as the Japanese adapted Western ideas on quality control to develop the QC circle, so will Americans adapt QC circles to fit the needs of American management and labor."[26]

More than 750 American firms which are not owned by the Japanese are also using quality circles. Some, like Westinghouse, have over a thousand circles and are adding them at the rate of five a week. Few failures are reported, while the financial returns in the first year or two are high, averaging two to six times the cost of the program. Eastern Airlines claims returns of eight times the cost.

But how long will a quick fix last once its salesmen depart? Cole's suggestion that Americans will adapt quality control circles to fit their needs still appears overly optimistic.

Wayne Reiker, president of the Quality Circle Institute and a leading promoter of circles in the United States, sees their acceptance being hindered by two basic problems: middle management resistance to letting workers solve problems that managers used to solve in the past; and logistics, such as the difficulty of finding time for a group of assemblers or nurses to meet for an hour without bringing an assembly line or a hospital floor to a complete halt. A third problem is that the companies do not share the gains from productivity increases fairly with the employees, and this causes resentment. Two additional difficulties are that: top management does not understand and support the circles approach; and the circles, after a year or two, begin to run out of problems to solve.[27]

An important distinction needs to be made between the typical quality circle program and a Quality of Work Life program which includes participation groups or circles. The normal quality circle effort is only for developing solutions to problems; management makes the decision whether or not to accept the solution.

The average QWL program is closer to autonomous groups which solve problems and usually do not need management's permission to implement the solutions. At the beginning of the typical QWL program, the shopfloor circles may go to management to get approval of most of their decisions. Over time, however, they take on more authority for making the decisions that affect their work. Both approaches give the employees more participation and control over their work than they had before, since they usually were not even asked to solve problems. But the QWL approach sets fewer constraints on the kinds of problems that the group can work on, and lets it make more decisions about solutions to be used. One approach is not necessarily better than another for a particular organization.

One manager who worries about a possible letdown from emulating the Japanese is C. Angus Wurtele, president of the Valspar Corporation in Minneapolis, Minnesota. He warns, "Quality is the catchword now, but that's really a cover for a whole lot of other things. I think many companies are going to be in trouble touting the quality theme as the Japanese have done. The Japanese haven't stumbled on this overnight. It's been a long, deliberate cultural phenomenon and there's a very different perspective on it by the workers." Wurtele predicts a "comeuppance" for the quality control circle fad that will "probably be worse than almost any other we've had in American business management."[28] Americans who are tempted to reproduce too faithfully every detail of Japanese management methods would be wise to recall the proverb "The crow imitating the cormorant drowns in the water."[29]

One interesting aspect of Japanese industrial success is the lack of a clear division between manager and managed. Many Japanese managers have worked their way up through the ranks and truly believe that everyone contributes to the well-being of the company. The adversarial system of labor-management relations is not nearly as entrenched there as in this country. An estimated one-fifth of company presidents of large Japanese firms were formerly presidents of the company union.[30]

Several aspects of the Japanese system of management need to be remembered. Only one in seven Japanese workers belongs to a quality control circle. Only 28 percent of the workforce has "lifetime employment," and then just until the age of fifty-five. The other 72 percent work in smaller firms, which have the highest bankruptcy rate in the world, three times the American rate. Women workers in all firms are hired and fired before men are, as demand for products rises and falls.

By early 1982, the quality control circle movement was in full swing. One conference limited registration to 800 people, but 1,200 showed up. Managers were desperate to hear about this new technique which seemed to promise packaged motivation.

Understandably, American managers long for the discipline, devotion, enterprise, and skill that the Japanese seem to get from their workers. Quality control circles packaged and peddled by consultant-salesmen seem to offer these managers a quick and easy resolution to many managerial problems. Just add a few drops of the milk of human kindness, stir in a little overtime pay, warm the concoction with a big "presentation" to management, and *voilà!* instant employee involvement. It's cheap. It's quick. Management doesn't have to surrender any real power.

But fads are endemic to our society, in management fraternities as well as with the public. Are quality control circles just the latest managerial "hula hoop," as one skeptic suggested? In 1981, some signs appeared that earlier quality control circle programs were developing problems.

First, after experiencing the excitement of problem-solving, a number of circle projects ran into the walls of managerial indifference or worker boredom. Both parties lost interest when the circles could not (or were not encouraged to) move on to tougher problems.

The second problem arose from the first: quality control circles or employee motivation schemes are not usually at the center of the company universe. When a company is most concerned with a tight production schedule, for instance, the question arises of whether participants must be paid overtime. Do superfluous workers have to be built into the process so that output can be maintained while the circle meets once a week? American managers usually want to know the immediate financial cost of participation. Workers also want to make sure they are paid for any extra effort. As consultant Tom Rohlen said, "One can't make hard and fast rules or say, for example, 'No overtime should be paid.' It has to have a quality of voluntarism and spontaneity to be of much motivational interest. It may mean that the company has to give up some regular time to it. That's a real leap of faith."[31]

In Japan there seems to be a greater "belief in human potential, sincerity and trust. Americans often don't give the other person the benefit of the doubt. It is more fundamental than fairness: if you believe this person really does want to do as well as he or she can and you let them know that, it's likely to encourage them to do a little better."[32]

Richard Danjin, an auto worker at General Motors's Chevrolet Gear, who is deeply commited to the GM-UAW participation teams, offered the following counsel to instant Japanophiles: "Over there, I take you into my company, I see to your wedding, I see to your children, I loan you mortgage money for your house. I take away all those distracting things that go to survival so that when you come to me to build whatever it is I'm manufacturing, you're trouble-free.

"The American mind will never get to that point. We're all too egotistical. We're all too busy trying to make a million dollars."[33]

[7]

Participation But Not Control

Vermont Asbestos
and South Bend Lathe

In the wake of the 1973–75 recession, many communities in the Northeastern United States were devastated by the loss of major firms. Most did not have the resources to respond, but in a few places there were efforts to save the companies and the jobs.

Communities abandoned by their corporate citizenry usually did little beyond wringing their hands, hurling a few choice epithets at the departing factory owners, lobbying for unemployment benefits with their local congressmen, and searching for some new business to come to the empty, dirty brick shells. After all, how else could they fight a corporate financial policy which focused on short-term success? Who could prevail against decisions to drop subsidiaries that didn't fit corporate guidelines?

In the communities of South Bend, Indiana, and Eden, Vermont, however, such cold financial logic met with fierce resistance. Employee and community anger distilled into enough resolve to find the money to buy the companies and save the jobs. These communities refused the "inevitability" that workers must either follow capital to the Sunbelt or go on welfare. The employees, managers, and community leaders in both places were not particularly interested in industrial democracy or broadened employee participation. Their concern was economic survival.

The creation of the Vermont Asbestos Group (VAG) was one of the most publicized employee takeovers in the 1970s. There was some-

116

thing affecting about the plucky miners in the desolate northern Vermont hills raising the money to buy their own jobs. The situation warmed hearts across the political spectrum. On the left, it was seen as an assertion of worker control, a spontaneous collective decision to take charge of their lives against conglomerate heartlessness. On the right, it showed that the capitalistic desire for ownership was the principal drive motivating individual workers.

Before analyzing what happened at VAG, it is worth remembering that none of the major participants had any desire to break new organizational ground. They were not out to prove that industrial democracy could flourish. To a man, they believed that work under an authoritarian style of management was infinitely preferable to no work at all. As one miner remarked when told that asbestos might kill him in thirty years, "Starvation will do it in less than one."

Lamoille County, Vermont, contains both the wealthy playgrounds of Stowe and the hardscrabble farms around Eden, near the Canadian border. In that section of the county, one resident observed, "Poverty may be our most important product, because it brings in the most money."

The largest employer was the General Alkaline and Film (GAF)–owned mine in Eden, which supplied about 80 percent of the United States production of chrysotile asbestos. This kind of asbestos is used primarily in chlorine manufacture and friction products, such as auto brake linings. Early in 1974, worried about the extent of remaining reserves, GAF announced it would close the mine in one year. Company officials added that they were unwilling to install $1.25 million in additional anti-pollution equipment required by the Environmental Protection Agency. The decision made good corporate sense, but for the miners and the surrounding economy, which received $3.6 million annually from the mine, it was a devastating announcement.

It didn't take long to rouse both managers and the rank-and-file to action. Within ten days, the president of Local 388 of the Cement, Lime and Gypsum Workers Union called a public meeting at a local bowling alley owned by state representative Alvin Warner. Calling themselves the GAF Employees and Friends

Committee, they elected maintenance supervisor John Lupien to explore the options. They were: (a) appeal to the EPA to relax its regulations to permit GAF to continue running the mine without the pollution control equipment; (b) search for another company to buy the mine; and (c) find out if the workers were interested in purchasing the mine and running it themselves. This last was Lupien's suggestion.

For the next several months, the committee explored these options. EPA refused to relent on its requirements—the agency had already extended the deadline three times for GAF—and no other corporation seemed interested in taking over the mine. It became clear that the employees would have to buy it themselves to keep it open.

At first the notion seemed ludicrous. Miners, managers, community leaders, and state officials were disbelieving. But Lupien pushed the idea in every forum. More than any other single person, he was responsible for the creation of Vermont Asbestos Group, the new stockholders' association. Friends and foes later acknowledged that without his unquenchable optimism and drive, the mine would have closed down. After a feasibility study showed that rising asbestos prices would enable the company to repay loans guaranteed by the state, Lupien led the effort to enlist support of local and state industrial development officials to assemble a sensible financial package.

The final package was a complicated mix of state and federal guarantees, a GAF mortgage, and 2,000 shares of stock priced at $50 per share. With a maximum of 100 shares per person, employees bought about 80 percent of the stock. Each employee acquired at least one share; the average was six. One mine accountant purchased the maximum of 100 shares. Rank-and-file employees took just over 50 percent, but they did it as individuals, not as a bloc. Members of the community bought the other 20 percent. One of the latter was Howard Manosh, a local contractor and well-driller.

Financial arrangements were not completed until the last moment. So much time and energy went into the financial preparations that the employee-owners-to-be gave little thought to the structure of their future company—in retrospect, a fatal error. They turned that job over to a Montpelier corporation lawyer, Andrew Field, whose first reaction to the notion of employee ownership was "My God, the monkeys are going to run the zoo!" For philosophical and practical reasons, Field was adamantly opposed to the idea of any democratic oversight of the operation of the company, so he drew up the by-laws and articles of association as he would for any regular corporation. "The workers were not investors; they bought the stock to save their jobs. They had no desire to manage the company," he said. "Companies survive in the long run because they are based on profit-making and traditional-line management responsibilities. Management needs to practice good friendship and good stewardship; it has to build trust. But it can't be buddy-buddy with the workers."[1]

On March 31, 1975, before the eyes of local and national media, the employees took possession of their $7 million mine. John Lupien, the indefatigable spearhead of the takeover, proclaimed, "We made us all little businessmen today!"[2]

The first board of directors included seven workers, seven management representatives, and one outsider, Alvin Warner, the state legislator. (To his great disappointment, Lupien was elected chairman of the board of directors, not president of the company as he had hoped.) A year later, this changed to five workers, eight managers, and two outsiders.

In the first year, as one miner remarked, it was "paradise in Eden." Everyone shared joy and relief at having saved the company. Productivity rose. Workers and managers cooperated on maintenance problems as they never had before. "We all felt we had a piece of the action," said one miner.

The new owners also received a totally unexpected gift. Strikes and a rockslide at the Canadian mine which was their principal competitor and a boost in the demand for their fiber pushed prices up almost 50 percent during the first year. VAG was able to pay off its $1.25 million loan in the first nine months. The value of the shares soared to $700, then to over $1,800 in the second year.

The first year of employee ownership was filled with understandable pride and satisfaction. The management team, which remained largely intact, saw a new mood of enthusiasm and commitment among the miners. But in the fall the union bargaining committee, noting the explosion of company profitability, asked for a substantial increase over the base wage of $2.97 per hour. Management balked, even though it was realigning its own salaries according to the national averages outlined by a paid consultant. When workers asked for those figures, the board (on Andrew Field's advice) refused.

Discontent about the board grew among the miners. Repeated requests for open meetings and more information were rebuffed as being inappropriate. Chairman Lupien developed a standard reply to inquiries: "Just because you own a couple of shares in General Motors doesn't mean you can run the company." The information distributed came in the form of sanitized minutes posted on company bulletin boards. Alvin Warner argued in vain for more open disclosure of the board's activities. A public official for twenty years, Warner was used to working in the public eye. "Secrecy is where distrust begins," he warned prophetically.[3]

The rank-and-file members on the board were in the most uncomfortable position of all. They were asked, for example, to sit in an "advisory" position on wage negotiations. There was no guidance for them on learning how to wear four different hats, those of worker, union member, owner, and board member. They did their best, arguing about things they had firsthand knowledge of. But they were caught in the middle between the suspicions of their fellow union members and their directors' oath of secrecy. Their loyalties wavered constantly, and from time to time they took it upon themselves to share information they thought important.

Several months later, Lupien called a general meeting to propose an Employee Stock Ownership Plan. He gave very few details, but assured the workers they would get $60,000 to $70,000 worth of stock upon retirement. The proposal was so sketchy and novel that the employees rejected it out of hand and Lupien never brought it up again.

At the second annual meeting, the employee-owners were given an enormous amount of information to consider without any preparation. President Gerald Hammang said that "the biggest problem we face is the potential for internal strife that is so prevalent in the operation today." At the same time, he revealed that he was now the head of a group of investors interested in buying the company to "protect it from outsiders."[4] It was the first time the idea of selling the company had been raised. The elusive question of asbestos reserves brought a 50-year estimate from management, a figure few of the miners believed, and at the very end of the meeting, as an unannounced item, the board proposed a stock split of twenty to one, which the miners voted down.

Several board members pointed out that the uncertainty of the reserves meant they should look for some alternative investment that would give the company life after the asbestos gave out. Even if there were a half century of reserves, retrieving them through hundreds of feet of tough overburden would require major capital investment.

In 1976, Lupien suggested using the mine tailings as the base for fireproof wallboard. There was no lack of tailings near the mine —an estimated 15 million tons' accumulation from thirty-five years of mining. The crusher plant looked like a fragile whaling boat next to the hundred-foot-high Moby-Dick pile of gray-white tailings.

Lupien brought in a consultant who said the wallboard idea was feasible, though such a project had never been attempted anywhere else. That was enough for the chairman, and he went about preparing for it as single-mindedly as he had worked on the creation of VAG. He dismissed all voices of caution and disapproval, including those of the state development agency, which rejected his "naïve" and "fragmented" proposal.

Backed by corporate counsel Field, the board asserted that the wallboard investment was part of its day-to-day managerial prerogatives, which didn't need employee approval. In July, 1977, after a shareholder vote on the issue (which was variously billed as "binding" and "advisory") had gone against the board, it pushed on and committed $800,000 to the project.[5]

The miners saw the decision to build the wallboard plant as arrogance, and as confirmation that owning shares gave them no more significant control than when GAF had called the shots from New York. Monte Mason, who later became union president, said he and many of his fellow miners were angry because their vote had been disregarded so many times.[6] They were not opposed to the subsidiary *per se,* but they felt that VAG should not be saddled with the financial guarantee for the wallboard plant when the company was facing straitened circumstances. In retrospect, it appears that the vote signaled the approaching end of worker ownership at VAG.

In the late summer of 1977, just before the union contract was due to be negotiated, the board cited declining sales and poor production quality as grounds for cutting workers' coffee breaks and Saturday (overtime) shifts. No management salaries were decreased and workers came within an ace of striking their own company, with wages as the immediate issue. The union president, in an unconsciously ironic confirmation of Lupien's remark, said he saw nothing unusual in the idea of a strike. "We're no different from men at General Electric who own a couple of shares."[7]

By now, employees no longer felt the pride of ownership, even though they collectively owned a significant percentage of the company and their representatives sat on the board. After two and a half years of being ignored, they had fallen back on a traditional view of labor-management relations. They seemed to confirm Lupien's assessment that the only thing of importance is the "long green. When you have money, you can buy anything you want; otherwise it's only promises."[8]

The mortar of employee-ownership solidarity was obviously weakening. The rank and file had lost confidence in the leadership. They felt prey to fluctuations in the price of asbestos, continuing uncertainty about the reserves, and competing offers for their shares.

That fall, four different groups of investors toured the mine and pored over the accounts as the book value of shares fluctuated around $2,000. Potential buyers included President Hammang, the local banker who had given the original loan, and a Utah investor brought in by Lupien.

An informal survey of the shareholders found that over 50

percent were interested in selling their stock. The union president at the time, Clifton Thompson, speaking for a majority of his membership, said he didn't care if the mine was sold. "Either way, I'd have a job."[9]

Many shareholders were increasingly nervous about threats to their newfound wealth, which for some was more than they had invested in their homes. Orders for asbestos fell 20 percent, there were technical problems with new equipment, and the company had to absorb an $80,000 cost of shipping an entire order back from Germany because of poor quality.

In January, 1978, Howard Manosh, a local contractor who had made a fortune in well-drilling and construction, entered the bidding. He was well known, personable, and highly respected, if not universally liked. "Howard can sell you a six-pack of beer for ten dollars and make you think you got a bargain," said one worker.[10]

Manosh said he was interested in buying a few shares from workers "as a favor." The word got out that "Howard is buying" and by the end of the month, he had 220 shares worth $225,000, having purchased 20 shares originally. He then made a tender offer of $1,834 per share, provided he could obtain 15 percent of the stock.

In February, the board of directors, exasperated by Hammang's offers to buy and his opposition to the wallboard plant, fired him as president and brought in the head of the wallboard plant to fight a public relations and legal battle against Manosh. The showdown came at the company's third annual meeting, before which Lupien suddenly resigned as chairman of the board. With 98 percent of the stock represented in person or by proxy, the shareholders listened to the competing appeals of the board and Manosh, as well as two additional expressions of interest in a purchase.

Duane Brown, a former rank-and-file board member, spoke with passion of the "fallen animal" of VAG beset by the "vultures" bent on takeover. But his pleas brought no response. When the votes were counted, the employees had chosen the "firm guiding hand" of Manosh by accepting fourteen out of the fifteen people on his slate for the board.

Janette Johannesen, a graduate student under William Whyte

at Cornell, spent four years studying the VAG case. She concluded that the workers became interested in selling out when their demands for more information and involvement were rebuffed. "It was this fundamental issue of the rights of worker-owners, the degree of power of the board, and how much information must or should be shared," that led to the slow buildup of tension "within the company which culminated in the Manosh takeover."[11]

Commenting on the end of worker ownership, Monte Mason said he had sold his two shares back to the company because he was angry at Lupien for going ahead on the wallboard plant, and because he wanted to buy a house. In retrospect, he thought the workers might have been able to block Lupien with some legal action, but it didn't occur to them at the time. "None of us ever owned stock before. We just got mad and sold our shares." Duane Brown added, "Greed and jealousy killed this thing."[12]

Manosh's victory was hailed locally as a victory for "woodchuck power," the Vermont equivalent of "red-neck power." It was clear that the workers were sick of the bickering. They preferred to get their hands on their nearly 4,000 percent profits and be ruled by the familiar figure of Manosh.

The same media that had celebrated the worker purchase now arrived to proclaim its demise: "WORKERS BUY, RUN, SELL MINE" said the Washington *Post*. "The headiness of financial success was apparently harder to wield than a 15-pound miner's pick. . . . The experiment has turned into a sort of Frankenstein monster."[13] That no VAG miners use picks reveals the depth of that particular analysis. More seriously, it was only an "experiment" to outside observers; to the miners, it was saving the only jobs there were.

Decision-making at VAG did not change with employee ownership, because those who held the power—the board and the larger stockholders—did not want it to change. There were simply too many forces on the side of convention and tradition. Most of the board members were strongly influenced by their lawyer and local bankers. One observer pointed out that "the workers' expectations were based on their assumption that the general atmosphere of togetherness and equality that existed during the organizing year would continue after the change in ownership. Management had no such expectations. They intended that the company should operate as a 'traditional' one."[14]

There was no effort to teach the miners to think down the road, to balance the legitimate desire for short-term financial gain with the longer-term needs of the business. As University of Vermont Professor Lauck Parke said, "The miners never understood, as owners must, the notion of an income-producing asset. There was no effort to educate them."[15]

In 1980, when VAG lost $227,000 on sales of $8.9 million, the miners had a sense of *déjà vu*. Company debt had increased from zero to $4 million; the wallboard plant (which never used the tailings and never made a profit) was leased to another firm. The plant was shut down twice for a total of over two months because of high inventories. Miners grumbled about Manosh's inexperience and his "high-grading" of the ore, which meant using up the quality reserves more quickly. In six years, the miners had come full circle on the future of their jobs.

In January 1975, a machine tool industry trade journal carried a small item announcing that Amsted Industries of Chicago intended to liquidate its seven-year-old lathe-making subsidiary in South Bend, Indiana.

In 1969, Amsted had taken over the Studebaker engine plant, then only five years old, for its lathe-making operations. The company had suffered five straight years of losses, and officials, led by president J. Richard Boulis, had premonitions that the parent company might want to be rid of it. The notice in the journal was the first concrete evidence for the 500 employees that their jobs were threatened.

On the shopfloor, men like Stanley Kwiatkowski were both angry and fearful. They were proud of their lathes, which were sold throughout the country and placed on board almost every U.S. Navy ship. Kwiatkowski had worked for the Studebaker Auto Company for thirteen years before joining South Bend Lathe. Studebaker had once employed 25,000 workers at its sprawling South Bend works, but in 1963 the company closed for good, idling the last 8,000 employees, Kwiatkowski among them.

There wasn't much that he and his fellow steelworkers could do if Amsted closed down the plant, but Richard Boulis was convinced he could run the plant at a profit if given a free rein. He went to see Robert F. McGinty, a development officer at the First Bank and Trust Company of South Bend, to discuss the possibility of local financing to buy the company. Coincidentally, McGinty had heard that the federal Economic Development Administration (EDA) was looking for an area of high unemployment in which to experiment with an Employee Stock Ownership Plan (ESOP).

San Francisco attorney Louis Kelso had developed the idea for ESOPs in the 1960s. In books such as *How to Turn Eighty Million Workers Into Capitalists on Borrowed Money*, with Patricia Hetter, he argued that one way to economic equity and industrial peace lay through broadened stock ownership among employees, giving them a "piece of the action."[16] He promised that dividend checks and a retirement nest egg of company stock would assure much greater worker participation, loyalty, and productivity.

Kelso's faith found a significant convert in 1973, when Senator Russell Long (son of "Share the Wealth" Governor Huey Long) became a born-again ESOPian and began to promote the idea through tax code revision.

In some ways, an ESOP is simply a deferred-compensation plan. The company establishes an employee stock ownership trust, and then makes annual, tax-deductible, cash or stock contributions to it. With that money the trust, in turn, buys company stock or other assets. The stock is vested in the employees' names over a period of time, usually ten years, according to a formula based on wages and length of service, and is distributed to them upon termination of service. In a "leveraged" ESOP (such as South Bend became), the tax benefits are greatly magnified, because the trust may also borrow money from a bank using company assets, credit, and stock as collateral. Both interest and principal are then tax-deductible. Assuming the company is in the 50 percent tax bracket, it needs only about half as much income to service its debts as with conventional financing.

Among ESOP advocates, a fundamental split has developed over whether the ESOP trustee should have discretion in exercising voting rights. While some say the trustee should solicit instructions from participants before voting the stock, others, probably the majority, disagree. Unquestionably, the requirement of passing through the vote to the individual stockholder has made many companies shy away from this first step in increased employee participation in ownership.

Through his sponsorship of the Employee Retirement Income Security Act of 1974, and the insertion of a clause permitting a stock bonus plan to borrow money to buy employee stock, Long helped give a big boost to the number of companies establishing ESOP's. Whereas conventional stock bonus plans had been permitted to invest in employer securities, ESOP's were now, under ERISA regulations, required to do so.[17]

For its proponents, the ESOP offered something to companies as large as Sears, Roebuck, and as small as Allied Plywood, a lumberyard with 20 employees in Arlington, Virginia. By 1981, there were an estimated 5,000 ESOPs in the country. Only 250, however, had a majority of voting stock owned by the employees.[18]

The motherhood brand of enthusiasm that ESOP supporters feel for their financing device is shown in this rhetorical question that Long put to a Washington *Post* reporter in 1975: "Can you predict anything other than a future of socialism when so many people get so little out of a life of hard work? If you believe in capitalism, there ought to be more capitalists in this country."[19]

In February 1975, a radio commentator discussed ESOPs as a way for capitalism to use its "best tool of all in its struggle against socialism—capitalism itself. . . . Over the next ten years, there will probably be five hundred billion dollars' worth of new investment for businesses and industrial expansion. It can also be five hundred billion dollars' worth of corporate ownership by employees. An ever-increasing number of citizens thus would have two sources of income—a paycheck and a share of the profits. Could there be a better answer to the stupidity of Karl Marx than millions of workers individually sharing in the ownership of the means of production?"[20]

The commentator's name was Ronald Reagan.

In South Bend, McGinty and Boulis worked with federal and local city officials on a package to raise the $10 million purchase price. The Economic Development Administration would lend the city of South Bend $5 million for 25 years at 3 percent interest, and a consortium of local banks would match this figure at conventional rates. As the federal money was paid back, it would be loaned out again to provide a sort of revolving fund of seed money for other businesses in the South Bend area.

When McGinty was reasonably confident the plan would find federal acceptance, he went to the West Side Democratic Club on a Polish holiday and, over quantities of sausages and beer, sold the local union leaders on the ESOP as a way to save their jobs. The plan did not call for workers to invest their own savings in the new company, but they were asked to provide significant "negative collateral" by surrendering over $2 million in pension claims against Amsted. Boulis told them the company could not otherwise get off the ground.

To ease some of the sting of this concession, management distributed copies of a *Newsweek* article telling how Charles Valentine, a warehouse laborer at Lowe's (a Southeast building supply chain) retired with $660,000 in stock gained through an ESOP.[21]

The new company issued 10,000 shares of stock and placed them in an Employee Stock Ownership Trust, whose board consisted of Boulis, two union members, and two managers (handpicked by Boulis). Over a ten-year period, the shares were to be transferred to the employees, so that by 1987 the rank and file would control approximately 66 percent of the voting stock. Boulis and his management team made the changeover intact.

During the first year, aided by several millions in inventory, pre-tax profits went up 9 percent, while productivity, measured by dollars of shipments per employee (adjusted for price increases), rose 25 percent. The company gave its workers two bonuses, one a week's pay and one $50. The company also won the largest ($1.5 million) contract in its 70-year history, to supply 236 lathes to industrial arts classes in Tennessee.

A study commissioned by the Economic Development Administration for the Institute for Social Research at the University of Michigan eighteen months after the takeover found that almost all employees, managers, and workers felt that morale had improved, and that people were more conscientious about their jobs and had a greater sense of community. "You have everyone more united," one worker said. "You have a better outlook on coming to work. You just don't come in and put in your eight hours. You work like any other job, but it's a psychological thing where you are working for yourself, like you're in business for yourself."[22]

There was also a reduction in waste and absenteeism. "Everybody is not so willing to throw a part away, which is one of the first signs they care about the company. . . . A ten-minute break is now a fifteen-minute break, where it used to be a half-hour break."[23]

The survey found that 53 percent of the workers interviewed thought managers' attitudes toward workers had changed for the better (45 percent said "No change"), and 73 percent of the managers said workers' attitudes had improved (18 percent said "No change"). Managers thought this improvement was mostly due to better communications and cooperation. One manager said, "We now look at the worker as a source of improvements. Before, we did it our way and that was that, but now we ask for ideas."[24] However, while 36 percent of the managers said workers had more voice in making decisions, only 3 percent of the workers agreed.

One manager noted that stock ownership and increased influence were not necessarily synonymous. "Stock ownership does not really give stock owners influence in the company. Today it's a one-man corporation—the President. He appoints the Board of Directors [which] appoints the Employee Trust Committee. It's one continuous circle. . . . I'm a bit skeptical about the ability of management to change. This is not a criticism of ESOP; it's a comment about the company."[25]

Everything went so well those first two years that the union and the company worked without a contract. The local came within 27 votes of decertifying from the United Steelworkers.

Then cracks began to appear in the façade of this "model" ESOP. Seeking more rank-and-file involvement in company decisions, the union proposed an increase in the number of its board members from two to three, to equal management representation. Boulis and the other board members rejected the idea.

Meanwhile, the union international filed suit in federal court to recover the conceded pension funds. The regional and international United Steelworkers representatives had remained at best lukewarm and at worst downright hostile to the concept of employee ownership, because it threatened to blur the distinctions between their members and management. In 1979, the company's financial position weakened, and management gave out no annual bonuses for the first time since the buy-out.

These difficulties provided the workers with an introduction to one of the vagaries of investment: fluctuating stock values. With a pension plan, they knew they could look forward to a fixed amount of money. But, as the Research Institute of America pointed out in an analysis of ESOPs, "ESOP backers have vacillated over whether to describe an ESOP as a retirement plan. As critics have been quick to note, such a billing gives rise to false hopes among employees. Unlike defined benefit plans ["regular" pensions], the future level of benefits is not guaranteed by the ESOP approach. Nor does it permit the diversification possible in profit-sharing and other defined contribution plans. ESOP's, which must invest primarily in employer stock, could be wiped out by a single bad decision over which the average employee has no control, particularly in smaller firms."[26]

For some skeptics in the union, the shifting value of stock proved that ESOP was little more than "funny money." This perception reinforced their suspicions about secret decisions made by the board, controlled by Boulis. John Deak, the local union president and one of two hourly workers on the board, finally resigned, saying he could not wear the hats of both union representative and board member.

Employee ownership does not insulate a company against inflation any better than conventional ownership. At the 1980 contract bargaining session, union negotiators demanded an unlimited cost of living allowance (COLA). Management said the company couldn't afford it, and countered with a flat 10 percent raise and a $225 Christmas bonus. Neither side would budge.

On August 23, 1980, the 300 members of the United Steelworkers Local No. 1722 went out on strike against their own company. Ostensibly, the quarrel was about wages, but there was an underlying dissatisfaction about the venture as a whole.

The strike lasted for nine weeks, pickets outside complaining about the lack of worker influence at "their company," Boulis inside berating the strikers for not acting "like owners." The workers called Boulis a Captain Bligh and complained that "management doesn't give you credit for wanting anything but money." As one striker said, "The biggest ESOP fable is that we have anything to say about how this company is run."[27]

The strike was finally settled, with the union getting a modified COLA amounting to a little over 10 percent. Boulis pointed out that individual workers had lost $3,000 in order to end up with roughly management's last offer before the walkout.

Deep bitterness and misunderstanding remained after everyone had gone back to work. On the picket line, workers had shown a certain schizophrenia, saying that they "didn't want to run the company," and yet they wanted to see the company, their company, "run right." One problem was that there was no mechanism for educating the employee-owners on how to "run the company right" other than the board membership by two union members (later, one). Boulis claimed that in the crush of turning the company around, he didn't have time for "human relations . . . to go around patting people on the butt. . . . I didn't think about anything except keeping this business going and making money."[28]

Boulis also pointed out that the company had offered evening classes in financial statements and the workings of the ESOP, but out of the five people who attended, only one was from the floor.

"I think the average guy in the shop wants to have a good job, do a good job, know he's got good management, and see a good return," he said. "Employee ownership should be a way of letting people achieve wealth and participate in the benefits of it. I don't think it means some kind of worker democracy, because, first of all, you can't get three hundred to five hundred people to agree on a decision. And frankly, in today's economy you really don't have time for that kind of stuff. Management has to keep fighting the fires all the time to keep the business going."[29]

The workers' vague but intense conviction that their relationship with management would change with ownership ran afoul of management's traditional practices. Boulis said that when he circulated a questionnaire asking if the workforce wanted to participate in management decisions, only 26 out of 500 said yes. On the other hand, he acknowledged that many workers wanted more information. To satisfy them, he established a communications committee of twenty-five departmental representatives who met with him monthly. He would discuss the balance sheet, backlog, profit and loss, even possible acquisitions, then take questions. A transcript was posted on company bulletin boards, together with quarterly financial statements.

"Not too many guys in the factory really understood what all those things are," he said. "Unfortunately, too often it boiled down to 'Why don't we have parts back on the assembly line?' Not the kind of meeting I had anticipated, where people really want to know what was going on in the company, or how their ESOP is doing."[30]

By the end of the strike, Gerald Vogel, the union vice-president and the only rank-and-file member left on the board, was the quintessential "man in the middle." He knew his position made him suspect in the eyes of his fellow workers. "It was natural that some of the membership would accuse me and John Deak of going to bed with management," he said. He added that he still felt that someone from the floor ought to be on the board.

In the wake of the strike, Vogel led a push to explore participation groups along the Japanese model of quality control circles as a way to change the adversarial atmosphere. The board agreed to conduct a survey of the workers and found 86 percent in favor of the idea, with 60 percent actually willing to become participants. Management then agreed to try it, and the board decided to bring in a third-party consultant "to get us off on the right foot and not suffer through it like we did with ESOP."[31]

Vogel hoped the small participatory groups could give more workers experience in and exposure to the complexities of running the business. They would function like baseball farm teams, providing material for the major leagues—in this case, board membership.

After the strike, many observers, including the South Bend *Tribune*, noted that "because the system [ESOP] does not alter traditional attitudes of unions or of management," mere settlement of the economic issues would not solve the underlying problems.[32]

Since 1978 at South Bend there has been a "limited pass-through" of voting rights on major company decisions, such as acquisitions, but Boulis and others oppose even this amount of stockholder influence, because of its potentially stifling effect on management once a majority of shares passes into employee hands. Others, such as Washington attorney Norman Kurland, who helped set up the South Bend ESOP, have said that full pass-through voting rights are the very heart of "industrial democracy" and the only way to insure that ownership will translate into control. "You can't treat workers like second-class stockholders by preventing them from voting their stake in the business," he said.[33]

"ESOP is like a marriage" were Vogel's words. "You have your quarrels. We have to find out if we can get back together or whether we will have to get a divorce."[34]

The rescue missions at South Bend Lathe and Vermont Asbestos were not examples of workers taking control. At first the air was steamy with the confusing rhetoric of blue collar capitalism, workplace democracy and worker control, but the fundamental purpose of the buy-outs was still to save jobs. Purchase by the employees would never have occurred had the rescue crews been able to find conventional buyers. The atmosphere of crisis left no time or energy to investigate concepts of economic redistribution or self-management. Ownership, the workers learned, was not the same thing as control.

The union locals were as ill-prepared for their new roles as were the managers, and they got no support from their internationals. They had no experience with a cooperative alternative to the adversarial "us against them."

In both cases here, management and community leaders held traditional views on the respective roles of labor and management. With the exception of Norman Kurland at South Bend Lathe, the prevailing attitude was that these were changes of ownership, not changes in management style. To Andrew Field and Richard Boulis, the suggestion that workers have a say in management was like worrying about a new boiler before the plant was purchased.

William Foote Whyte of Cornell University has said that employee and community buy-outs usually go through two distinct stages in the conversion process. The first is the period of euphoria and general self-congratulation that "we have saved the plant." For several months, or even a couple of years, the excitement of a successful purchase keeps the mood buoyant. The second stage is when the workers begin to resent the fact that managers have not changed their attitudes and practices. The implicit promises contained in the word "ownership" begin to wear thin as workers are upset about not being consulted or included in company decisions. As far as managers' notions go, "If they give any thought to union-management or worker-management relations, they are likely to assume that workers, now being co-owners of the firm, will appreciate the wisdom of management decisions and will comply more effectively with management orders."[35]

These cases demonstrate that without education, training, and some kind of participation in day-to-day control over one's own work, employee buy-outs run a great risk of disappointing the new owners. Worker board members have the toughest job of all. Their directors' oath of secrecy clashes with union loyalties. How are owners to bargain with themselves?

None of the managers at either company made much effort to educate workers about the business or the rights and duties of stock ownership. Workers who had always lived close to the financial edge had little sense of what an income-producing asset was or how to balance short-term and long-term business needs. There was no organization or body of experience to help them adjust to their new roles. At VAG, with a huge price increase in the value of shares in just two years and sharp fluctuations in the price of the product, changes in the company finances were dizzying.

As Norman Kurland said, "The [economic] education of American workers is very, very limited. And until we address that, we're not going to be very effective in participation in decision-making."[19]

"Acting like owners" was the attitude Boulis asked from the workers at South Bend Lathe, but it was useless to expect people to exercise the responsibilities of ownership without giving them some access to the levers of power, directly or indirectly through representatives. Kurland pointed out that "you need structure. Industrial democracy, or any other form of democracy, does not work without structure, without checks and balances, without a clear delineation of the roles that people play in performing different functions within the corporation."[37]

[8]

Full Participation

Mondragón, Moose Creek, and Fastener

Hidden in the mountain valleys of northern Spain is the world's most extensive system of employee-owned and -managed firms. Virtually unknown to outsiders until the mid-1970s, the Basque cooperatives built around the village of Mondragón have been a salvation to advocates of cooperation searching for success in this field. As Robert Oakeshott, an English journalist, has said, "Without Mondragón, the evidence is that we [co-op supporters] might have to call it a day."[1] In this chapter we examine three examples of full employee participation in management and ownership.

Since 1956, the Mondragón cooperatives have grown from five employees to a network of more than 87 cooperatives, with 18,000 employees and $1.7 billion in annual sales. Their five-year average return on capital is 18 percent. One of the co-ops is the largest producer of stoves and refrigerators in Spain. Others manufacture electronic equipment, foundry products, and building materials. The core of the cooperation has been a savings bank, the Caja Laboral Popular (the Bank of People's Labor), with assets of $2.1 billion in 1978. Funds from the accounts of 300,000 depositors have provided much of the backing for the phenomenal growth of the cooperative network.

If the idea for the co-ops had a single source, it was the fertile mind of Father José María Arizmendi, a priest who was sent to the

Basque region at the beginning of World War II. The area had been strongly Republican during the Civil War, so Franco's victory meant a reduction in federal government support. Arizmendi knew that the people there would be thrown upon their own resources for jobs and education.

The Basques are characterized by a strong inclination toward saving money and a centuries-old tradition of craftsmanship. But Arizmendi soon found that, except for an apprenticeship program at Unión Cerrajera, the village's largest business, there was no formal structure to provide much-needed technical education. The establishment of a vocational school was obviously a high priority. Arizmendi persuaded the villagers that they could raise enough money for a school through subscriptions. In a matter of days, one-quarter of the town's families offered cash or kind toward building the school, and in 1943 a new technical high school, overseen by a committee that the parents elected, opened its doors to 24 students. By 1980, the school had over 2,000 students, and offered instruction up through the college level.

Twelve years later, five members of the first graduating class, all of whom worked for Unión Cerrajera, decided to start a firm to make oil stoves. They bought an existing stove company, and over the next three years, under Arizmendi's tutelage, developed a democratic ownership and management structure that has remained stable, yet remarkably flexible, for more than twenty years. The board of directors is elected by the employees on a one-person-one-vote basis, and the board then chooses the chief executive.

The five men had some savings of their own, but additional money was needed, so they sought help from friends in their *chiquiteos*—drinking clubs—a distinctive Basque institution, each of which has about fourteen members who eat and drink together regularly. Friendships made in the clubs are deep and lasting; thanks to this fraternal trust, the five men were quickly able to raise capital on the basis of a handshake.

Through the company's early years, Arizmendi remained in the background, but he urged the five founders to think of their mission as partly economic and partly social—developing jobs for the region, as well as succeeding financially in a cooperative. Management and ownership structure was not designed in advance, but grew out of Arizmendi's response to specific organizational problems as they arose. His primary goal was to provide the maximum number of jobs, and each decision was made with that in mind. He wanted the job creation program and capital formation to be as locally controlled as possible.

In the first three years, two co-ops were spun off from the original oil stove company, and three others were started from scratch. Arizmendi did not participate actively in the formation of the co-ops, but provided much of the legal research. As the five original founders realized that their financial requirements had outgrown the informal network of *chiquiteo* brotherhoods, it was Arizmendi again who suggested a solution: create a bank.

At first the founders thought he was crazy. "We told him yesterday we were craftsmen, foremen, and engineers. Today we are trying to learn to be managers and executives. Tomorrow you want us to become bankers. That is impossible."[2]

Arizmendi persisted, arguing that future expansion would depend on a steady, secure source of credit, something that couldn't be found in private banks. He convinced them by his research that a cooperative savings bank could profit from the Basque propensity to save by offering 1 percent more interest on savings than commercial banks, and in 1959 the Caja Laboral Popular was born. It was to become the key institution for sustaining the growth of the Mondragón cooperatives.

The bank was one of those practical ideas that appear brilliant in retrospect. As Oakeshott noted, by investing entirely locally the Caja stood on its head the hoary conventional wisdom of not reinvesting locally. It took an "explicitly inter-co-op coordinating role," enabling the co-ops to avoid the financial isolation which has crippled or destroyed so many others.[3]

The bank has two divisions to serve its two purposes: the economic section, which gathers in local savings; and the management section, which serves as nursemaid, guardian, coach, financial confessor, and "godfather" to new co-ops, covering unexpected cash-flow problems or losses. "Money buys time, corrects mistakes, and, in difficult circumstances, helps survival, just as in favorable times it aids development."[4] A bank officer serves on the board of new co-ops for the first several years, and returns to an established one if it gets into deep trouble.

Between 1961 and 1976, the Caja aided in the creation of 56 new co-ops, which added about 800 jobs annually. Not one failed. The management division is now the heart of Mondragón's success. Co-ops have developed either by splitting off from existing organizations, such as those making parts for the stove or refrigerator companies, or by starting afresh. A group of workers usually comes to the bank asking for help in establishing a new enterprise. The bank first tries to dissuade them by explaining how difficult starting a co-op is, how uncertain the markets are, and how much commitment they will need, both financially and emotionally. Each will have to put up about $2,000, the total amounting to approximately 20 percent of the initial capital investment. The bank furnishes the rest.

If the workers remain undaunted, they choose one of their number to represent them with the bank, and eventually to manage their company. Two bank employees are selected to help the manager develop the co-op's product, business plan, financial projections, and site location. Along the way, the workers are given several chances to back out.

Finally, after as long as two years, the project is launched and the real work begins. "The hardest part is always when that cooperative has to confront the market, has to save, has to produce, has to arrive at the level of competitiveness. That is its real difficulty, because it's easy to fight with paper, but it's not easy to fight with the market."[5]

Even after the co-op has started production, the bank does not let go. It requires monthly financial statements and assigns a two-person team to continue monitoring the co-op's progress. Any serious difficulties will bring a bank staff member back to the board.

Two kinds of groups evolved: primary co-ops, such as the stove, machine tool, and agricultural ones; and secondary co-ops, whose basic purpose is to serve the industrial and agricultural co-ops.

These include the bank, the school, and the research and development center (Ikerlan). Secondary co-op boards have half their members from their own enterprise and half from other co-ops. In addition, there are 100 primary schools managed by teachers and parents.

Ana Gutiérrez Johnson, a Cornell University graduate student who has studied Mondragón, said there was a "lot of trial and error" along the way. "The development was more random than it appears in retrospect. Arizmendi kept the projects going because he moved so self-effacingly through time and space. What he did was just to get people together to talk about their problems."[6]

Most co-ops are governed through a general assembly, where the workers elect a governing board to oversee management. In what Oakeshott calls a "highly sophisticated attempt to reconcile the need for genuine democratic structures with the need for efficient management and management continuity," the board appoints a manager for a term of at least four years.[7] The employees are also represented through a social council, which considers health, safety, and working conditions in the manner of Germany's works councils.

One of the major reasons for Mondragón's financial success is its reinvestment policy. According to Spanish law, 10 percent of the profits from co-ops must be donated to some civic or social organization. It is easy to satisfy this requirement and keep the money in the community by investing that 10 percent in schools or other civic associations.

It is what is done with the other 90 percent that demonstrates the pragmatic genius of the Mondragón system. Co-ops worldwide have exhibited a chronic tendency to underinvest as the members' short-term needs have been given priority. At Mondragón, individual needs have been balanced with company goals by reinvesting 20 percent of profits in the co-ops, and depositing the remaining 70 (of the 90 percent) in individual worker accounts. This money, too, is reinvested in the co-op. When workers leave or retire, they take the accumulated proceeds of their internal accounts with them. In the late 1970s, workers were retiring with about $50,000 apiece. There is provision, too, for hard times: up to 70 percent of individual accounts may be debited to cover losses.

Mondragón has not been without its problems. In the early 1970s, a number of co-ops experienced increased rates of absenteeism and a drop in product quality. Several of the larger ones were afflicted with the worker alienation that had appeared in other Western industrial societies: many of the Mondragón factories had been set up along conventional, Tayloristic "scientific management" lines, and the workers began to chafe at the restrictions.

After watching production and quality fall for several years, the staff at the bank sought assistance from the Norwegian management expert Einar Thorsrud. He helped establish a number of successful work reform projects to give the individual worker more control over his or her job. Worker morale and productivity improved as a result.

The successful self-government of the Mondragón co-ops is now buttressed by principles that define their goals. They include:

- Provisions to insure democratic, from-the-bottom-up self-government.

- Requirements for the contribution of capital by all worker members.

- Protection of job security and a regime of work behavior and discipline that promotes inter-co-op solidarity and coordination.

- Pursuance of open-door policies of maximum job creation and acceptance of new members.[8]

There are two vital elements in the success of Mondragón: one is the sophisticated management and ownership structure of the individual firms, which balances managerial effectiveness and employee participation. The second is the combination of profit-sharing for the employee-owner with the reinvestment needs of the firm. Taken separately, the ideas do not appear new, but when combined, they have produced competitive and self-renewing organizations. Equally important is the management and financial support the co-ops get from the bank. It is as if a small American

firm could afford financial advice from Morgan Stanley and could
keep Arthur D. Little on retainer.

The roots of employee ownership in the United States are long but
fragile. Probably the most famous examples of cooperative ownership were the Utopian communities of New Harmony, Brook
Farm, and religious settlements such as the one at Oneida, New
York. The statement of principles at Brook Farm proclaimed the
desire "to combine the thinker and the worker, as far as possible,
in the same individual . . . to achieve a more wholesome and
simple life than can be led amidst the pressures of our competitive
institutions."[9]

Another strain of employee ownership both antedated and
outlasted the Utopians. These were the non-agricultural producer
co-ops that flourished in cycles beginning in the 1790s. Most of
them were clusters of firms in cooperage, plywood, shingle, and
other craftlike industries.

The golden age of American producer co-ops occurred in the
quarter century following the Civil War. During those years, the
idea of workers buying out their bosses appealed to both locked-
out employees and political liberals such as E. L. Godkin, editor
of the *Nation* for thirty years. Godkin praised co-ops as a means
to abolish "wage slavery" and let the workers "see for themselves
where wages come from [and] what the necessities of capital
are."[10]

The Knights of Labor, under Terence V. Powderly, enthusiastically endorsed producer co-ops and formed over 100 of them in the
1870s. But few lasted more than several years. Powderly's own
postmortem on them included "lack of business qualifications, lack
of confidence in each other, hostility of those engaged in a similar
line of business, the boycotting of the wares of cooperative institutions and a lack of the necessary funds . . . among the causes of
failures of cooperative institutions."[11]

American co-ops, by and large, have never developed either
the ideological or the structural cement necessary to hold themselves together for long. They have not found ways to extend

initial enthusiasm, to forge financial links with other co-ops, or to pass membership to the next generation. The powerful solvents of individualism and acquisitiveness have invariably loosened the glue of ethnic, religious, or political solidarity. American co-ops have tended to be what Professor Jaroslav Vanek of Cornell University calls "mule firms," because they can't reproduce.

There is, however, at least one American organization that is trying to plant the cooperative Mondragón seed in the individualistic soil of America. In 1978, a small group of progressives founded the Industrial Cooperative Association in Cambridge, Massachusetts. Most of ICA's members had backgrounds in political or community organizing, but had eschewed working within the existing economic system. "The United States is so different from Western Europe, where there is both a cooperative tradition and one which aims for greater worker involvement in the running of business," coordinator Steven Dawson said.

The ICA model, like that of Mondragón, is based on the cooperative principle of one person, one vote. Only employees may be members and all members must be employees. Most of the profit is retained by the cooperative in individual accounts, and when a member leaves, he takes his account with him. For Dawson, Mondragón's most impressive accomplishment is to have "institutionalized the entrepreneurial process, the risk-taking. There is no reason the entrepreneurial process has to be totally individualistic."[12]

As envisioned by ICA staff, the fundamental difference between an employee-owned business and a producer co-op lies in the division of ownership rights. In an employee-owned firm, both the right to membership—i.e., to vote—and the right of ownership—i.e., possession—are included in the same piece of paper, the stock certificate. The people who own the most shares, therefore, have the right to the most influence and the most financial return from the firm.

In the ICA model, "The internal structure of the co-op allows each member to eventually [recoup] the net amount of capital supplied to the co-op [membership fee plus accumulated retained earnings] without any 'leakage' of membership rights to outsiders, and without requiring the newcomers to individually come up with the accumulated 'savings' of the retiring members. Hence, the company can maintain its integrity as a workers' cooperative over the course of time and avoid the 'suicidal' tendencies of employee-owned corporations."[13]

In both Mondragón and ICA co-ops, the rights of ownership and rights to profit and control are personal rights deriving from the individual's labor within and for that firm. Thus the firm is a "human institution, not just a piece of property."[14]

The ICA is well aware of the lack of an American equivalent of Mondragón's Caja. The National Consumer Cooperative Bank was chartered in 1979 primarily to aid consumer co-ops, but with only 10 percent of its loans reserved for producer co-ops. The ICA has patterned its function on the management division of the Caja. In its search for funding, ICA has relied on loans from both conventional lending institutions and the co-op bank. In the future, they hope to have a third financial source—their own revolving fund for venture capital.

Once a week, on the average, Steven Dawson receives a call from a group somewhere in the country of grocery workers, poultry cutters, machinists, looking for a way to save their livelihoods. Staff members meet with delegations from the groups that seem to have some potential. Often in a bare two or three weeks, they guide them through a complex and usually unfamiliar analysis of the company's viability, and assess the financial and human resources available for conversion to a co-op. They also stress the demanding nature of democratic decision-making under the gun of economic necessity.

Dawson said, "It is tragic that people who have worked their whole lives for a company come to this moment and want desperately to save their jobs, but don't know as much about their own business as we do from the outside."

Hard work and dedication are not enough, the staff tells the workers. Virtue is not its own reward. Having a good cooperative structure doesn't guarantee a successful business. It is no protection against human failings, nor is it security against the vagaries of the market. Nine times out of ten, ICA recommends against going ahead with a buy-out.

Most of ICA's clients come to them *in extremis:* a printing press in Massachusetts, textile workers in North Carolina, broom makers in Oklahoma, poultry workers in Connecticut. One company that came for help in less desperate straits was a construction company in northern Vermont: Moose Creek Restoration, Ltd. It was already employee-owned.

Moose Creek was founded in 1972, when Greg Jeffers came to Burlington, Vermont, to visit two fraternity brothers, Sam Johnson and Bruce Andrews. Jeffers was looking for fulfilling work outside the corporate environment. Having worked summers on construction, and being handy with tools, he founded a small construction company with Johnson and Andrews. During the first years, they concentrated on what Jeffers calls the "hippie residential," but then moved into Burlington for more commercial work.

The first big job was a $350,000 contract to convert a century-old icehouse into a restaurant. The company suddenly had to double its workforce. However, with the new work came some of the drawbacks of too rapid growth: $30,000 worth of debt, half of it from work on a new saloon whose owners never paid.

"We were pretty loose," Jeffers admitted. "We had no planning, no accounting procedures, no standards of quality control, no job descriptions, no decision-making policy. Everyone was working in the field; no one was in the office even to answer the phone. Some days if we didn't feel like working, we went to a bar and drank most of the day. We finally decided we had to get serious about the business. We held long brainstorming sessions to see what we wanted to do, and found that our problems boiled down to two categories: communications and organization."[15]

The company also had to satisfy a bonding company whose accounting and reporting requirements permitted no haphazard procedures. "It was a struggle," said Eric Hanson, another fraternity brother and a banker, who joined the Moose Creek board. "The bonding company was always looking for some one person to nail if anything went wrong. They weren't used to dealing with a group of employee-owners."

As the number of workers increased, the company began to

hold monthly meetings to discuss current problems. Since projects were spread out over three counties, not all employees came to the meetings, but they were an important way for the office staff to stay in touch with the masons, the bricklayers, and the carpenters.

The Moosers developed trust based on years of shared experiences, but as Tom McCarthy, the chief mason and one of eight children from a poor rural family, said, "A lot of us have shared a similar experience—it's called poverty."[16]

Jim Young, the shop foreman and a childhood friend of Jeffers's, described the bond that seems to hold them together. "This work is what we have all been looking for. Many of us have come from places and jobs where the bosses always want you to make something as fast as you can with no attention to quality. If it isn't right, screw it, you'll still get paid.

"I believe that everything we do reflects on the company and therefore upon our income. It's just not like other jobs where you have one guy hammering and three guys telling him how to do it."[17]

Moose Creek has tried to keep the wage range as narrow as possible. In fact, it is narrower than the one-to-five ratio of lowest to highest in the Mondragón co-ops. Everyone is paid by the hour, in a deliberate attempt to fortify company morale and reduce tension between the office staff and those doing the "hard work" in the field.

However, by late 1980 there was discontent at Moose Creek over the "self-perpetuating" board. There were three classes of employees: the founders (Jeffers, Johnson, and Andrews), who together held a majority of the stock; those who had obtained some stock over the years (about 45 percent of the total number of workers); and the new employees, who were told, in effect, that if they worked hard they might have a chance to buy some stock after a year's satisfactory service.

The greatest dissatisfaction came from the small shareholders, who saw no chance of ever gaining significant voting power over company decisions. Meanwhile, Moose Creek's problems were intensified by a deteriorating financial condition.

In response to the complaints, the three founders began to

explore means of sharing some of the ownership with the other workers. At first they didn't want to surrender control. Johnson said the prospect of sharing stock and eventually losing control was "really scary." The "gang of three," as they were called, attempted several different ways to distribute stock, each more complicated than the last.

After repeated rejection of the various stock-sharing plans, one new employee suggested moving to a cooperative structure. For guidance and help, the board went to ICA, which persuaded them to try a one-person, one-vote co-op in the style of Mondragón. Provisions were made to buy out the assets of the founders gradually, and internal accounts were set up for the employees.

At the first meeting of the newly elected co-op board, the members voted Jeffers out as president. They asked him to remain as chairman of the board (a largely honorary post), but he refused. He had always said that the most important issue under employee ownership was that of "power and control." When unexpectedly relieved of his power, Jeffers chose to leave the company entirely.

The Moosers have their work cut out for them. They are like the hive that has to raise a new queen after a swarm, but their new leaders must be chosen democratically. The cooperative structure will place more responsibility on all the individual members, replacing the fraternal feelings of the founders. Tom McCarthy observed that even in a co-op, "Most people want to see leadership and they are happy to let management manage. When Greg Jeffers left, there was a loss of creativity and a lessening of morale in the field force. I am looking for a leader, someone with charisma, but many of the field workers are looking for job security."[18]

In the year since Moose Creek became a cooperative, ICA has worked with the firm to help the membership in two areas: building up what might be called a democratic infrastructure and reorganizing work in the field along more formally democratic lines. In addition, ICA helped set up a series of committees to "process the chaos," as one staff member put it. These committees were personnel, governance, and an employees association serving as a committee of the whole. They worked hard not to let the members feel "committeed to death."

The personnel committee had a fairly easy time the first year because they had concrete problems, such as establishing a raise policy. The governance committee, composed of two members from the board of directors and two members from the employees association, wrestled with defining the limits of power and authority between various levels of management and the employees. Although the committee had the vital educational task of leading the transition to a democratic structure, its members fretted that it had no continuing function. However, they did make some practical suggestions such as bringing all contracts over $100,000 to the board for approval. After lively discussion, this measure was approved.

The ICA model of separating membership from ownership rights has a strong practical and philosophical justification, but it is not clear how widely the model can be applied. A cooperative structure needs, indeed requires, a level of commitment far greater than does a conventional corporation. A co-op levels the hierarchy, depends on a collective decision-making process, and provides fewer concrete rewards such as promotions or money, while a traditional organization is based on the principle that he who puts in the most time, money, risk, and energy should be able to take out the most.

The cooperative structure will continue to attract interest and adherents, but it requires a double leap into the unknown. The new owners must learn the rights and duties of ownership and they must also adjust to a consensus about individual financial rewards and be willing to follow a different kind of leader. Bruce Andrews of Moose Creek said, "I think that unless you found a cooperative on some really sound economic reason that is either related to job security or profit, then you are totally lost. The ideological component of a cooperative, nice as it sounds, is not enough to blow a fly off your nose."

There is now a small body of experience in democratic control of conventional business through employee ownership, which most often occurs when an owner is attracted by the tax benefits of an ESOP. Of the more than 5,000 Employee Stock Ownership Plans operating in the United States in 1980, a third had trusts owning 20 to 30 percent of the stock; only about 150 were 100 percent employee-owned.[19] One of the companies entirely owned by employees with full pass-through voting powers is Fastener Industries in Berea, Ohio.

While most of the enthusiastic proponents of ESOPs have been silent on letting the employee-owners have the right to vote their shares, the president of Fastener Industries is clearly in favor. "If employees don't have voting rights," says Richard Biernacki, "they don't own the company. . . . Having the vote is the key. The employees really feel they own the company here because they are assured of the board of directors they want. I realize I could be out on the street next year if that's the way the vote goes, but that's the only way this place is going to work."[20]

Fastener Industries was founded in the 1920s by Roderick Whelan, Sr. It produces high-quality fasteners for over 5,000 customers in the metalworking industries. From the end of World War II until 1980, it was run by Whelan's son Roderick, Jr. The workforce was steady; some were even third-generation employees. Sales in 1980 were just under $10 million. The Whelans paid wages at the prevailing rate, but for over thirty years Fastener employees have worked 35 hours a week while being paid for 40. The reason for this was pragmatic. As Whelan said, "A fastener plant, by its very nature, is not an attractive environment. It's noisy, it's dirty. I don't care how good a machine operator you are, you stay in that environment too long, you're going to start making mistakes. A man can chew up ten thousand dollars' worth of machinery or material in a very few minutes. If you don't get tired, you don't make mistakes."[21]

Whelan was also uncomfortable with a pyramid organization which "shut the employees out of involvement." He oversaw the decentralization of the business into separate cost centers to increase employee participation and provide long-term responsibilities. He speculated that he was less fearful of giving up power than some of his contemporaries: "Many of them come to think they are both infallible and omnipotent. They don't feel their employees have enough sense to come in out of the rain. I have just one question for them: how come you have them working for you? Our assets per employee are eighty thousand dollars to a hundred thousand. You give a man eighty thousand dollars and he's *got* to know enough to come in out of the rain."

In 1979, Whelan decided to retire, but there were no direct descendants to carry on the family business. The board of directors discussed ways of selling the company to the employees, since, as one of them said, "they are the ones who gave us what we have." In consulting with lawyers and accountants, they learned of ESOPs. The board favored this method, and broached it to the employees, including full voting rights and full pass-through dividends from the start, because "if ownership is spread far enough it will work."

As management was well aware, circumstances were beneficial for a conversion to an ESOP. They had a long-standing and success-ful profit-sharing plan, part of which was used to make the pur-chase. Local bankers were supportive because they knew the com-pany well. A sense of trust had existed between management and employees for many years.

Only six of the 120 employees declined to transfer their profit-sharing money to the ESOP, and two of them left the company. Although managers held a significantly larger amount of stock than the rank and file, Biernacki did not feel there was any dis-crimination against blue-collar workers: no one employee owns more than 6 percent of the company.

As soon as the conversion took place, Biernacki noticed an increase in unsolicited suggestions. The factory's appearance was spruced up, and interviews with a number of Fastener workers confirmed that the conversion to employee ownership had made a difference in the way they went about their responsibilities. Plant manager Joe Sapara said that the change of ownership had shown up on two levels: people attacked their individual jobs with more energy, and displayed greater interest in the financial condi-tions and decisions of the company. There was a greater readiness to correct the behavior of fellow workers by appealing to the instincts of ownership instead of being bossy. The new attitude was "I'm watching out for mine just as well as yours."[22]

In the first year under the ESOP, the board of directors held an interim election to fill two vacancies on the board. Fourteen candidates came forward, mostly first- and second-level supervisors. The employee-owners voted for the chief accountant (later named the corporate treasurer) and a plant manager. The board also voted to make its terms co-terminous. It was felt, according to Biernacki, that if a dissenting group had the employees' support, then "it was just as well that they take over at once rather than prolong the turmoil for two elections."[23]

The company to date has made little effort to develop formal programs of shopfloor participation, on the premise that it already exists. The president has always worked closely with his subordinates, and company-wide meetings are a tradition. One innovation, however, was that when the managers discussed the development of a new machine, they brought in one of the best operators, something that would not have been done before the conversion. "It works both ways," Biernacki said. "The worker owns the place and *expects* to be involved. You respect him, and you *want* him involved. You know he knows best and he can save you a lot of problems."

For maintenance mechanic Dale Zelinski, the changes have meant that now everyone is "paying the bills. When you goof up, that's money out of your pocket. Before, it was someone else who paid."[24]

Another effect of the conversion has been that workers are more willing to accept additional duties rather than hiring more people. "It's not that people have to work harder, but they seem to see the fat more clearly. They find that where an outsider might say 'you need another man,' they can get along without him. They are the ones who know whether they need a man or not."[25]

Mondragón's success demonstrates that cooperatives need the same sound managerial and technical skills and financing as those required in conventional businesses. American co-ops have never possessed the financial linchpin of a strong bank that could provide both money and financial training, as does the Caja. The National Consumer Cooperative Bank may in time be able to fulfill that role, but as long as its primary mission is to help consumer co-ops, producer co-ops will find it hard to get backing.

One question hanging over the future of co-ops in the U.S. is the possibility of a new kind of entrepreneur. Traditionally, in the American economy, the entrepreneur takes the most power and gain as the reward for the greatest risk. Co-ops will need to find ways to mute that winner-take-all attitude. Steven Dawson envisions the evolution of a "social entrepreneur" who is well equipped with business skills and puts group rewards ahead of self-aggrandizement.

Without doubt, the Mondragón and the ICA models of full democratic control are attractive to anyone seeking substantial equity in the workplace. However, it appears that in the present political and economic climate the move toward more employee participation in ownership is more likely to spread through employee stock ownership on the Fastener Industries model. As company shares are distributed, employees should develop a greater sense of proprietorship.

The acceptance of stock as a measure of both ownership and membership rights is deeply ingrained in American thinking. A few ESOPs exist with a one-person, one-vote provision, but they remain a small minority. Fastener adopted full voting rights with its ESOP because the Whelans thought that was the right and proper thing to do. They had nurtured a cooperative environment, if not a cooperative structure, for thirty years.

[IIII]

PROBLEMS ON THE WAY
TO PARTICIPATION

In the descriptions of participatory management and ownership in Part II, we did not intend to imply that shifts of perception and power occurred effortlessly. On the contrary, the process is long and difficult.

The field of participation is still young, yet it is old enough to have spawned its share of snake-oil salesmen who promise that for $1,000 a day, their magic formula will make workers happier, keep unions out, reduce the workforce, and boost productivity. At the other extreme are the "new Wobblies," who claim, with the old labor radical Bill Haywood, that the managers' brains are really under the workmen's caps and that all they need to do is turn the business over to the rank and file and economic justice—and efficiency—will prevail.

Genuine participation in management and ownership is time-consuming, difficult, complicated, and emotionally wearing. It requires a shift in values, and faith that both the employees and the enterprise will be better off as the former gain more control over their jobs. Participation is a long-needed balance to the American fascination with the technological fix.

Before introducing reform, it is imperative that managers and workers ask themselves several simple, but vital, questions. If they can answer them honestly and clearly, they will save time and heartburn:

- Why are we doing this and what do we hope to accomplish?

- What are the first steps in carrying out a program of increased participation?

- At what organizational levels will participation occur?

- What kind of leadership is required to plan and implement the proposed changes?

- How will increased worker participation affect lower-level managers?

- If the firm is unionized, what role will the union play in a participation program?

In trying to answer the above questions, we have broken down Part III into two sections. The first three chapters, "Conflicting Objectives," "Getting Started," and "Sharing Decision-Making," address the first three questions. We examine the organizational process and structure needed for introducing increased participation. We point out some of the tactical and mechanical issues while trying to avoid the contradictions and simplicity of an instruction manual. We want potential travelers to determine their destination and be familiar with their equipment before starting off on this journey.

The second three chapters deal with three important travelers on this expedition: leaders, middle managers, and union officials.

Participation involves a dual change in the way organizations function. It means changing the way work is structured, and the way people work together. It has been called a change in philosophy because the changes go to the heart of human values and behavior. Participation has come to describe the umbrella of thought under which people go about those changes.

[9]

Conflicting Objectives

Much of the discussion of employee participation in recent years has been rife with such phrases as "human development," "self-actualization," "quality of work life," "the marriage of human and business outcomes," and "everyone a stockholder." What these expressions are trying to say is that genuine participation requires the goals of an organization and the interests of the people who work in it to become more congruent and mutually supportive. If objectives are in conflict, there can be no common economic purpose.

Before discussing the problem of conflicting objectives which exist for both individuals and organizations interested in participation, it is important to remember that such participation involves the redistribution of power. For some people, this realization alone may be enough to dampen their interest in the subject. To better understand this reaction, it may be useful to say a word about what attracts people to power.

Power is the ability to say "Jump!" and have others ask, "How high?" Power is both the carrot which tempts and the stick which drives people up a hierarchy. Its possession can be more intoxicating than money. Power means being able to ask for advice and not having to take it. The powerful can say, "Be reasonable, do it my way."

Lack of power is the exasperated General Motors executive who found no entourage to greet him at an airport and yelled,

"Goddammit, I served my time picking up my bosses at the airport. Now you guys are going to do it for me."[1]

Abraham Zaleznik, of the Harvard Business School, has written: "Whatever else organizations may be (problem-solving instruments, socio-technical systems, reward systems, and so on) they are political structures. This means that organizations operate by distributing authority and setting a stage for the exercise of power. It is no wonder, therefore, that individuals who are highly motivated to seek and use power find a familiar and hospitable environment in business."[2]

The sharing of information is a key factor in genuine participation, and critical to sharing power. "Too often we ask for employees' attitudes and opinions in great detail, but in most cases, once we have the data, nothing is done with it. And this is because the employees are telling management what it doesn't want to hear, so management ignores the finding. Then they wonder why we continue to have discontent, grievances and strikes. It would be better not to ask the employees what they believe and feel than to ask them and do nothing."[3]

It is difficult to find a statement of corporate objectives which does not include some ritual celebration of "people power" or "people, our most important asset." Managers and owners trip over their financial print-outs in their eagerness to tell their employees and the public that they are "listening" and they want to make "every worker a manager." The distance between preaching and practice is often farther than that between the pulpit and the last pew.

There is also a question of how much power workers want. Some unionized workers are demanding decision-making powers in their national contracts. Other unions have asked for seats on the board of directors. Most employee concern, however, is concentrated on decisions that directly affect their own jobs. Many academics and labor relations specialists espouse the idea of participation, but there doesn't appear to be a great groundswell of desire for it yet. Part of the reason may be that management has a clearer idea than labor of what it means to redistribute power. Managers and owners are also clearer on what they expect to get out of participation. Workers have not evaluated the implications, and some who have do not want to take managerial headaches home with them.

Power can be shared to varying degrees in stock ownership plans. In closely held corporations, according to legislation passed in 1981, workers do not have to have voting rights attached to their shares. Alternatively, owners have the right to delay for years giving the workers the right to vote their shares. Owners who wish to share power can do this. Richard Biernacki, president of Fastener Industries, believes that giving the workers the right to vote their stock as soon as they get it is essential to developing better individual commitment and corporate performance.

A key requirement for effective democratic management is that those in power view its diffusion as sharing, rather than surrender. If they believe there is a finite amount of authority that has to be guarded at all costs, then they will view increased participation in ownership or management as a threat. If they believe, with Douglas McGregor and Einar Thorsrud (as discussed in Chapter 3), that there is enough power for everyone, that managerial prerequisites and self-esteem are not under siege, they may be more receptive to change. Sharing power, however, is not for everyone.

If no one questions a management style, if the company is achieving the required rate of return, if managers are keeping the troops in line, why should they change? The answer is, they don't. One proponent of workplace participation ruefully quoted a worker as saying, "Authority is the way we are used to working."[4]

"The 'good' manager seeks power not for himself but for the good of the organization," wrote Professors David McClelland and David Burnham of Harvard. "We think the bogeyman of authoritarianism has, in fact, been wrongly used to downplay the importance of power in management. After all, management is an influence game. Some proponents of democratic management seem to have forgotten this fact, urging managers to be primarily concerned with people's needs rather than with helping them get things done."[5] One of the secrets to effective participation is setting objectives to resolve the conflicts between individual and organizational needs.

Some managers or owners do not want to engage their employees in a discussion of objectives, whether organizational or even career in nature. They feel that those issues are their prerogative and that discussing them would only create friction. The rapid diffusion of the Management by Objectives technique in American organizations reveals not only the lack of discussion of objectives in many organizations, but its continued payoff when properly used. This technique helps people set short- and long-term job objectives with supervisors, which are used in the evaluation of job performance. Employers would also prefer to avoid a discussion of objectives with representatives of community groups. They see both types of discussion as an invitation to conflict best avoided by all parties.

Employees want job security, but promising such security could jeopardize the organization's performance. Employees want better working conditions, including flexible working hours and better safety conditions, but employers see this as changing the rules and costing money. Employees want a greater say in decisions that affect their work, but managers find this a threat to their power. Employees would like to become shareholders and owners, but owners are often reluctant to share wealth and status.

There are substantial problems with meeting employee objectives. If their job is machine-paced, it is difficult for people to have more control over it. If the company's procedures and discipline treat people like children who need to ask permission to go to the bathroom, as the operators do in most Bell Telephone Companies, then it is hard to achieve greater dignity at work.

The community—really a range of interested groups whose objectives may often conflict with one another, such as the chamber of commerce and "no-growth" groups—would like to keep at least existing jobs in the community. It would like to control air, water, and noise pollution. It would like to reduce crime, which is often a result of unemployment and large disparities in wealth. It wants members of private firms to become active members of the community rather than commuting to their distant suburban bedrooms, leaving their responsibilities as citizens to the "community relations department." Given these differing objectives, there is little reason to expect that many organizations would consider serious discussions about them, let alone attempting to reconcile them. Table 2 below shows some of the conflicting objectives of the individual, the organization, and the community.

Table 2

Conflicting Objectives

Individual	Organization	Community
· Income and job security	· Improve profits and net worth*	· Maintain full community employment and income
· Better physical working conditions	· Improve efficiency and productivity	· Increase the influence of consumers over what they buy
· Greater dignity	· Improve quality and provide for service	
· More satisfying work		
· Satisfaction of need for power and achievement	· Expand share of market	· Decrease crime and violence
	· Increase automation	· Control environmental impact of workplace
· Increased control over the job	· Maintain the hiearchy	
· Participation in ownership	· Discipline/control	· Reduce disparities in wealth and status
	· Lay off workers when market declines	
· Protection by union		
	· Avoid unionization	

*For nonprofit organizations, substitute "increase of number of products or quality of service."

In a small but growing number of firms whose leadership feels that there may be better ways of management and ownership, discussions about these objectives have begun. In some, like General Motors and South Bend Lathe, a crisis of survival has forced the discussion. In others—a very few—like Hewlett-Packard and the Mondragón cooperatives, people have decided that such discussions are in the best interests of all parties. For all of them it took a leap of faith that it would be time well spent. Some have failed, while others have discovered that there are often objectives that they can agree on.

While many organizations give lip service to objectives and policies that "people are our most important asset," or that they are "decentralized," their daily actions seldom match their on-paper assertions. The Dana Corporation and the federal agency Action, which administers the Peace Corps and Vista, are two organizations that support such objectives with appropriate management actions and organizational structures.

Dana, with 30,000 employees, is increasingly recognized as a leader in new approaches to management and ownership. Dana's objectives and policies are listed on a single page, which replaces a 23-inch stack of "corporate procedures." After four short paragraphs on the importance of profits for shareholders and of a steady rate of growth, the eleven remaining paragraphs are devoted to "People."

These state that at Dana, "We are dedicated to the belief that our people are our most important asset."

Managers have extensive autonomy. "We believe in a 'store manager' concept." For example, if a plant manager wants $4 million to increase his capital budget for the next fiscal year, he would not have to tell the chief executive officer, Gerry Mitchell, what he wants it for. "And I don't want to know what he wants it for," says Mitchell, "it's his plant."

Higher pay follows job performance. "We believe that people respond to recognition, freedom to contribute, opportunity to grow, and to fair compensation."

Dana believes that everyone in the organization should be involved in planning. Managers are required "to keep people up-to-date constantly through newsletters, bulletin boards and group meetings." Mitchell says "It's much better to talk to a person than write a memo. Personally, I hate memos. I've no use for them."

Corporate policy urges supervisors to "encourage opinions and ideas from their people. Supervisors shall implement those ideas and suggestions that have merit *or explain the reasons why* certain things cannot be done. This is not the old style, do-it-my-way-or-get-out supervisor."[6]

As former Dana CEO Rene McPherson, now Dean of the Stanford Business School, has said, "We don't motivate people. They are motivated by their upbringing, education and other things. . . . What we are doing is taking the handcuffs off by giving the workers responsibility and a voice in how their jobs are done." He added that since the company began encouraging employees to "talk back to the boss," productivity of production workers has gone up significantly.[7]

Mitchell summarized the Dana approach: "We let people manage themselves" because the best kind of control is self-control. The *Financial Times* of Canada concluded that the "tough, but democratic, style pays off," alluding to the fact that Dana ranks second among the top two hundred U.S. industrial companies, based on a five-year rate of return to equity.[8]

What is the best way to mesh competing objectives of individuals and the organization? There are no panaceas. The people at Dana find that the ways of doing it vary from plant to plant and supervisor to supervisor. One of the common threads, however, is the sharing of authority and responsibility so that people can help solve their own problems. Sharing ownership is another. Participation in setting objectives helps establish a basis for trust among fellow workers and thus improves cooperation.

Different groups within a given organization may also have conflicting objectives for a participation program. When the staff of the Federal Government agency Action began discussing the agency's management problems in 1978, they soon realized that involving people more in decisions that affected their work made good sense. They studied what they might do about it, and what other organizations had been doing, and established a Participation Work Improvement Program. A list of seven statements about workplace democracy was drawn up:

1. "Workplace democracy is an attempt to develop ways for staff to increase participation, equity, security and creative individual development. It is not an intellectual

process of discussion or a new management style or system which will enhance the Agency at the expense of the workers.

2. "Workplace democracy is an opportunity for workers to have more input into decisions affecting their work and work environment. It is not workers taking over the operation of a Unit and the job of the manager.

3. "Workplace democracy is all workers and supervisors putting their heads together to get the work done in the best possible manner. It is not an abdicating of individual effort in favor of group achievement.

4. "Workplace democracy is democratic principles being applied to work production and authority/responsibility relationships for the well-being of all staff. It is not efforts for communal or leaderless work environments which are paralyzed from lack of direction or decisive action.

5. "Workplace democracy is as important for middle managers in relation to their superiors as for lower-echelon workers in relation to their supervisors. It is not a technique for getting various levels of employees together to lobby for change or to resist the goals and decisions of high level managers.

6. "Workplace democracy is an opportunity for each staff person to learn to understand why things happen the way they do, and why people react to them in certain ways. It is a chance to let others know your ideas and how you feel without jeopardizing your job. It is not a pre-set or distinctly defined process for all work situations or staffs, and must be discussed, shared and adjusted to fit the needs of different offices, as well as different workers.

7. "Workplace democracy is an attempt to develop a place to work that can fulfill the needs of employees as well as the needs of the agency. It is not another way to get more work from people at the expense of their well-being."

This list of principles provides the basis for a democratization program within an organization. As it is a public agency, ownership is not an issue.

Several questions related to objectives may help clarify whether or not the benefits of greater participation outweigh the risks.

FOR MANAGERS AND OWNERS

1. How far are you willing to go with participation? Where do you draw the line on "management prerogatives"?
2. Are you looking for a quick, low-cost boost to productivity with a return of the work ethic of Calvin and Carnegie?
3. Are you trying to stave off or starve out a union?
4. Are you willing to let workers participate in the design and implementation of the proposed changes?
5. Are you prepared to commit yourselves and your organization to a process lasting ten years or more?
6. Are you looking for a way to make some workers happy while the jobs of their colleagues are automated out from under them?
7. Do you believe that workers respond solely to financial incentives?
8. If you like the idea of ESOPs, do you want to distribute voting stock?

FOR WORKERS AND UNION OFFICIALS

1. Do you want broader control over your jobs and your firm?
2. Are you prepared to deal with problems of management like the selection of supervisor, the disciplining of co-workers, and planning your work?
3. Do you have the stomach for making decisions, especially when it means judging your peers?

4. Do you want to put your savings at risk in the company which employs you?
5. Can you be both union members and company owners?

FOR BOTH GROUPS

1. Do you really want to seek a better way to build a common economic and social purpose?
2. Can "every worker manage and every manager work," as enjoined by James Lincoln, founder of Lincoln Electric?

Most of the time, an organization will be interested in these questions only because internal or external crises have forced it to look for "a better way." Employee participation, as such, is not a widespread business goal, because linking "human needs" with "business needs" runs counter to the traditional way to achieve a satisfactory bottom line.

The purpose of management is to find ways to design and manage organizations so that the conflict between the goals of the organization and the interests of the people who work in them is resolved. Participatory management is one way to begin to build bridges among individual, organizational, and community objectives.

Different promoters of participation have different objectives. Some people who are pushing these ideas feel that universal capitalism, proposed by Louis Kelso and Mortimer Adler in *The Capitalist Manifesto*, where every worker owns a share in the business where he/she works, will reverse the trend toward socialism. Others feel that the shrinking size of the "ideal" plant—at Dana and Mondragón, that equals 500 employees—and the growing number of smaller autonomous units within an organization are confirmation of E. F. Schumacher's idea that small *is* beautiful.

Some people feel that participation will begin to help labor regain the control over jobs and the firm which was lost in the onslaught of Taylor's scientific management, and will be a major step in establishing democratic socialism. Others feel that participation is a way to introduce consumers directly into the decisions which determine the nature of the goods and services they find in the market.

It is all very well to set up a company philosophy which promotes the "company's motivating spirit," but the proof is in the practice. Statements of corporate philosophy in an executive suite may gather as much dust as the Declaration of Independence on a post office wall. In some companies, officials have operated long and successfully without feeling the need to formalize their statements of purpose. Their "philosophy" is in their behavior.

James Lincoln, founder of Lincoln Electric, by all measures one of the most financially successful companies in the country, and perhaps the only one with a public guarantee of life-long employment, said, " 'As ye would that others would do to you, do ye even so to them,' is the complete answer to all problems that can arise between people. This philosophy of life is complete. Our reaction to it is the problem. We do not easily change our developed habits. The acceptance of such change is the problem, not the development of a proper program."[9]

[10]

Getting Started

Between 1968 and 1972, the Valspar Corporation, a paint company in Minneapolis, had two major strikes totaling twenty weeks of lost production. C. Angus Wurtele, the president of the company, described what that meant to him. "It's particularly distressing when you have a strike at the place which is also your headquarters. You walk through the picket lines every morning and you realize that once you're in a strike situation, it's really too late to do anything. Those experiences indicated to me that there *had* to be a more productive way to work with a unionized workforce in this particular case and, in broader measure, with all our employees.

"I was just forty and I'd been president of the company for ten years at that time. I realized that it really would be beneficial to me and my family and the business to step back and observe what was going on in the world." Valspar employs 1,300 people at 11 production facilities and additional warehouses. Net sales were $136 million in 1980 from paint resins and molded plastics.

Angus Wurtele decided to take a sabbatical to visit the major corporate work reform experiments. He went to the General Foods dog food plant in Topeka, Kansas, and to Donnelly Mirrors in Holland, Michigan. He visited IBM and Procter & Gamble facilities which "were doing lots of interesting things but not talking about [them]." He then went to Europe and looked at a number of companies in several countries there.

"I had two concerns at the time. One was corporate behavior, how to manage ourselves, and the other was external behavior, what society was expecting of corporations. I came back full of ideas, and we started our process of reform in late 1974.

"There's a philosophical dilemma that says theoretically these things should rise from the bottom up. So, from the position of management, how do you let them? Do you use old-style 'you'll do it this way' techniques?

"We tried to create an environment where we would let things happen, where we could encourage individual managers to try things and then back [them] up, then record the results, and circulate them within the company to open the eyes of other managers. For instance, our billing process used to be an assembly-line-type process. Instead of doing it in a sequential way, with each person doing one step, we assigned an individual to a group of customers and had him do *all* the steps [so that] each person began to have responsibility for a group of customers. They've got their own monitors in the project and we've eliminated the supervisors. It was a good, successful experiment."[1]

"We're a small company in a highly competitive field," Wurtele told a Minneapolis *Tribune* reporter in 1976. "We're not going to out-research or out-mechanize a Sherwin-Williams. The key for us must be our management of human resources."[2]

Angus Wurtele's experience is comparable to that of many managers who have introduced more participative management. They experience a crisis such as a strike which offends their personal values of cooperation, trust, and dignity. As a result, they begin to search for a better way to run their company or agency. This chapter reviews the problems of getting the philosophy of participation launched in different organizations.

One June morning in 1970, the 5000 employees of the Handelsbanken in Stockholm woke up to read in their newspapers that the bank had been involved in some questionable currency speculation, and was in serious financial trouble. Several weeks later, the chairman resigned, and the board chose Jan Wallenda to take charge. Dr. Wallenda, a distinguished economist, had been the chief executive of a bank of five hundred employees.

The basic problem, Wallenda learned, was that the organization had "trouble making decisions." Although the bank was organized into 500 branches and 20 district offices, too much authority was concentrated in the 1000 staff people at central headquarters. "Like most organizations, we were decentralized on paper, but not in practice." The decision-makers were too far away from the customers. Wallenda realized that all employees had to take more responsibility for improving the effectiveness of the bank. The board of directors agreed with that objective.

Wallenda then went to the staff, who were worried about the future of the bank, and to its union, to ask what should be done. They began to develop objectives. He met in small groups with a large portion of the staff. Other managers began to do the same. The tasks became clearer. They saw, often to their surprise, that they shared objectives. The level of trust between management and staff improved.

Management and the union then agreed on two objectives: first, that all employees become more involved in decisions that affected their work, and second, that all employees become owners of the bank.

After this agreement, a trickle of ideas about how to improve the efficiency of the operation grew to a flood. For the first time, tellers and branch managers were given full authority to make loans. The dress code was abolished; peer pressure was much more effective. Job rotation was introduced. Training, a key to the success of the program, was expanded. Seventy percent of the headquarters staff either went to the district offices or branches or retired voluntarily.

The venerable loan committee was abolished; big loans went to the board for a decision. When old customers came to Wallenda for a quick decision on their loans as they had in the past, he told them, "I can no longer decide. If I had not decentralized myself, the sharing of authority would not have happened." Stock ownership and profit-sharing were introduced for all employees. By 1978, employees owned the largest portion of the stock.

Within five years of that June headline, Handelsbanken moved from thirteenth in profitability out of the fourteen major Swedish

banks to number one. Wallenda reviewed what they had done.
"We did not have the idea to democratize management, but just
to use our resources more efficiently."[3]

Democratization of the organization was the process which
raised the level of trust, and released ideas and energy which
transformed the organization, and its performance. Managers at
Handelsbanken learned that there was no trade-off between the
objectives of democracy and efficiency. In fact, more democracy
led to better performance.

If employees are going to have genuine "ownership" of a new
working relationship, they have to take "possession" at the beginning. That is the advice of John Beck, a staff member of the Michigan Labor Studies Center in Ann Arbor. "Know the project," he
tells his colleagues. "Find out how it is run, so it doesn't appear as
if top union and top management are *telling* the worker to participate. People underneath have to understand that they have to
come up with a lot of new ways things should be done. That's the
whole idea, isn't it? We are using the intelligence of workers that
has never been tapped before. Well, dammit, tap that intelligence
at the beginning. Don't wait!"[4]

After the top executives of an organization decide that they
want to adopt participatory management, and before their thinking advances too far on how to implement it, they need to raise
the issue with their employees. Are they interested? A program
featuring a "cooperative approach" can sound like something for
nothing—like a plan for getting the employees to make a greater
effort, while receiving nothing from the company in return. Employees may not trust management, and such a program may only
deepen their skepticism of management's motives. Building mutual respect and trust, therefore, is an essential step in getting
started.

When Charles Brown, chairman of American Telephone and
Telegraph, decided to explore labor-management cooperation, his
staff approached one of the unions, the Communications Workers
of America, with the idea. The union was more than a little skepti-

cal. It looked like one more program to eliminate jobs and raise productivity, while the CWA wanted the reduction of what its members called "job pressure."

The computerization of the telephone business was turning people at AT&T into newly Taylorized workers. They felt dominated by *"the count"*—the average number of seconds they spend with a customer. This average is reported on a computer printout to supervisors every fifteen minutes during a working day. A survey of their feelings on this subject gathered comments like these:

- "They say they're interested in quality, but really the only tune they sing is productivity."

- "Before, we never had time clocks. Now with the 4E machinery, the computer asks you why you weren't there."

- "Now they measure everything but the pressure of your left cheek on the chair—and soon they'll be able to do that."[5]

Perhaps most galling to the operators was the secret surveillance by supervisors. The company called it "objective remote performance evaluation." The operators called it spying. When AT&T announced its new interest in cooperation, the Communications Workers said, "Show us! Give us a sign that you are really serious. Eliminate that eavesdropping and prove you really mean it." According to Glenn Watts, president of CWA, when AT&T did agree to stop some surveillance, a major cornerstone of trust was laid. Watts did not expect decades of adversarial relations to end overnight with a QWL clause in the contract, but it was a beginning.[6]

A basic problem in initiating participation is deciding who should participate in planning the shift in management approach, and how to work together. People at Chevrolet Gear, Rath Packing, and the Dana Corporation have used different approaches to reach a common goal. After an agreement was reached about the objectives for a program in labor-management participation, this goal was to appoint a committee of top management and employee representatives.

At the Rath Packing Company, the board of directors, to which the employees had elected the majority of the members, authorized the establishment of voluntary problem-solving groups in the offices and on the shop floor. At Chevrolet Gear, each side chose the other's representatives: the employees selected the four management people, and management the four worker representatives. At the Dana Corporation, as elsewhere, Scanlon Plans have a two-tier joint committee structure, shop floor and top level.

Top-level committees and shop floor problem-solving groups provide one basic structure for participatory management and ownership. All members participate in awareness sessions, and practice running meetings and solving problems to improve their skills. The existence of the committee and group structure is one of the basic differences in approach from the "organizational development" efforts, which stressed changing the attitudes of the people first, and leaving the structural changes to follow the attitudinal change.

It is the cooperative structure that reinforces the desire to cooperate. Its very formation demonstrates deepening respect and trust. It is a clear statement about the shared responsibility of management and workers for the future of the organization. We now turn to the initiation of shop floor groups.

Gaining understanding of and commitment to a new philosophy from the employees working on the shopfloor and in offices is another essential for starting a good program. After several meetings with their supervisor about the nature of the QWL program, the employees at the Chevrolet Gear plant were required to sign the form shown in Figure 4 on the next page indicating their interest in trying such a program. When a high percentage of the people working with one supervisor had signed the forms, which was part of a four-page brochure describing the program, a circle would be started. Only then did all the members of the group get their first training session, which lasted six hours on company time, to learn how to conduct and participate in meetings to raise and solve problems. The twenty percent who did not want to join were not required to or pressured into coming to the meetings.

At the Dana Corporation, when a plant manager introduces

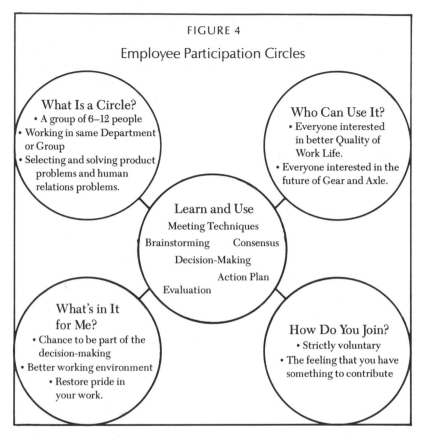

FIGURE 4

Employee Participation Circles

What Is a Circle?
• A group of 6–12 people
• Working in same Department or Group
• Selecting and solving product problems and human relations problems.

Who Can Use It?
• Everyone interested in better Quality of Work Life.
• Everyone interested in the future of Gear and Axle.

Learn and Use
Meeting Techniques
Brainstorming   Consensus
Decision-Making
Action Plan
Evaluation

What's in It for Me?
• Chance to be part of the decision-making
• Better working environment
• Restore pride in your work.

How Do You Join?
• Strictly voluntary
• The feeling that you have something to contribute

the idea of a Scanlon Plan, employees are not required to accept it. After an involved and time-consuming period of sharing information about what a Scanlon Plan is, the entire workforce votes on whether to accept the plan or not. Approval must exceed 70 percent of the workforce. One year after the plan's introduction, a second vote is taken, and again, 70 percent of the workforce must approve it. Eight years after adoption of the first plan, only one-third of Dana's American plants have Scanlon Plans.

According to Rene McPherson, the former president of Dana and now dean of the Stanford University School of Business, "one of the reasons it has worked so well is that it took us five years to get it installed. It involved everyone in an operation, from the sweeper to the plant manager. It made you stop once a month and talk to everyone about how you were doing. If you couple that with promotion from within, with stock ownership, and with education, it's a total philosophy, not a program. To get somebody's philosophy moved around takes two, five, ten years. If you jam it down their throats, if it's somebody's special idea that he's trying to install for you, then it won't work. Nobody pushes you. To get seventy percent approval . . . you've really got to believe. That's why it works."[7]

Most successful programs establish a set of principles which provide the foundation for the new approach. Statements of principles, however, can ring as hollow as advertising slogans or political promises. The test comes in the practice. Nonetheless, the exercise in employee-management cooperation of jointly writing down some guidelines is an excellent first step in building a common economic purpose. Drawing up guidelines may be easier for union and management representatives than for employees and management in a non-union plant, as the former are at least accustomed to looking at each other across a bargaining table. They know each other's strengths and weaknesses and have confidence in their abilities to deal with each other.

Establishing a set of principles takes many different forms:

- At Moose Creek Restoration, Ltd., a subcommittee of the Employees Committee developed a "constitution" which became a general philosophical document under which members would operate.

- At the Rath Packing Company, bought by its employees in 1980, one of the first actions of the board of directors was to empower a joint steering committee of labor and management to draw up a "Charter" to govern relations among the employee-owners.

- At the Jamestown Area Labor Management Committee, Chris Meek, a staff member, asked that, as a first step, each in-plant committee write a set of principles for goals and behavior. If it did not do so, he would decline to serve as its third party.

One of the first—and subsequently widely copied—set of principles was developed by workers, managers, and consultants in rural Tennessee. Sidney Harman, president of Harman International Industries, bought an auto-mirror factory in Bolivar, Tennessee. He described its physical plant with its leaking roof and extreme temperatures as a "Dickensian anachronism."[8] While president, Harman, holder of a Ph.D. in psychology, had introduced some participative techniques in other non-union company plants, and he wanted to see if he could apply the principles he had learned to a unionized plant.

At a 1972 Senate hearing on worker alienation, Harman met Irving Bluestone, UAW vice-president for General Motors, and Michael Maccoby, director of the Harvard University Project on Technology, Work, and Character. During the following year, the three put together the skeleton of a Work Improvement Project (WIP) for Bolivar which, in Maccoby's words, was meant "to create an American model of industrial democracy; a model that is acceptable to unions and that might stimulate further union efforts. The project is based on the view that a national movement to improve quality of work is unlikely to succeed without union support."[9]

One of the first things Harman did under the new project was to conduct a detailed survey of employee attitudes and expectations. He found deep worker suspicion of management in general, and of the new Work Improvement Project in particular, since it was seen as another productivity-boosting gimmick. When the consultants offered to discuss the results of the survey, only three or four of the company's 1,000 workers turned up.[10] However, with Bluestone's personal urging, the local union came to an agreement with management to pursue a range of participation experiments on a purely voluntary basis.

Eventually, the structure of the WIP and the people involved helped to allay some of the union's fears. There were two levels of committees. The top was the working committee, composed of an equal number of union and management people and outside consultants. Below that were a number of departmental core groups, which almost always included shop stewards and foremen as well as two to four workers.

Management and labor adopted a set of four principles on the advice of Maccoby and Neal Herrick, of the University of Arizona. They stated that *any* workplace change should insure the following:

Security— creating conditions which free workers from the fear of losing their jobs, and which maximize their income.

Equity—guaranteeing fairness in hiring, promotions, and pay; an end to discrimination against women and minorities; and profit sharing if productivity increases.

Individuation—understanding that each worker is different. Individuation, as the participants describe it, means that changes in the workplace should be structured to allow each worker to satisfy his or her individual development. The employee must not be forced to participate in a way that executives and social scientists have deemed "satisfying" for them. Changes in the workplace should accommodate everyone as much as possible, and permit workers to get the job done at their own pace.

Democracy—making free speech, due process, and workers' participation in decisions which directly affect them a way of life in the corporation.[11]

The first tasks set by the core groups came from rank-and-file suggestions on ventilation and parking-lot traffic jams. In 1974, Maccoby brought in Einar Thorsrud from Norway to help design other shopfloor improvements and techniques.

It took many months to develop a modicum of worker trust. A number of small suggestions, such as having a backup screwdriver available for certain jobs, were adopted. Then, in one department, workers asked if they finished their quotas early and satisfactorily, could they go home? For people in this rural area, working on their farms and gardens was more attractive than extra pay in a factory. When management and the union agreed, this was the beginning of the concept of "Earned Idle Time," which eventually spread to the entire factory. By 1980, it had reached the Chevrolet Gear Plant in Detroit.

The American Center for the Quality of Work Life, a non-profit organization supported by labor and management, runs seminars to give managers and union officials a chance to explore the theories and ideas of Quality of Work Life. "Many organizations are incapable of coping with the QWL mode of operation," said Ted Mills, the Center's chairman.[12] The Center gives people, through the two-day course, a whiff of the QWL powder before having to make a decision and use live ammunition. Mills said, "Many failures we have seen could have been avoided if senior management had been better informed," but senior management support, or lack of it, is only part of the problem.

The Center's "Entry Process" has four parts, each of which allows either executives or union officials to terminate the program. A half-day meeting devoted to "policy determination" is the first phase of the entry process. Managers are briefed on what QWL is, how it can be achieved, its potential risks and benefits, and its possible contribution to enhanced organizational effectiveness. If the officers agree that these ideas deserve further examination, the "feasibility phase" can start. Selected officers from the company or union visit peers in other organizations which already have programs. At the end of this phase, the officers meet to decide if they would like to enter the third one—planning a program for their own organization. Planning includes asking such questions as whether there is a need for outside consultants, who will have responsibility for implementation, what training is needed, how much money and time must be spent, whether QC circles are desirable, and what is the structure of and process for setting up labor-management committees. The final phase is implementation.

Some of Mills' greatest wrath is reserved for those who think that QWL is an off-the-shelf item, something which can be installed like a new sparkplug. Changes often create "damaging expectations in the employees." He railed against the impatient managers who "don't want it right: they want it Thursday." New product development, new construction, acquisitions and mergers require months or years of meticulous study and preparation before approval, but many Quality of Work Life projects are adopted in haste. Mills blamed this on the continued precedence taken by "business objectives" over "human objectives." The result is that managers do not think about Quality of Work Life until after they have made their investment decisions.[13]

People cannot be expected to "solve problems" in new ways unless they are taught to do so. They cannot lead meetings to reach decisions without the appropriate skills. High-quality training is essential to the effective introduction of the more advanced forms of participation: QWL, Employee Stock Ownership Plans, or cooperatives. Within five years after the GM QWL program had been launched, 700 employees had been trained as QWL specialists and placed in the plants. All the employees at Chevrolet Gear, for example, who volunteer to join an employee participation circle receive a day of training in problem-solving. All of the 3,000 employees at GM's Tarrytown assembly plant had three days of training in problem-solving on company time as the QWL program was being introduced there.

For every graduate of Mills' familiarization programs, there are those who decide to explore new techniques in managing human resources on their own. Urged on not by shop floor complaints or some corporate crisis, but by a desire to work with people more effectively, they investigate the range of programs and then quietly implement them.

Frank Cirillo, senior vice-president for operations of Simmonds Precision Instrument Systems Division, was such a manager. His was a textbook case of top-down analysis and initiation of reform. He decided on his own to study ways of improving the productivity and quality of working life at his plant in Vergennes, Vermont. No crisis pushed him to action: the division and company, which makes a variety of systems instruments switches and high-quality area space fuel gauging, was doing very well. Indeed, between 1977 and 1981, Cirillo's division increased annual sales from about $20 million to over $50 million. More than 1,200 people worked in Vergennes, the largest division in the company.

In 1978, Cirillo first introduced "Flex-time"—flexible schedules built around a core of six-hour workdays. (In Vermont, that means you can see some daylight in the winter.) He had seen it in operation in Europe. He tested it on a small group at first, but had such success that he extended it to the entire 1,200-person division. He says, "Flex-time is a form of participatory management in that the employee is deciding what 'I' am going to do about the time that 'I' spend at my little business in the Simmonds Co. work station."[14]

Cirillo then looked for other ways to improve the workplace. "It really was not top-management-directed at all. It came as a revelation, or an understanding, that looking into programs formally, rather than catch-as-catch-can, might be a good approach. I discussed it with our division president and he encouraged me to follow it up. Essentially, the study took me through a number of compilations of what other companies and other countries are doing, and a lot of personal contact with people who have lived through the experience or are about ready to embark on it."

His research came down to a choice between employee suggestion systems or group participation schemes. "In sharing information with my colleagues, I concluded that I could get a 'bigger bang for the buck' or more employee participation with the Quality Circle concept. I believe that what captured my attention was that the suggestion system tends to cater to the individual in the organization who is outgoing, takes initiative, is aggressive, and might have a leg up on thinking power. So, if I want to get maximum employee participation, I might be inhibiting some people by using the suggestion system. Don't misunderstand me. I think the suggestion system is in our future as well, but I wanted to fire off a first shot that would give me the broadest coverage of employee involvement."

Groups of ten volunteers were established, built around first-line supervisors as team leaders. They met "once a week to brainstorm about change and how to improve the quality of work life, but also to help productivity and all the other good things that go with a group of people trying to change the way they are doing work." The five initial groups were in both blue- and white-collar departments, such as assembly, machine shop, and purchasing. Cirillo said, "I think we are raising the entire consciousness level of people at all levels in the division. One of the hidden by-products of this will be the emergence of another wave of natural leaders that are somewhere out there in the organization. Developing leadership and improving productivity go hand in hand. It's going to take time, but I'm going to bet on its success and I plan to double the number of circles next year." By September, 1981, the division had fifteen active circles.

Cirillo is a very matter-of-fact manager who points with approval to a quotation from the great English scientist Lord Kelvin: "When you can measure what you're speaking about and can express it in numbers, you know something about it. But when you cannot measure it, when you cannot express it in numbers, your knowledge is of a meagre and unsatisfactory kind. It may be the beginning of knowledge, but you have scarcely, in your thoughts, advanced to the stage of science."

And yet, though Cirillo has been guided by such pragmatism all his business life, he said, "I have also been very much interested in that which is not tangible. My common sense tells me the returns [of work reform] have got to be there."

When Cirillo decided to introduce more participation in his division, he had little to fear and nothing to lose. He set about his task like an engineer, doing the measurements and reading the literature. He had no pressure from above or below. He was interesting in ratcheting up productivity by a couple of percentage points, not starting a revolution from above. He had an established workforce with a strong, traditional work ethic in a growth industry. In his experiments, first with "Flex-time" and then with quality control circles, he really was doing what he thought was any good manager's job, developing the climate and people at hand.

While there are the exceptional managers such as Hewlett, Harman, Donnelly, and Lincoln—who, it is important to note, are both founders and owners as well—or the exceptional organizers, like Father Arizmendi of Mondragón, most people have neither the understanding nor the skills to effect such a transition. It is hard enough to establish that employee participation is something you want to try, let alone have the ability to plan and implement it.

A third party, either an individual or a team, not only helps the different groups to change their behavior; it can be a sort of benevolent termite in the organization, chewing into an existing organization's structure and processes so that managers and workers build new ones together. At its best, the third party helps people within an organization gently rotate the kaleidoscope of their relationships until they have settled on new structures more to their liking and comfort.

A third party may serve as a mediator, confessor, peaceful agitator, "change agent," or pot watcher. He or she may be "internal" or "external." But consultants, like chefs, come with a variety of cuisines and a range of talents: there are four-star chefs, and there are those who grill hamburgers. They must be chosen as carefully as any other element that contributes to work reform. "Third parties are vital," John Beck says, "because people have a tendency to undervalue what insiders say. We are talking about role changes, and a role change is often helped by someone who doesn't know the parties in their old roles."[15]

Consultants are almost always brought in and paid for by management. Workers trying to save their jobs or improve their working conditions usually have little time or money to spend on organizational development. A notable exception is the joint sponsorship of consultant Michael Maccoby by the Communications Workers of America and AT&T to establish a strategy for work improvement.

Those who look for a simple plan for participation, however, do not realize the importance of taking the leap of faith. "Often you are faced with situations where you let things evolve, and every day brings a new mystery. You simply have to have faith in mankind and your own capabilities and that managers and workers of organizations will be responsible enough to work things out."[16]

One of a consultant's most important functions is to teach the new skills of participative management, such as problem-solving skills and the art of conducting a good meeting—basic democratic behavior.

Nowhere is the need for consultations and training greater than in employee-owned businesses where, in the case of plant shutdowns, workers are suddenly asked to take on double burdens as owners and supervisors of management. Tove Hammer and her colleagues from Cornell's School of Industrial and Labor Relations, were crucial to the formation of a structure for employee ownership at the Rath Packing Company in Waterloo, Iowa. After a year's work with the union and management, they came up with a plan for members to buy 60 percent of the stock through an Employee Stock Ownership Plan, and to obtain a majority of the seats on the board of directors. Hammer joined ex-Senator Dick Clark as an "outside" representative on the board.

Lee Ozley, president of Responsive Organizations in Arlington, Virginia, and a consultant to businesses and unions on participatory management programs, summarized the lessons he has learned about getting programs started. The basic problem is how to encourage people to do something differently. First, they need an intellectual understanding of the new approach; then they must have an operational understanding of it. Finally, they need to learn the behavior which is required to implement it. Ozley, who was formerly an executive in the clothing industry, helps his clients to understand where they are now and where they would like to go. They then have to define the barriers to achieving their objective, and how they can use participatory methods for removing those barriers.

Many of his clients, according to Ozley, have overly high expectations of quick results. Neither management nor employees understand that such programs take months to initiate and years to nurture to sustained growth.

Consultants sometimes create problems for themselves, abandoning their neutral position and taking sides with either management or employees. Consultants may think they know all the answers to the organization's problems, and they may have an idea what process and structures make sense for their client, but that does not make them omniscient. Consultants go to training sessions and they come away thinking that "process" is God. Ozley has occasionally been too slow to confront his clients when they are "straying from the agreed values," and so has set up the following guideline: ". . . we see people make two mistakes; then when they do it a third time, we say you have just stubbed your toe a third time, and here are the previous two examples."[17]

Careful planning is critical to establishing a viable program in participatory management. But as the staff of the World Bank in Washington, D.C., learned, good planning and early employee involvement were not enough. The full understanding and active support of the chief executive were also needed.

In the spring of 1975, several middle-level staff members at the Bank began discussing the fact that bank management practices were impeding the set of objectives approved two years earlier by the board of directors. The board had decided, with President Robert S. McNamara's encouragement, that poverty in developing countries would be tackled more directly than in the past.

The staff discussions, with the help of Dr. Douglass Carmichael, a consultant, continued over two years of regular lunch-hour meetings. Two suggestions about changing management practices resulted. The first was to encourage the leaders of the teams which designed and supervised the Bank's loans to include the potential beneficiaries of those loans in both the planning and the management of them. The second suggestion was to tackle the problems relating to headquarters management. These were serious and of long standing. In the previous five years, the value of dollar lending had quintupled, and the staff had doubled, with a concomitant increase in organizational stress.

In 1974 a communications task force, approved by McNamara, documented the failure of managers to keep staff informed and involved in relevant decisions. Although a communications adviser was appointed to work on this problem, the effort was abandoned in 1976. Another report to the president in 1977 identified "an inappropriate management style . . . reflected in many decisions coming from the top of the pyramid without participation of the staff." A report in 1978 called attention to the "assembly-line style of work in the Bank." Lower level staff felt constrained and underutilized by management structure and procedures, including the several layers of middle management. Staff mistrusted management. Personnel and administrative policies were felt to be inappropriate. Job satisfaction and morale were falling.

In the spring of 1978, the discussion group went to the Staff Association, the Bank's employee union, and proposed a study of the strengths and weaknesses of the Bank's management and of greater staff involvement in making decisions as one way to solve these problems.

When the Association presented the plan to senior management, it received a lukewarm reception. McNamara said that participation was "just good management . . . but the approach would take too long." He would, however, welcome the study. At the same time, he advised his vice-presidents not to join the newly founded Participation Advisory Committee (PARTAC), whose members were a cross-section of the staff, including management, and which was to undertake the study.

After six months of effort, much of it on their own time, and with the help of five outside consultants and two full-time staff selected for the purpose, PARTAC's 40 members, including two vice-presidents who decided to join despite McNamara's warning, completed a report. It recommended using the Bank's staff more effectively by increasing their participation in making decisions. The report confirmed the previous assertions that the Bank was "over-controlled and undermanaged," meaning that the staff was being constrained by the very procedures which were supposed to improve its effectiveness. PARTAC concluded that as a result, staff "believe that open communication is not valued and acted upon, and managers may be insulated from the real problems of the Bank's operations."[18]

The report was distributed and widely discussed among the 5,000 staff at the headquarters. It recommended a work improvement program which would help groups to work in a more open, trusting, and effective way. By the time the report was finished, six work groups had already started to identify their management problems.

The vice-president for personnel strongly backed the report. A special consultant from Sweden, requested by McNamara to work on union-management problems, also endorsed it. Within five months, more than 40 of the Bank's 350 divisions held formal discussions on its implications. But six months after it had appeared, only 10 groups had gone beyond discussion.

What had happened? Participation was not a priority issue for McNamara, as he had made clear in his response to the Association's proposal. He didn't want to change his management style or techniques, nor did he have to. The crisis was small enough for him to dismiss the report as the bleatings of a few discontented middle managers. Although several managers and their staffs have initiated successful participation efforts for the introduction of office technology and team development, it is clear that, despite extensive planning, lukewarm support from the chief executive and his colleagues was not enough to launch a strong Bank-wide program.

Ninety-six percent of American companies are family-owned. This includes 177 of the Fortune 500. Many of them face a future with no appropriate family-connected successor to run them. The law relating to closely held companies, as interpreted by the Internal Revenue Service, is another problem.

Ed Sanders, president of Allied Plywood, Inc., of Arlington, Virginia, had no children to take over the firm he owned when he was ready to retire. When he sold some of his stock back to the company and took a substantial capital gain, the sale was taxed as regular income, not as a lower-bracket capital gain: under the law, the firm was "closely held," so appreciation in the value of the stocks was considered a dividend. The only alternative to paying the higher tax rate was to exchange stock with a large public company to qualify for the capital gains rate, but Sanders felt that solution would leave the employees at the mercy of a new owner. He had watched conglomerates which bought family firms fire their employees, milk the company of its cash and depreciation value, and then shut the plant down. (Allied's employees could not buy the stock themselves because they couldn't raise the capital.)

Then Sanders read a letter to the editor of the Washington *Post* from Norman Kurland, defending Employee Stock Ownership Plans (ESOPs). He called Kurland, who helped him set up an ESOP for Allied.[19]

.   .   .

A range of options faces anyone wishing to change an organization using principles of participation: these are summarized in Figure 5 on page 186. The options range from quality control circles to cooperatives. The more participation in management decisions or company ownership that an option offers, the further it is along the axes.

Three different types of Employee Stock Ownership Plans (ESOPs) demonstrate their flexible character. ESOP I gives the employees some ownership, but less than a fifty percent, or controlling, interest. Employee stockholders may or may not have the right to vote their stock. While ESOP II gives the employees controlling interest, only a small proportion of the employees, usually managers, holds the majority of the shares. ESOP III, a democratic ESOP (like the Rath Packing Company's), gives controlling interest to the majority of the employees, not just managers. It is also possible to have an ESOP where each employee has only one vote; this is identical to the "cooperative" option, or a cooperative ESOP.

On the management axis, QWL and Scanlon Plans usually give employees more decision-making authority than do the typical quality control circles. It is important to note that employee representation on the board may not, in fact, provide participation in major decisions, since the board does not participate in most decisions made in an organization. Board membership, however, is at the top of the axis because of the influence of the few decisions that a board does make.

It is important not to see these separate options as mutually exclusive. In fact, companies are rapidly combining different elements of them. General Motors has QWL and TRASOP, an ESOP cousin. Chrysler put an employee representative on the board and has begun quality circles. Eighty percent of Dana's employees are stockholders, and many of them are in Scanlon Plans.

It is clear from the illustrations cited above that there is no one way to initiate thought and action in the field of participation. Successful efforts, however, share several common elements. One is management understanding and commitment. Second, developing trust among the future partners is essential. Third, a cornerstone of the philosophy of participation is that people's participation be voluntary. Fourth, learning some new ways of doing things

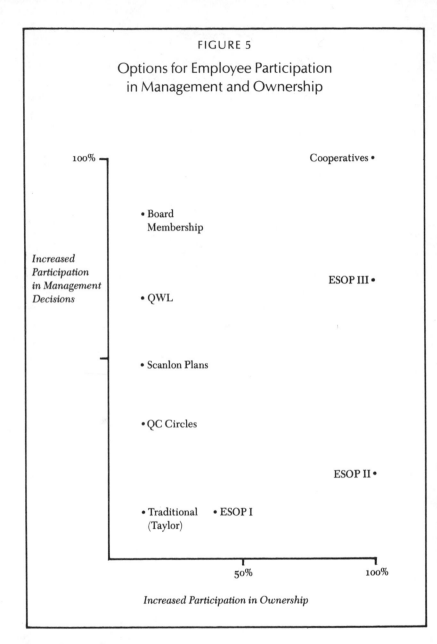

FIGURE 5

Options for Employee Participation
in Management and Ownership

100% ‒

Cooperatives •

• Board
Membership

*Increased
Participation
in Management
Decisions*

ESOP III •

• QWL

• Scanlon Plans

• QC Circles

ESOP II •

• Traditional   • ESOP I
(Taylor)

50%   100%

Increased Participation in Ownership

Note: ESOP Definitions:
   I. Minority Control of Common Stock for Employees
   II. All Employees Stockholders, but Managers Majority Control
   III. Employees Majority Control, but not one person/one vote.

like group problem-solving is usually essential. And fifth is the presence of a skilled outsider.

It is important to emphasize the pitfalls of getting participatory programs started. Top executives get so enthusiastic about the process that they want it done yesterday. The president of Motorola said in early 1981 that he wanted QWL in every department of the company by the end of the year. He subsequently changed the date to 1983, but that showed that he did not understand the critical voluntary aspect of QWL.

Executives may think they can buy a package and have someone install it for them, and that they themselves will not need to change. At the other extreme, they may try to provide too much direction for the program. Managers at all levels in an organization need to distinguish between the need for leadership and the chilling effect of domination. Rene McPherson says that his role at Dana was to "create the climate and get out of the way."[20]

Taking the first steps toward participation is not an orderly process, like buying a major appliance after reading *Consumer Reports.* Uncertainty is inevitable; only in retrospect does order appear.

Changes of any magnitude frighten people. Those with power are reluctant to give it up, and find lots of reasons why they shouldn't do so, or say the workers don't really want more responsibility. For those contemplating workplace democracy, the most important thing to keep in mind is that genuine participation means an inevitable change in power relationships. Business under more democratic systems will not be "as usual."

What is the toughest thing that people have to do to make these kinds of programs successful? "Ask people to behave differently," replied Lee Ozley, "and they don't know how to. They find QWL a threat to their authority, and it attacks their stereotype of subordinates. They wonder whether or not they will be seen as a failure if they use participatory management."[21] They must be reassured that this will not happen. They need to take the leap of faith, to achieve the perception that "the more power I give up, the more I get."

[11]

Sharing Decision-Making

As soon as many managers hear about "democracy in the work-place," they worry about "running the company by committee." In their minds, it is both absurd and dangerous to let workers make decisions about the management of an enterprise, its investments, its hirings and firings, or its product or markets. When the notions of democratic participation and consensus-seeking come in at the front door, efficiency and decisiveness are bound to be driven out the back.

Peter Drucker, the doyen of American management thinkers, is emphatic on this point. "I have very little interest in what is known as worker democracy because I believe you need decisions that are made exclusively in the interests of the enterprise. The moment you put workers into management decisions, you build rigidity into the economy." At the same time, Drucker is almost as adamantly in favor of "pushing the maximum of decision-making responsibility down the furthest possible [distance] to the things that the individual understands, which have a direct impact on him and which he is better qualified to handle than anyone else."[1]

On this second point, Drucker appears to have strong support from workers themselves. In a 1979 U.S. Chamber of Commerce poll of employees across a spectrum of employment, eighty-four percent said they would do a better job if they were involved in decisions affecting their work. Drucker believes in worker participation in shopfloor decision-making, but he calls it "citizenship," not "democracy." He abhors even the phrase "participatory management" as an "often futile attempt to disguise the reality of impotence through psychological manipulation."[2] Many workers and managers, however, believe that participatory management, at least the way they practice it, has removed rather than disguised the "reality of impotence."

Managers in organizations which have successfully implemented a philosophy of participatory management or ownership spend little time talking about "making decisions." Rather, they are concerned with "solving problems," as they have learned that people have to make decisions because there is some sort of problem. This chapter reviews the different degrees of participation in problem-solving that exist in different organizations.

The questions unanswered by the Chamber of Commerce poll are what issues do workers want to participate in, at what level, and what degree of control they do want over them. In his book *Workplace Democratization,* Paul Bernstein breaks participation in making decisions into three elements: the degree of control employees enjoy over a single decision, the issues over which that control is exercised, and the organizational level at which it is performed.[3]

What determines where a particular company or organization falls along a spectrum of greater to lesser participation is the amount of control management is willing to share. Bernstein's formulation provides a way of distinguishing between the superficial and the substantive, between the immediate and the remote. A decision taken for granted by a secretary at IBM about when he or she may go to the bathroom is an issue of participation for AT&T's telephone operators. Turning over control of the company's recreation program to the employees is not the same thing as involving them in a capital expansion plan. Being consulted about the colors in the cafeteria is different from having a veto over the introduction of new, labor-saving equipment. Management may retain final authority over the firm's policies, yet allow within those policies a great deal of worker autonomy and participation in making decisions.

Most discussion of workplace reform has dealt with voluntary problem-solving on what Irving Bluestone of the UAW called the "management of the job." He and other observers believed that problems in the 10- to 20-square-foot space used by workers on a daily basis were so manifold and manifest that it would be a long time before workers would want control at other levels in the organization. Worker involvement in "management of the firm" is rare, except in cases of employee-ownership or of a major crisis such as that at Chrysler. However, as workers gain more control over their immediate jobs, it seems inevitable that eventually they will see the links between their decisions and those made at higher levels and will want more substantial control.

Some proponents of workplace democracy say that the only real power is veto power. If you can't prohibit a company from shutting down a plant, then you have no real power. Participation in plant redesign is a snare and a delusion if the new design throws 50 workers out of their jobs. However, the shift in power or sharing problem-solving does not have to be absolute to be real. It need not be earth-shattering to be meaningful. It can be as simple as the ability to throw a switch.

Since Taylor's time, the fundamental symbol of the industrial era has been the inexorable assembly line and its relentless "count." This image of industrial life continues today despite the fact that today less than two percent of American workers labor on assembly lines, and their numbers decrease every year.[4] Human powerlessness and the dehumanization of work remain, however, something to fight against.

In the last few years, a number of companies have allowed workers to push the start-stop buttons which control the line. Previously, the line had always been kept moving regardless of the quality of the final product. In the face of competition for their goods, some companies opened up this closely guarded management prerogative to try to improve both quality and productivity. It's a small thing in the overall operation, but some workers described their new authority as they would a first communion. Agnes Bogarz, a grandmotherly "utility person" in a Matushita television factory in Illinois, was one of them. Her line produced 500 televisions per shift.

"The first time I stopped the line, I was scared. I thought I might get fired. I think it was the wrong parts they were putting on the panels. But nothing happened to me. It made me feel good to think that I could do it and solve the problem. You just feel more involved. This company strives for quality and you just want to help them."[5]

In the 1970's, many management-initiated work reform projects accompanied the construction of new factories. Managers and personnel directors believed that a new factory, location, and (non-union, many of them hoped) workforce would create an atmosphere conducive to improved relations between workers and managers. They sought to implement some of the socio-technical ideas developed in Europe.

Among the European pioneers in work redesign and participation was a giant British chemical company, Imperial Chemical Industries, Ltd. When its American subsidiary decided to build a new plant on the Texas Gulf coast, company officials were already familiar with the parent company's participation projects.

"I think it came about as a realization by ourselves and a lot of other companies that there's got to be a better way to operate a plant. . . . When you build a new plant, you get all your best engineers [to] go over all the equipment. But you never really do that on the people side of it. So we said, OK, here's a chance. . . . We've got 250 acres of scrub and mesquite in Bayport, Texas. Let's start questioning every fundamental assumption about what we're going to do on the people side."[6]

This is how James C. McCarty, a manager, explained the way management thought in 1976–77, when ICI Americas set out to build a $70 million, highly automated plant to make the herbicide Paraquat.

ICI managers were not interested in changing the world, or in creating a new era in worker participation. They sought to involve workers in decisions not because they wanted them to "self-actualize" but because the more alert and committed the workers were, the better operators they would make.

"The dread of any manager in a chemical processing plant is

emergencies, so that is what you have to prepare people to handle," said Donald Kotrady, the former Bayport plant manager. "You have to do things to motivate people because you can very easily fall into a routine of being stale and not learning. One of the things we try to do is to have total flexibility, people learning a number of jobs so they continue to use their brains."[7]

The planners at ICI, which included Kotrady and McCarty, were confronting what has sometimes been called the "Three Mile Island Syndrome," the tendency for routine jobs to produce inattention and boredom. When a process is so highly automated that people only watch dials, they can neither anticipate problems nor respond quickly enough when things go wrong. With expensive equipment and a volatile product, an incorrect reaction is not only costly but potentially catastrophic.

As Richard Hoots, ICI vice-president, said, "We start by asking ourselves, why should the guy running the distillation column be any less motivated to do a good job than the site manager? And we set up the whole program to provide that kind of motivation."[8]

To do the job, ICI Americas had a clean slate—a new $70 million plant and 57 jobs to fill out of a large applicant pool. They chose chemical engineers with B.A. and M.A. degrees as their first-line supervisors with the full knowledge that they would be promoted out of those jobs. At the same time, they brought those supervisors directly into the hiring process by having them interview those who would replace them. In his interviews with applicants, McCarty stressed that to work at ICI was to give up the notion of identifying with a particular job. "We're trying to get everyone to understand what's behind the gauge. And so what you need are guys who are very flexible, and have a wide job description, who don't have the 'Chico and the Man' syndrome of 'Hey, man, that isn't my job!' but who say, 'What do you want me to do?'"

Job rotation was required: in addition to each employee's primary responsibility, he or she had to learn two subordinate jobs, as well as basic maintenance skills from several other fields.

To achieve the initial phase of flexibility and cross-training, Bayport borrowed the idea of a "fifth shift" from one of ICI's plants in Canada. A chemical processing plant usually has four shifts which rotate in a variety of ways. Adding a fifth shift meant that for one week a month, each operator is rotated out of his or her job and spends the week being trained in maintenance or another specialty. Operators take over many of the maintenance tasks, which cuts down on the need for and the cost of calling in outside maintenance crews. For the employees, a "fifth shift" means two consecutive weeks on day shift and a four-day weekend. "For two weeks, it meant the operators could live like normal people."[9]

Next, everyone was put on salary; the company also instituted a program of "discipline without punishment." If a worker persisted in some proscribed behavior—absenteeism, smoking in a non-smoking area—through a series of steps, the supervisor would send him/her home *with* pay to think it over. If the employee came back, agreed to abide by the rules, and broke them again, firing would result.

Even with this high degree of participation, management never abdicated its right to manage, McCarty hastened to say. "Management has to make the basic decisions. But once you set your parameters of what the company can handle, why not let people decide the rest?"

A visit to the plant found that employees seemed to feel adequately consulted, and were not demanding more participation than the company offered. The company was treating "every worker like a manager" without much self-importance.

Not all the workers, however, were convinced that the fifth shift was the way to make every operator as concerned about the distillation column as the plant manager, and they feared that too much job rotation could be harmful. Further, some worried that some workers were taking advantage of the "discipline without punishment": when a worker was sent home for smoking "funny cigarettes," they felt old-fashioned punishment would have been in order.

ICI set out to build a plant that would give it the most flexible, responsible workforce it could find and train. It had the pick of the crop. In the first four years, not one worker quit to join another chemical company, and the number of operating employees had been reduced by 27 percent. Direct maintenance costs dropped by 15 to 20 percent, and the company decided to use the same general techniques in another new plant being built next door.

Workers at the plant enjoyed freedom and challenge in their jobs. "They put more trust in you than in most plants," said one. Chris Wright, a technician, said, "The fact that you can do a variety of things makes it less monotonous. Solving your own problems is good. It makes the time pass faster when you can do it yourself."[10]

One of the most famous cases of work redesign in the 1970's was the Gaines Dog Food Plant of General Foods Corporation in Topeka, Kansas. Within five years of start-up, however, its new ways of empowering workers to make decisions had upset the corporate management in White Plains, New York. They forced Topeka management to take control back from the workers and refused to talk to outsiders about the project.

To return to the beginning: In 1969, General Foods had endless problems at its Kankakee, Illinois, dog food plant. Racial tensions were rising, the union was fractious, absenteeism was up, sabotage was high. But the dog food business was booming, and there was a need for another plant.

General Foods' top managers thought they perhaps could avoid some of their current headaches if they went to a "green field" site, built a new plant with the latest technology, and hired new workers. They decided to use the plant as a laboratory for some of the socio-technical principles which seemed to be working so well in Scandinavia. The "Topeka system" of organizing the plant was based on the premise that "bad quality is inevitably a product of alienation."[11]

To make the most of the new facility, the company carefully chose the initial 63-person workforce out of 1,200 applicants. Through a battery of tests, people were picked for their initiative, intelligence, and ability to work in a group.

All the latest principles were applied to the "Topeka system." There were no demeaning time clocks. Employees were organized into 8- and 16-person teams, which were given significant control over hiring and promotion of fellow workers. The teams did a variety of jobs on a rotation system. Some laboratory processes were deliberately not automated, to permit workers a chance to participate at different levels. Team leaders were chosen to be coaches, not foremen; to lead by example, not direction. For a time, workers set production quotas.

As Lyman Ketchum, the manager of the Kankekee plant and designer of the Topeka plant, said, "If people are to have self-esteem, you have to do things to satisfy them. If they are to have a sense of accomplishment, they have to be able to finish their tasks. Autonomy means they have to be able to plan the work, check the quality, change the design of the jobs. They have to have real control, and not just over simple stuff, like when to take a coffee break—its the real guts of the job."[12]

The "enabling legislation" for this experiment was the corporate document entitled "Topeka Organization Systems and Development," which said in part: "Humans will best respond . . . when there exists a high feeling of self-worth by the employee, and employee identification with success of the total organization . . . an organization which more fully utilizes human potential of employees can pay off in dollars and cents."[13]

Eighteen months into the experiment, plant manager Edward Dulworth painted a rosy picture: "People have more responsibilities here, broader jobs, more authority, a lot of freedom. There are very few written statements as to what is expected in terms of behavior. . . . People are free to come and go when they wish. In the plant, the operators are free to arrange the tasks among themselves. The scheduling—who does what and when—is all handled by the people in the plant. Everybody is involved in all aspects of the business. We have committees on safety, fire and disaster, spare parts, welfare and benefits, recreation and so on. Almost everyone has some part in the committee work."[14]

After four years, Richard Walton, a designer of the new system and professor at the Harvard Business School, reported that the plant had saved about $1 million a year, with unit costs running about 5 percent less than at conventional General Foods plants. Absenteeism was below 1.5 percent and the plant required only 70 people, compared to the 110 it had been designed to employ.[15] "Topeka" showed that workers could take control over management decisions and the company still make a profit. Yet, by March, 1977, *Business Week* magazine reported that the "Topeka System" was cracking and company officials were "Stonewalling Plant Democracy."

What had happened? Was General Foods losing money? Apparently not: through 1980 the Topeka plant ranked number one in corporate performance every year but one since it had opened. Was it fighting a unionizing drive? No. Was too much democracy somehow the problem?

Four of the managers who had been identified with the experiment at the beginning went to other General Foods divisions or left the company during the first three years. They were replaced by managers far less sympathetic to the experiment. Walton observed in late 1976 that there were "doubts about the [corporate] hierarchy's understanding [of] or commitment to the Topeka innovation" from the start.[16]

Daniel Zwerdling, a writer who specialized in work reform projects, blamed much of the lack of management interest on the "threats" to the jobs of corporate specialists and technicians: the personnel manager, the laboratory chemists, the quality control personnel, and the engineers at corporate level were unhappy when they didn't have their professional kinsmen to talk to at the plant. Here were all these *workers* doing jobs formerly held by managers. It had been very disconcerting for a General Foods manager at another plant to call up the Topeka plant, ask for the personnel manager or lab technician, and hear a voice say, "I'm it for this week."[17]

There was also disillusionment in the ranks. The workers found that after the TV crews and reporters left, they were still dealing with dog food, and it was dog food manufactured to management's specifications, in amounts determined by management, and shipped according to orders developed by management.

Part of the problem lay in inflated expectations. After listening to the publicists, journalists, "change agents," and sympathetic managers, workers may have come to believe all the positive rhetoric of the "Topeka System." When the enthusiasm wore off, many workers looked around and asked what the benefits really were. "We were in the clouds for a long time," said one worker, "but 300 tons of dog food a day, every day, can bring you down to earth in a hurry."

They wondered if General Foods was just rotating their jobs to reduce labor costs. Their frustrations were exacerbated by the difficulty of judging and being judged by their peers, especially on matters of pay.[18]

As one employee observed bitterly, "You get right down to the fact that they [management] can do whatever they want. They run it. They own it. What's to stop them? What right do I have? I mean, they didn't have to let us do this whole thing in the first place. That plant is there for one reason—to make money."[19]

However, the main problem with the Topeka system was at corporate headquarters in White Plains. Senior management there lacked commitment to the project's stated objectives. While Chauncey W. Cook, chairman of the board at the time the plant was being planned, was a strong supporter of it, few managers went along with him. Willis Easter, the assistant manager of the plant who left in 1978 and is now with McNeil Customer Products Company, said that "senior management did not understand what they were doing. When they got some bad publicity about the plant, they clammed up."[20]

Corporate spokesmen have refused to discuss what happened. In September 1981, however, they permitted the current plant manager and five employees to attend an international meeting in Toronto on the quality of work life. Their remarks were guarded, but the audience did learn that the plant still had the highest performance of any General Foods plant, and the best safety record. Further, the two levels of middle management that the corporate office had put into the plant about 1976 were taken out again eighteen months later; the original project design is virtually intact.

Donnelly Mirrors in Holland, Michigan, comes close to what Peter Drucker had in mind when he pictured a self-governing plant community. Founded in 1905, Donnelly has been a closely held corporation manufacturing auto parts. Over the years, the company has evolved a sophisticated yet practical system of employee participation in the governance of the plant. By all accounts, it is one of the most advanced systems of participation in the United States.

Much of the credit goes to John Donnelly, who left the priesthood to become president of the company in 1932 when his father died. Over the years, Donnelly has worked constantly to expand the role of all employees in the running of the company.

In 1952, the employees voted to adopt a Scanlon Plan as both a participative style of management and a company-wide bonus system based on cost reductions. Within a year, Donnelly employees modified the bonus system: instead of limiting the savings pool to labor costs, which set departments against each other, they included savings on materials and operating supplies as well. In another divergence from regular Scanlon Plan practice, the company decided not to recalculate the monthly bonus when new machinery was introduced, because the decision to purchase the machine would have been made by the employees. In effect, all employees would contribute to the constant upgrading of equipment without fear of being replaced. The result would combine a guarantee against technologically induced layoffs and a retention of machine improvement in the bonus base.

In 1964, Donnelly added another level of participation. With the help of University of Michigan sociologist Rensis Likert, the company installed a system of interlocking work teams, so that worker experts could join together to fashion a whole larger than the sum of its parts. The teams of eight to twelve people were built around specific tasks, with leaders chosen by a cross-section of peers, subordinates, and superiors. Each leader was also a member of the team at the next higher level of management. The teams try to make decisions by consensus, but if they can't, the leader makes the decision. There is no abdication of management responsibility.[21]

A new engineer told Donnelly he was awestruck by the willingness of shopfloor workers to share expertise readily and openly. Donnelly explained that this happened because the workers "expect that you're not going to abuse the information, and that if you want to do something with it, you will talk it over with them and that if there are any problems, you'll work them out together."[22]

One of the most interesting innovations is the Donnelly Committee, a plant-wide assembly of all employees in which every thirty-five employees elect one representative to serve a two-year term. The body handles all personnel matters such as fringe benefits, pay policies, and grievances. Recommendations by the committee have the weight of board decisions. They must be unanimous, and the entire workforce votes annually whether to continue this policy of unanimity.[23]

Jo Ann Czerkies, an employee in the molded products department, called the committee "the heart of the company" where "very big decisions are made and where we've got management people, production people, office people—everyone—represented. The company *is* everybody, you know."[24]

What Donnelly has developed is a parallel and interlocking system of participation: an executive system of management built on the teams and a representative system that deals with the human "frictions that normally develop in the course of the work."[25] The cement for the system's success is trust and participation in the financial rewards.

Donnelly recalled the Hawthorne experiments of Elton Mayo, when researchers found that "if you pay attention to people, they perform better. And what we are trying to do is pay attention to people on a constant basis. So, in a way, what we're trying to do is have a continuous Hawthorne Effect."[26]

In the Pacific Northwest are a group of cooperatives which are the most successful and long-lasting combination of democracy and efficiency in the United States. Because many were started as cooperatives, they resemble "green field" plants. They are the twelve cooperatives which produce about 12 percent of the plywood for the American market. While Bayport and Topeka are advanced examples of increasing the decision-making authority of workers, management there still retains final authority for policy decisions. In the plywood cooperatives, the workers—and the managers—*indirectly* control all decisions including those concerning policy. Control is indirect because each employee owns a share of stock in the firm, which gives the right to elect a board of directors.

Not only have the plywood coops competed successfully with giants like Weyerhaeuser, but they have proved that their payment of wages 25 percent higher than the competition's is justified by their 25–60 percent greater productivity. They have shown that they can not only survive in a tough market, but, due to their greater efficiency, pay higher wages as well. Some of the companies have become so successful that they have been picked off by the large lumber companies anxious to get their hands on the plywood firms' forest reserves.

Some mills were started from scratch by woodworkers who wanted to control their own jobs. Others were taken over from conventional firms which were closing their mills. In almost every case, the individuals chipped in equal sums, customarily $1,000 to $2,000. There is no outside ownership.

Based on a one-employee, one-vote principle, ultimate control of decisions is vested in a General Meeting of the members. In two or three meetings per year, they set overall policy, may remove the general manager, vote on capital expenditures over a certain amount ($25,000 in some cases), and elect an odd-numbered board of trustees from their own ranks.

Day-to-day management is handled by a non-member manager hired by the board of trustees, to whom he is directly responsible, reporting at weekly or bi-weekly meetings. In the plywood coops, the manager is caught in the middle, since he is deliberately chosen to reduce friction among members and to give the coop expertise. He does not have an ownership stake, but carries the hopes, fears, expectations, and demands of those who do.

Turnover among plywood coop managers is high. Berchal Montieth, manager at the North Pacific Plywood Company, voiced their dilemma: "If this were a privately owned corporation, I'd make different economic decisions. I'd take more gambles, make more investments, try different pay scales and that sort of thing. But here, the men have bought a job and they want to take the money home with them. I can't say 'the hell with it,' because it's *their* mill. Most corporate managers don't give a goddamn what the workers take home. They just want to see some big profits."[27]

Calvin Lloyd, manager at the Everett Plywood Company, added, "Suppose I think we need a new barker, which I do, and suppose you have three hundred people out there in the mill who want a twenty-five-cent raise. Now who wins?"[28]

In some cases, the board rubber-stamps the manager's decisions, but in others, boards watch the managers closely on everything from disciplining workers to small capital investments.

The board members, in turn, are under constant scrutiny by the membership, who work next to them in the planing mills or warehouses. Board members are elected to one-year terms and those who act against the wishes of their members are simply not re-elected. Just what those "wishes" are, of course, varies widely. There is a tremendous amount of informal discussion between board members and those they represent.

Diffusing information on a timely basis is crucial to any business, but in coops, it must be shared particularly thoroughly. "If you stay aloof and don't communicate with the owners, you don't get much of the information you need," commented Leamon J. Bennett, then chairman of the board of the Puget Sound Plywood Company.

"It's not so much a matter of being influenced by what the owners think, and doing what they want . . . as it is knowing the information for making the right decision. We've always got that bottom line to worry about, just as any other company does . . . the primary thing is communication. I don't think you'd be on the board long if you communicated well, but couldn't defend your decisions before the other owners. But no matter what your intellect, you wouldn't get re-elected if you don't continually talk with them about what's going on."[29]

The darker side of the communication coin is the complaint that sometimes there is too much of it. "There's too many chiefs and not enough Indians in this place. Everybody thinks [he's] boss

. . . everybody stands around and tells everybody else what to do. We get to arguing among ourselves, then we don't do nothing. I think that's a bad thing," one worker said.[30]

Bennett and other board members say that one of the key benefits of shopfloor board membership comes with turnover of members. The terms are staggered so that there is time for new members to learn their duties gradually. Over the long run, more members become familiar with the sometimes conflicting demands of a business.

As democratic and efficient as they are, the plywood cooperatives have been unable to solve the problem of how to bring in new workers as owners, as Mondragón has done. As the companies have prospered and the average stake has increased 20–50 times in value, the original members have been reluctant to dilute their holdings. A worker would now need to stake up to $100,000 to become an owner.

For all the plywood coops, the solution has been to hire outside workers who cannot be shareholders. Thus, a two-class system has formed, not as extreme as that of ancient Athens with its citizens and slaves, but embarrassing to the members and galling to the non-members.

It would be wrong to dismiss this genuine dissatisfaction, but given the plywoods' patent financial success, one must conclude that they have learned to cope with the tensions of both long-term and short-term demands. They do not suffer unduly from excessive delays in making decisions.

Many different ways exist to solve problems and share decision-making. Different methods, ranging from secret and unilateral to public and consensual, are appropriate for different circumstances. Both extremes are used by people in both authoritarian and participatory organizations. Bayport, Topeka, and the plywood coops illustrate the opportunity for participation in decision-making where management could start from scratch with the "green field," building the plant or hiring the people to fit the new management system it had in mind, rather than patching up the old as at Donnelly.

Bayport and Topeka show how far plant management can go in giving up some decisions to the workers and sharing others. In both cases, however, management retained control of basic policy decisions. In the Topeka case the changes were so threatening to the corporate management philosophy of General Foods that company headquarters management forced the plant manager to change his approach. Bayport did not have these problems because corporate management of ICI had a better understanding of what participation involved. They were committed to providing a supportive environment for their managers, and judged them by the plants' performance.

The plywoods were also "green fields," with one important difference from Bayport and Topeka: the employees were also the owners, and elected the board of directors. Therefore, they had control, albeit indirectly through their board representatives, over the firm's major policies. The employees at Bayport and Topeka did not.

The plywood and Mondragón coops have built a sophisticated means of combining democratic oversight with efficient delegation of authority for day-to-day operations. In these coops, managers have found that their mandate to concentrate on the firm's economic priorities is not compromised or unduly constricted by their being selected by the employees. Under this division of labor, the manager can be the guardian of efficiency, the member-workers the guardians of fairness, and the board the honest broker.

These illustrations should begin to dispel the myth that even advanced forms of participatory management and ownership mean that everybody gets involved in every decision. In firms with over ten employees, it just does not happen that way. People do not like to sit in meetings all day long, and they do not. They trust their colleagues and they delegate authority to them. While workers would like to have their ideas heard at the highest levels of an organization, most prefer to put their energy into those decisions that directly affect their own jobs.

[12]

Participatory Leadership

From Warlord to Colleague

David K. Easlick, the president of Michigan Bell Telephone, thought that his company could be better managed. He asked an outside consultant to interview the company's forty-five top managers about this question and to report to him their consensus. Easlick reported on his discussion with the consultant. "I expected to hear a whole range of ideas and complaints; and I was prepared to change the way we did things in any way that seemed reasonable and useful. But as I listened to the consultant's report . . . it became depressingly obvious that he was telling me that the major problem was *me*, the way *I* was managing: *my* management style! Inside, I remember being angry, hurt and faintly sick. I had an urge to throw him out of my office. But the case was documented. He had it from the people who knew, and had the biggest stake in my management behavior. . . . After we got our own act together in the Executive Group, we got a number of things going at Michigan Bell. . . . I began changing myself from supreme warlord, order giver, and chief idea man to someone closer to being a colleague, listener and cooperator."[1]

Easlick personifies three good qualities of the participatory leader. First, he had enough curiosity about how he might improve the organization to ask his subordinates for their advice, filtering it through a consultant. Second, he was able to acknowledge that he was a major part of the problem. Third, he was willing to change his management style and practice.

The difficulty of changing management style cannot be overestimated. The solitary ascent through the ranks of an existing hierarchy is, by definition, success. Why should people who have struggled to the top think of changing? While it may occur to them that there are more participatory ways of managing, it is usually hard to find the time to give them a try. As Rene McPherson, former Dana Corporation president, said, "The typical manager is over-educated, over-energized, pretty confident and dynamic. *That* is the person to whom you are going to say, 'Let the people decide'? That is like asking a Senator or Congressman to be concerned about all the people, not just his constituents. It doesn't happen very often."[2]

Most managers, if asked, would say that they are already participatory. They consult their subordinates about many decisions, and, if they are senior executives, talk about the importance of decentralized authority. Consultation and talk, however, are a long way from the more advanced forms of participation which some organizations are using.

The most paradoxical figure in the move toward workplace democracy is the leader. In every situation, top management support is vital for the initiation and ultimate success of reform. A basic characteristic of the participatory leader is that he or she views the redistribution of power as sharing, not surrender. Good managers "must possess a high need for power, that is, a concern for influencing people. However, this need must be disciplined and controlled so that it is directed toward the benefit of the institution as a whole and not toward the manager's personal aggrandizement."[3]

Management experts Robert Tannenbaum and Warren Schmidt have classified different management styles which they illustrate with four actual quotations from managers about their use of power.

1. "I believe in getting things done. I can't waste time calling meetings. Someone has to call the shots around here, and I think it should be me."
2. "Once I have decided on a course of action, I do my best to sell my ideas to my employees."
3. "It is foolish to make decisions oneself on matters that

affect people. I always talk things over with my subordinates, but I make it clear to them that I'm the one who
has the final say."

4. "I put most questions into my group's hands and leave
it to them to carry the ball from there. I serve merely
as a catalyst, mirroring . . . people's thoughts and feelings so that they can better understand them."[4]

Twenty years ago, these researchers and others began to challenge the efficiency of "highly directive leadership" as illustrated
by statements 1 and 2. By 1982 the research evidence is conclusive
that participation can work in many organizations. (See Appendix
1 for productivity results.) This chapter describes the experiences
of senior managers who have been leading a shift to more participatory management and ownership.

Elsa Porter, a former Assistant Secretary of Commerce for Administration, would put herself in category 4. She observed that
many people are dependent on the leader for their own power.
"My predecessors had all been combative people, coming in and
fighting. The people under them drew a lot of this negative power
from a 'strong' leader. As I am a mediator, they view me as a 'soft'
leader. Since I try to resolve conflicts in a non-bloody way, this
does not do anything for their egos."[5]

For Porter, a basic problem of leadership *is* to define effective
power. Her predecessors' understanding of power was that of a
"warrior kind of power. My kind is conflict resolution—[a] mediat-
ing, caring kind of power. I see that as power to get people to do
things in a constructive way that gets them to grow and develop.
My predecessors didn't see that as power at all. They measured
power by how many notches in your gun, how many victims."

When Porter had to appoint a new director of the Audit Department, the excellent QWL project in that department ended.
The new director, said Porter, "does not understand what the
project is all about . . . she is so unsure of herself" that she can not
even maintain such an innovative approach to work. As a result,

many people left the department. Porter had been involved in selecting the new director, and had looked specifically for someone with the leadership skills to maintain the project. What happened? "We were under duress," Porter said, "and had to do it quickly. We misjudged."[6]

According to F. James McDonald, president of General Motors Corporation, the personal values of managers who excel in leading Quality of Work Life programs are those necessary in any good manager. Application of them, however, may differ. The most important is "personal integrity: you cannot say one thing and do another." In a participatory management style, "if you cut the legs out from under your subordinates once they step over the line, you haven't got integrity."

If QWL is so important to GM, why, after more than seven years, is QWL in only 80 of the 150 GM plants? "QWL," McDonald said, "is not something you can dictate. [You cannot] say to a manager, 'put this in your plant, or if you don't . . . you are not a good manager.' Or, 'Bob's operation has got QWL and he's doing great, so you better get going.' Those kind of efforts don't pay off. You have to find some way or other to get a manager to believe that this is the best way to run his business."

What role does GM leadership play in creating this belief? The manager has to know that it can work. McDonald said: "He's got to see the opportunity in his own operation. Unless he believes in it himself, he just can't get a QWL program off the ground. If the programs are forced on people, they simply won't work.

"You can work around a passive local union, but you have a heck of a time with a local that is dead-set against putting this kind of a program in [its] plant. That doesn't mean that the manager gives up; he's just got to work a little longer and harder to convince people . . . to create the environment. If there [has been] mistrust over the years between management and the local union, you don't turn that all around by all of a sudden saying, 'Hey, fellas, let's start out tomorrow doing things differently.' You have to build up . . . trust and credibility from scratch. When you have accomplished that, you then talk about a QWL program. If the manager believes it, it will come."

A chief executive must not only be supportive, but must promote the benefits of QWL to the maximum. He or she also has to demonstrate behavior that is consistent with the philosophy. McDonald had been president for only four months when we interviewed him, and he had already begun to improve communications between the Executive Committee and the Executive Group of GM. To demonstrate that he could improve his own behavior, he had initiated a two-day off-site meeting with the members of these two committees, and had used games to loosen people up and create a congenial environment.

Using QWL guidelines, McDonald was advised that he should not chair the meeting; instead, a "facilitator" with corporate QWL expertise, Dr. Howard Carlson, was recommended to take the place of a formal chair. During the meetings, a number of serious problems surfaced that had not been raised before. The members of the Executive Group, each responsible for combined Divisions generating several billions of dollars in sales, said they "felt like an information-gathering group that went to the Divisions for the information and passed it on to the Executive Committee to make the decisions. The Executive Committee didn't think that that was what the Executive Group did—we always felt that we had them participate. The key point was, *they* didn't think that they did. You want people that high up in the organization to take responsibility, but they have to have authority with that responsibility."

"We talked," said McDonald, "about how [to] improve the relationship between me and the group executives and [to] expand the responsibility and authority of the group executives. When you go off site and ask, 'What do you really think?', you find it out." That was the first QWL "off-site" for GM's top executives.

McDonald said that the meeting also helped break down barriers among people at that level: "It was the barrier to telling the person up above what you are doing wrong." In a participatory climate, it is easier for a subordinate to tell the boss, "Here are the kinds of things that you and/or the rest of the top group do which inhibit my ability to do the job."[7]

Few companies have been as profitable for as many years as the Hewlett-Packard electronics firm of Palo Alto, California. In forty years it has grown from a two-man company in a backyard garage to a firm with $2.4 billion in sales (1981) and a world-wide operation. Hewlett-Packard employs 50,000 people, who work at either research and development or manufacturing. It was one of the first American companies to use quality control circles.

William Hewlett, in a recent interview, described the important dimensions of his company's approach to participation, which had worked so well at unlocking the energy and creativity of the employees, including himself. Even as the company grew to multinational proportions, Hewlett would spend hours each month sitting at workbenches and drafting tables talking with technicians and engineers.

The "H-P Way," according to Hewlett, is based on the belief that "men and women want to do a good job, and a creative job. If they are provided the proper environment, they will do so." Hewlett says that the company has had a "tradition of treating each individual with respect and recognizing personal achievements."[8]

Job security is an important dimension of the H-P Way. "Both Packard and I were products of the depression and we saw what happened. We did not want a hire-and-fire operation." The two men also knew what it was like to do routine, menial jobs. "Dave and I had done everything, at one time or another, from sweeping the floor to keeping the books. We know the people and could sympathize with their problems."[9] When an employee came down with TB, at a time when the company did not have health insurance, the employers assisted him, and subsequently they took out catastrophic coverage for everyone.

When orders fell in 1970, and they faced laying off 15 percent of the workforce, they decided instead to cut one full day every two weeks. All employees, including executives, took a 15 percent pay reduction. Everyone shared the burden, and in six months, the company was on a full schedule again. "Dave and I saw the problems and tried to take care of them."

Hewlett was actually trying to make the lives of the employees easier; there was no "hidden agenda of increased productivity." Unnecessary rules had proliferated as the company grew, and he wanted to reduce the arbitrary treatment this encouraged. The time clock was removed early in the company's history: flexible hours worked in their German plant, so they were tried, successfully, in California. For years there was no personnel department; even now it is used only for administration, and does not affect the "relationship between a manager and his employees." With managers encouraged to be more responsible for employees, and as a result of making things easier for workers, Hewlett and Packard found "they all did better work."

Asking such flexibility and awareness from managers makes good candidates hard to find. While Hewlett believes in promoting from within the organization, the company's rapid growth has meant that a substantial number of outsiders have been hired, some of whom have to learn that they "just don't order people around." Hewlett reports that "we have had our aggressive managers, but the system kind of knocks off [their] corners. You need aggression, but it cannot be at the expense of everything else."

Hewlett feels that employees who are shareholders are better employees. They own more than fifty percent of the common stock. Participation in profit-sharing is also an important part of the Hewlett-Packard approach: the company offered profit-sharing to all employees from the establishment of the firm. When the bonus reached eighty percent of the average employee's wages, wages and salaries were increased by fifty percent, and bonuses reduced to about twenty percent. In the late 1950's, HP went to a scheme of 12 percent of pre-tax profits to the employees because it worked better for the multi-plant operation that they had become. For the first half of 1981, corporate earnings totaled $137 million, of which Hewlett-Packard paid out $38 million to their employees through profit-sharing; the stockholders got $12 million in dividends. There are no individual bonuses. "We felt that the employees would take a greater interest in work if they felt they were part of the company." Employee stock ownership has also provided more than $25 million in self-financing.

Hewlett offered this advice to managers interested in trying participation: "Don't let the system get away from you. Sometimes you have to forget . . . management by objectives, and have management by decree. You don't like to do that, but you have to be prepared to do it." For example, at the end of the 1980 budget process, in which he had been a full participant, Hewlett still felt that the weak economy did not warrant the size of the budget his colleagues wanted. His decree was, "Cut it back ten percent."[10]

For a democratically owned firm, the demystification of management is not even an option; it is a necessity. The leaders of a cooperative simply cannot remain aloof from either the board of directors or the worker-owners. It is often thought that the selection of officers in a democratically owned and managed firm would be a popularity contest and that workers could not select a good leader. Leamon J. Bennett, president of Puget Sound Plywood, a cooperative with 240 worker-owners and 130 hired employees, disagreed. The company has grown steadily since its founding in 1941, and sales in 1979 were $41 million.

Each owner has one vote to elect the board of directors. "The first time the members select a president, they may be looking for someone who is witty and has a good deal of charisma, which are probably not the best qualities to look for," said Bennett. The second time around, "they look at what the fellow has done, how he has carried the ball, whether they have confidence in him."[11]

Bennett distinguished between being liked and being informed. He felt that it was "not so much a question of doing what the owners want and being likeable, as it is knowing the information for making the right decision." In a recent election, one board member ran for re-election and did not make it. The membership felt that he had not "communicated enough."

The leadership demands of a cooperative are obviously different from those of a traditional organization with absentee owners.

Bennett, for example, often comes in early to have meetings which relate to his job as president. Then he goes on to his shift in the mill. There is a full-time manager. He said that his job as president is to be "an arbitrator . . . and a spokesman for the members." His function is to make recommendations at board and shareholder meetings.

The board of directors in the plywood coops plays a special role in addition to its normal function of setting policy and hiring the general managers. Board members have more sources of information from within the mill than the managers because "we work out there, most of us." At the board meetings, which are held once a week, "we match notes."[12]

Frances Heaps is the president of International Group Plans, a 180-employee direct-mail group health insurance company which is a subsidiary of Consumers United Group in Washington, D.C. Each employee, after a six-month probation period, has one vote in selecting the board of directors. Annual sales are $60 million.

Heaps described what it was like to be the president of a firm where the employees, acting through the board of directors, could fire you. "I have very little decision-making authority. I cannot hire and fire. The teams which work together do that, since they have to live with the people involved 40 hours a week. My role is primarily to coordinate, to provide technical expertise where I can, to provide initiative in problem-solving, and to sign contracts with the outside world—which needs a president."[13]

IGP organizes its employees into three decision-making levels. The work of the firm is done in teams which select a leader; leaders sit on the departmental committee. Departmental coordinators, in turn, select a representative to sit on the company-wide committee, headed by the president. Coordinators carry policies down the organization, and the concerns of the staff up.

Heaps does not consider health insurance by direct mail IGP's main product. "I consider our main product the participation of people in decision-making in their workplace. It is their right to grow as human beings." The real objective of the business is making life a little better for the people who are involved—the employees, the suppliers, and the clients—not corporate profits and employee income.

Heaps feels that there is nothing more boring than the insurance business, but "what's exciting is the personal relationships you build with the people you serve. Insurance is designed to meet the needs of people, and they are real people with real problems. Since we sell health insurance, we get them at a very fragile part of their lives. We get them when they are sick or recovering, and they are miserable. They are in pain and often frightened. We have an incredible building of personal relationships among our staff and our customers. That is exciting."[14]

Heaps worked 15 years in a traditional insurance firm, and has been at IGP five years. What were the most important benefits for her as the president of a democratically owned and managed company? "More than anything else, the most valuable thing is the freedom that I have had to grow as a human being. Another benefit for me is that we have hired and trained the hard-core unemployed from the ghetto of the District of Columbia. Finally, we call ourselves a community, and it is. It is a family with all the fights and all of the good times, and all of the caring that a family has. That is just an incredible benefit."

Five basic issues confront leaders in organizations moving toward more participatory management. They include the sharing of power, the reduction of rules and regulations, the shift of roles for managers from order-givers to resource people, dealing with entrenched middle management, the lack of training that people have had to function effectively in the new participatory environment, and finally the importance of being lazy.

Participatory leadership and management means the ability to share power without feeling that one is undermined by the delegation of authority. It is the ability to let people take the initiative, stumble, recover, and try again. In describing how Jones & Laughlin Steel Corporation increased steel production capacity at a Cleveland mill by 20 percent with very little expense and no additional employees, president Thomas C. Graham said success came from "deep delegation" of authority to superintendents which left them "free to make big mistakes." The company did not stop at the superintendent level, but also pushed decision-making down to the mill floor level.[15]

Sharing power and decision-making is not a sign of weakness but of strength, says Pehr Gyllenhammar, chairman of Volvo. "A leader must never mistake participation for laxity. There is a vital difference between positive delegation and the inability of the weak leader to accept his responsibilities . . . to have the strength to open up an issue, to debate it, and to resolve conflict—these are the qualities of true leadership. The weak are incapable of delegating and have every reason to fear sharing their power. The strong have the self-confidence that makes delegation possible and easy."[16]

More than that, the leader who shares power may find his own increased, not diminished. Paul Reaves, plant manager at the Harman International Industries plant in Bolivar, Tennessee, during its path-breaking worker participation project, said, "Since I started giving it away, I never had so much authority."[17]

Since Taylor's time, and the founding of the discipline of management both "scientific" and otherwise, managers have handed down the rules. Dana Corporation's Rene McPherson believed that managers were paying obedience to the procedures without ever asking what they meant. People worried about following the rules rather than solving problems.

At a meeting of the board of directors soon after he became president, McPherson took the 13-inch-thick stack of corporate procedures and set them down on the board table. Those policies, he said, were written for only 10 percent of the Dana employees and got in the way of the other 90 percent. Which ones should be retained? The chairman said there were several "important" ones to be kept and McPherson asked him to specify. "Oh, I never had the time to read them," was the answer. After a few minutes of discussion, McPherson dropped the entire stack into a wastebasket and promised to bring to the next meeting all that was needed on one sheet.[18] He did, and the Dana board never looked back.

Turning the organizational chart upside down is one way to

visualize the position of the participatory leader who serves as a resource, rather than order-giver, to other levels of the organization. That is what Dennis Butt did at Kawasaki. "Our hierarchy is just like that at any other plant. Our organizational structure is the same except that I just turned it upside down. My position is on the bottom of the chart and the hourly worker's is on top. We consider the hourly worker the top of the organization and everyone else is here to support him or her. There is no dividing line between management and hourly people."[19]

Increased worker participation frequently can lead to the elimination of whole layers of middle managers. "The problem," McPherson noted, "is entrenched management. If their job is telling people what to do, then they are not in favor of asking people what they think." The participatory leader delights in increased efficiency but is sympathetic to the people being displaced. Rene McPherson said, "You don't fire them. You put them somewhere where they can [handle the responsibility]. . . . You keep your arm around them in public and you don't lower their compensation. *They* didn't change the system. You did. It's not their fault. They are still good people. They are not the villains. You are the S.O.B. who is the villain."[20]

A basic problem leaders have is the lack of understanding that people have of how to work together democratically. For James Gibbons, who gave half of his $60 million insurance company, Consumers United, to his employees in 1972, the problems of being a participatory leader are based on the lack of training in democratic experience. "Most people have never had any democratic experience. Where do you get democratic experience? In school? In the army? When you're at work? In your family? No. Most people get it in some civic association. The only democratic experience you get is basically when you're a volunteer, and the only reason you volunteer is you agree with the goals of the organization. You say, 'I'll give this much, I'll do whatever you want.'

"The leader is generally the one who works the hardest, is willing to do the most dirty work and has the respect of the folks. He can't command anybody to do anything, he can only do it by earning their respect, by developing a consensus.

"That's the model I hold out to the leadership here. I always

tell people, when they come here, there is no model in the workplace for the role you're going to play. The model is outside, in the
civic organizations, the civil rights organizations. That means that
you're going to have to work the hardest, you're going to have to
know the most, you're going to have to get your hands dirty in
every respect."[21]

Participatory leaders refrain from thinking of themselves as
infallible. A tongue-in-cheek expression of this attitude comes
from coal mine owner Warren Hinks. Together with the United
Mine Workers, Hinks initiated a worker participation experiment
at Rushton Coal Company in the early 1970's. "First of all, you have
to be inherently lazy, and not want to do all that [management]
stuff yourself. I'm not interested in being part of the day-to-day
management," Hinks continued. "I want every man that works for
me to be as autonomous as he can be. I have lots of other things
I can think about and do, planning new things, just looking ahead,
trying to develop new properties perhaps. You can always do that
better if you're standing on the bridge of your ship and you know
the engines are working and that they're going to go on working.

"Leadership traits? Well, of course you have to like your people, and see them as people, not cogs in a wheel. I think it's
important to see them as associates rather than as employees. It's
also extremely important never to let up on the fact that a good
job must be done. We're appealing to whatever ideas might be in
a workman's mind that would make him be a true, autonomous
professional. A leader should not be a loner but one who can think
both independently and with a group to do the best thing."[22]

What have we learned from these men and women who are such
strong supporters of participatory management and ownership?
They came to the idea of participation through their work experience and personal values, not management theory. David Easlick
learned to his surprise that his subordinates did not find his management style as effective as he thought it was. James McDonald
was increasingly frustrated with GM's adversarial relations with
labor and the government, and felt that there had to be a better

way of working together. Frances Heaps had worked for a traditionally managed insurance company, and sought a position at a company that was owned and managed by the employees. These leaders found, as Rene McPherson has noted, that "people like to be treated as people, but they rarely are." This stated succinctly both a basic leadership problem and a solution.

These leaders learned that there is no formula and no model plan for participatory leadership, but that once managers have built a philosophy of management they must get programs in participatory management off the ground. They also must exemplify the kind of manager they want their subordinates to be. The participatory leader believes, with the irreverent but successful Robert Townshend, the initiator of Avis' growth and author of *Up the Organization,* that "true leadership must be for the benefit of the followers, not the enrichment of the leaders. In combat, officers eat last."[23]

The new leaders emphasize the importance of the right set of personal values. They look for managers with personal integrity. They are critical of authority. They are willing to question the purpose and structure of their organizations. They have caring and respectful attitudes about people. They recognize the importance of restructuring management and ownership. They have a willingness to share power, and do not try to control everyone. Finally, they place a high priority on personal development for others and themselves. They trust that their colleagues and subordinates who are closest to the problem will develop and implement a solution. They believe with Lao Tzu that "when the best leader's work is done the people say, 'We did it ourselves.' "

In his study of leadership, Michael Maccoby found that for most managers, "organizational development is evaluated solely in terms of productivity and profit." It is the total concern for profit that "causes distrust and limits efficiency. People only trust leaders who articulate a moral code and who care about people."[24]

These leaders are unusual because they believe that most employees can take greater responsibility for themselves and their firms—not less, as Taylor's approach proposed. They see their role as one of creating a climate in which people will take this greater responsibility for their lives at work, whether it is by throwing out useless procedures or by putting employees on the board of directors.

Effective participation requires strong, not weak, leaders, who can recognize critical issues, and see that they are fairly debated and decided. These leaders have not stopped making decisions: they cut the budget, as William Hewlett did, when they think it is too high. If they are proved wrong, they think twice before overturning consensus the next time.

These leaders do not all practice the same degree of participation. Some are with organizations that are farther along the scale of participation than others. An important demarcation on the scale is where a majority of the employees controls the board of directors. Heaps and Bennett are on one side of that mark, the rest on the other side.

The new leaders differ from the old in another significant way. A study of the executives of Dana and Hewlett-Packard shows that the top leaders of these two successful companies stressed continual self-improvement, experimentation, and autonomy of lower-level managers and employees. They were not charismatic leaders. The typical executive in other companies, the study found, made speeches in favor of these things, but did not follow through.[25]

The new leadership style requires that managers' roles at all levels be transformed from order-giver and warlord to "resource person" and colleague with more time spent on planning activities, initiating problem-solving among team members, and assuring coordination among the other teams. The resolution of conflict comes from helping people to grow into more effective management styles, not regular bloody noses. One purpose is to make the lives of the employees easier by reducing the arbitrary and inflexible treatment they receive at work.

These leaders did not set out to democratize decision-making; they were just trying to manage more effectively. Looking back at what happened, however, they find that greater participation and equality among people resulted. Today, even after their experience with the problems of transforming the organization's management philosophy, they agree with James McDonald that "there is no other way to manage."

The participatory leader has to feel like Sidney Harman, president of Harman International Industries, who said, "I don't want to be admired because of the spot I'm in or how the hell I got there. I want to earn the respect or admiration or recognition of all the people on the basis that I do things well, that I am competent, that my positions are defensible, not because *I* offer them, but because there is merit in them. I want them to respond to me in a way that permits me to say, 'I don't understand that' or 'I blew it.' In the end, what I'd like to feel is that if there were an election for the CEO of my company, I'd be elected!"[26]

[13]

Middle Managers
in the Middle

One aspect of Frederick Winslow Taylor's "scientific management" was what he called "functional foremanship." He believed
that an entire organization would benefit by separating the foreman's multiple role of taskmaster, time-keeper, planner, "straw
boss" and disciplinarian into its constituent parts and giving some
of these tasks to management. Taylor was not the first to attempt
to control the foreman's power and whittle away his independence. Foremen had been gradually losing the power to hire, fire,
and promote, and their control over quality and the speed of
production. In fact, the strongest resistance to Taylor's "scientific
management," understandably, often came from foremen, not
from workers, because the latter were able to find ways to outwit
and outflank the time-and-motion men, whereas foremen were
asked to ratify and implement their own loss of authority.

Today, many foremen, or first-line supervisors, as they are now
called, feel much the same pressure. The growing interest in participatory management, and the encouragement of "from-the-
bottom-up" responsibility have often made them feel that they are
facing a whole new set of demands. Psychologically, their situation
may be worse than under Taylorism, which transferred their powers only to other managers. The present drive to expand workers'
influence would give their remaining powers to their hierarchical
inferiors. They hear workers saying, in effect, "What's mine is
mine. What's yours is negotiable." This chapter reviews the basic
problems that lower and middle managers have with participation
efforts, and looks at some solutions.

. . .

Supervisors have always had to tread the middle path between labor and higher management. They are the last and most vulnerable outposts of management. As more and more responsibility is urged upon rank and file workers, middle managers fear the possibility that they are being asked to "participate" themselves out of a job. In the words of Rene McPherson, former president of the Dana Corporation: "They know instinctively that you don't need as many of them, that you don't need all those layers. If you're the first ones liable to lose [authority] how enthusiastic are you going to be?"[1] The stark choice for middle managers is between a new role or no job.

Striking evidence of the defensive attitude of some supervisors comes from a major survey conducted in 1979 by staff at the Opinion Research Center in Princeton, New Jersey. One manager said, "For the past twenty years I have been a hard-working and loyal employee for this company. [Now,] for the first time in my working career, I have a nine-to-five mentality. During the past few years, I have been bothered by so many younger and lower-level employees receiving too much attention. This leaves those of us who have run the company through its good and bad years feeling left out—as if our loyalty and years of service have been taken for granted."[2]

Another Opinion Research Center survey in 1977 found that "incredible as it may seem, managers now feel less informed than do hourly employees. Managers' response to the question, 'How would you rate your company on letting you know what's going on in the company?' dropped in the 'very good' to 'good' category from 54 percent in 1975 to 35 percent after 1977. The hourly workers' 'very good' to 'good' response rose from 28 percent to 43 percent in the same period."[3]

The researchers make it clear that lower-level managers do feel threatened by workplace reforms: "Make no mistake about it; managerial discontent is growing. . . . If managers are unable to respond to the increasing demands of the work force, they will have failed in one of their primary roles as managers. If they do respond to these demands successfully, they will soon realize their success also means that other employees have new prerogatives—prerogatives that were once managers' alone. The irony is that the successful manager, by lessening the discontent of his or her subordinates, may be left to contend with his or her own feelings of increased discontent."[4]

Particularly vulnerable are those first-line managers who have come up from the ranks and have "gone over to the enemy." Seeking more pay, status, and power, they arrive on "the other side of the fence" to find the authority they have been promised hollow or fleeting. As they move up, they see their supervisors paying more attention to those they have left behind. It is not surprising, then, that some foremen have undermined participation experiments, by faking data, "stonewalling," or simply not cooperating, while actually counteracting orders from above.

There is also evidence to support supervisors' fears of being "participated" right out of their jobs. AT&T has cut one or two entire levels of middle management in some of its operating companies.

Matsushita cut 25 percent of its white collar employees, including one whole layer of first-line supervisors, when it took over the Motorola factory in Franklin Park, Illinois, in 1974. The company's solution to a cumbersome hierarchy was to give more responsibility to the "utility person" as a combined worker and manager. This freed other managers to "go anywhere in the plant to get help in solving the problems of the people on the line, who are, after all, the money-makers," said superintendent John Westell.[5]

The first-level supervisor is caught directly in a crossfire of values and priorities (as detailed in a paper by W. Earl Sasser, Jr., and Frank S. Leonard):

- "The supervisor often does not know the objectives and policies of top management, but heavily influences what management can accomplish.

- "The supervisor is not part of the work force, but depends heavily on its acceptance.

- "The supervisor is management, but has little authority.

- "The supervisor is a member of management, but is far removed from the locus of decision-making.

- "The supervisor is limited by precedents and company custom, but serves as the agent of change without whose action little occurs in the company.

- "The supervisor must establish standards and precedents, but has little information or knowledge on which to base such decisions.

- "The supervisor is supposed to spend time on worker-management relationships, but finds that much of that time is needed for record-keeping.

- "The supervisor is supposed to have a position of leadership, but feels that leadership traits are suppressed because of the self-image associated with the position.

- "The supervisor is asked to identify with the values and aspirations of management, but is at a dead end in career progress and development.

- "The supervisor is usually young, and deals with a young, diverse new type of working person, but is evaluated, trained, and rewarded by older, more conservative, more authoritarian supervisors."

"This combination of role confusion," Sasser and Leonard conclude, "increase in staff services, overlap of power with the unions, and conflicting demands has reduced the position of first-level supervisor to just a shadow of its earlier form."[6] It was a difficult job even *before* senior management started talking about participation!

Over thirty years ago, William Foote Whyte and Burleigh Gardner, then at the University of Chicago, noticed the same uncomfortable ambivalence among foremen during World War II. Under normal conditions, foremen were able to develop routine methods of handling their production and responsibilities. The average foreman "is thoroughly familiar with the work and its problems and knows exactly what can be done. He also knows what to expect from his supervisors, how to satisfy their demands or protect himself from their pressure. But under present conditions, nothing is stable; the jobs change, what is right today may be wrong tomorrow, people come and go too rapidly to establish smooth working relationships with the foreman or each other. Management demands more and more output and the union demands more consideration of the worker's feelings at a time when the foreman is overwhelmed with problems of production. Is it any wonder that he often feels lost and helpless, that he develops extreme anxieties, and that he wonders if the job is worth the effort?"[7]

Peter di Cicco, a regional vice-president of the International Union of Electrical Workers in Boston, contends that a Quality of Work Life experiment at one of the plants his union represents was deliberately sabotaged by management "in order to reflect that the people were screwing up on the job. The reason they were doing this was obviously because it was *their* jobs that were going out the door."[8]

Technicians and engineers may also worry about the erosion of their authority as workers are given the freedom to redesign their jobs. Frank Cirillo, senior vice-president at the Simmonds Precision plant in Vermont, found this to be true when he introduced quality control circles. The members of the circle "sit down and do a distribution curve on something that is bugging them so they can make the operation better. And out may come recommendations that we ought to change this machine configuration. You know what they're doing? They're playing with the role of the industrial manufacturing engineer. What is the interplay going to look like when suddenly a group of ten non-experts is now making recommendations for change in something that is not their day-to-day province? Very interesting."[9]

As long as supervisors believe they are in a no-win situation, their frustrations will continue. Unless there is a way to ensure them attention from above, and responsibility for those below, they will remain a weak link in any company's efforts to diffuse decision-making. They must retain a sense of value and dignity in their jobs. The Norwegians, who have practiced participation for more than twenty years, were among the first to recognize the needs of the pinched, forgotten, first-line supervisors.

Einar Thorsrud, of the Work Research Institutes in Oslo, says that the time is now ripe for redefining the role of first-line supervisors. The original efforts of workplace democratization had to focus on the rank and file level, where dissatisfaction was most obvious. "If nothing was done on this level, very little could be done to reduce the need for close supervision, which in turn restricted the capacity of lower levels of management for coordination between departments. Foremen and supervisors were likely to be skeptical of any sort of organizational change since their status had over some time been reduced by new types of centralized control systems, by new groups of specialists. For these reasons, the supervisory level could not be the point of entry for democratization of the work-place. Today it can."[10]

If more and more foremen's duties are taken over by the rank and file, what will be left for the foremen to do? Thorsrud and others have suggested that foremen of different departments or sections should work with each other to break down the boundaries between their respective areas of responsibility. They would act as coordinators more concerned with interdepartmental cooperation than with sitting over their subordinates with stopwatches.

"In middle management, it seems both possible and desirable to organize collaborative relations on the horizontal level, as soon as group autonomy has been increased on the lower level. Extensive use of project groups will also absorb much of middle management's capacity which was previously used in line control."[11] They also can begin to help in planning new investments and job redesign.

An interesting modification of a middle manager's attitude toward his workers was described by Ola Haug, manager of Norsk Hydro's fertilizer plant. At one of the first factories involved in the Norwegian Industrial Democracy Project, the managers tried a number of methods to increase worker involvement. They used job rotation, a new pay system, and reduction in the layers of hierarchy through attrition and transfer. For a while, they even experimented with having no foremen at all, but the workers asked to have them back, this time as "foremen with whom we can communicate, with less dictatorial behavior."

Subsequently, the company decided to build a major addition to the plant and merge two control rooms, an immensely complicated process. On the day the new plant was started up, an excited manager told Haug how he had just spent the afternoon watching the first running-in of the vast new control room. An hourly employee had been in charge.

"The fantastic thing about this," said Haug, "was that this man had shown no special aptitude under the old system of work organization." An even greater surprise was that the foreman willingly and readily obeyed this man's orders in front of their own supervisor.[12]

In this country, the Buffalo-Erie County Labor Management Council tries to anticipate discontent. According to director Robert Ahern, the council paid particular attention to the defensiveness of first-line supervisors in its arrangement of exploratory discussions between labor and management in different companies. "We made a special effort to work with those middle management folks, kind of cater to them, let them cover up a little as the system changes.

"They are just terribly afraid they'll lose power. What actually happens is just the opposite, because now they are dealing with problems at their own level, doing the job they are supposed to do, and getting the hell off the backs of the workers."[13]

Recognition of middle management disaffection with participation experiments was confirmed by Pehr G. Gyllenhammar, chairman of Volvo. He wrote of the contradictory messages reaching his first-line supervisors under the new forms of work: "Foremen . . . risk being squeezed between higher management and the plant employees. . . .

"For decades we told them in essence that they had two main functions. The first was to supervise the pace of the work, to keep the line moving. The second was to give technical advice and assistance wherever necessary. Thus, most of the people promoted to foremen's positions had been skilled employees who could solve technical problems. To keep people working, they became disciplinarians, experts at saying, 'Thou shalt not.'

"Suddenly we asked foremen to develop a rather different set of skills. We wanted them to be good 'managers of people.' Instead of people receiving discipline from the supervisor, the new climate emphasizes self-discipline. We redefined the foreman's role rapidly, and this created problems during the change [which] were exacerbated by the fact that formal training for foremen was traditionally less important than on-the-job training so they tended to be reluctant to take courses at first."[14]

Volvo officials realized they could not afford to continue putting the square pegs of traditionally trained foremen into the round holes of broadened workplace democracy. As a solution, the company first gave all supervisors three to four weeks of training in group dynamics. Second, it developed ten-to-twelve-person groups, including foremen and workers from the shop floor, similar to quality control circles. Groups dealt not only with problems of production, but also with absenteeism and personnel decisions. The results have been favorable: first-line supervisors seem to accept their new role as coordinators, and to feel part of the overall plan.[15]

Two researchers at American Telephone and Telegraph have found that both managerial trainees and first-line managers are more interested in self-fulfillment than in being a part of the company hierarchy. They will not contribute time or energy to the company if it impinges on their "life-style." They confirmed that AT&T had not escaped hiring the "new breed" of worker. In their paper, "Today's College Recruits: Managerial Timber or Deadwood?," Ann Howard and Douglas W. Bray conclude that management trainees lack the achievement and advancement motivation that characterized their counterparts twenty years ago.

" 'The hierarchy be damned' is the joint message here.... They neither aspire to [higher level] jobs nor defer to those who have them. They don't want to lead; they don't want to follow. . . . The message now reads 'Love me, don't lead me. Furthermore, I'll do the same to you.' With all due respect to the virtues of human warmth and kindness, who is going to run our corporations in the future?"[16]

At the same time Howard and Bray barely question the relevance of the management style and structure of AT&T which their subjects experience every day. Like many psychoanalysts, they see that it is the patient who has the problem, not the organization. While, like good researchers, they try to cover all the bases by suggesting that the organization might try to "adapt to the new breed and flatten the hierarchy," they question whether this approach would work at all. They conclude by saying that they "wondered if it [such an approach] made sense for the coming decades as organizations prepared to meet the turbulence, ambiguity, and constant change expected in the 1980's."[17]

Fortunately for the more than 80,000 middle managers in the Bell System, and its other 950,000 employees, Charles Brown, Chairman of the Board of AT&T, had reached different conclusions from the same data. In a letter to all presidents of AT&T companies in March, 1980, he said that their "management style" was one of the basic problems, and had to change. He endorsed the Quality of Work Life approach, and asked that managers adopt these new principles of management. He wrote that the "end objective [is their] gradual spread to the whole organization."[18]

This was a not-so-veiled reference to the highly touted programs in job enrichment which AT&T had encouraged ten years earlier: they had failed to spread largely because management had not fully supported the program, and did not deal with the basic problems of the organization's inappropriate structure, such as the role of middle management.[19]

By late November, three joint union-management committees had been established at AT&T "to encourage greater employee participation . . . to make work more satisfying and improve organizational performance."[20]

By mid-1981, AT&T had decided to cut many middle management positions to meet the new competition. Some of the operating companies, such as Michigan Bell and New England Bell, would lose 15 percent of their slots. Others might lose up to 40 percent, all by attrition. The other part of the solution was to proceed with Quality of Work Life programs.

In the case of Michigan Bell, once the company committed itself to improve the quality of work life, some upper-middle managers took the initiative to establish a new work arrangement. A group of fifth-level managers decided on their own to address two major concerns: decisions were being made too high up, too far away from the problems; and decisions were usually made departmentally, which led to a lack of coordination within the same level. Managers from different departments within the same level came up with a set of shared objectives which boiled down to the phrase "one win all win, one lose all lose."

The most dramatic example of shared objectives came when different groups of fifth-level managers agreed to share their budgets. Traditionally, company officers would assess revenues against expenses and if they were not up to objectives, they would make cuts across the board. In this case, the managers went to the officers and said, "Let us do the cutting, and we'll get the fourth-level and third-level managers involved. We'll guarantee to cut the budget and you stay out of the act." The officers were skeptical, but let the managers go ahead. With the three levels of managers working together, they were able to make the cuts by trimming from some districts and giving more to those which couldn't cut.[21]

In its pioneering work to develop new organizational structures for increased participation, General Motors came squarely up against the problem of understandably suspicious foremen.

Ray McGarry, plant manager at the 7,000-employee Chevrolet Gear and Axle plant, wanted to restructure the seven component plants at "the Gear" into cost centers. At first, McGarry thought that reorganization of the top management would be followed logically by reorganization of middle management, but this did not happen, because middle management was "pretty intractable. So we decided to anchor the program at the bottom of the organization." The introduction of new products gave McGarry a chance to create new teams on the shop floor, and have each plant tailor-make its own changes. "You just can't buy a program off the shelf which works in a southern plant or in Japan."

McGarry's vision for the Gear was based on self-governing groups of 20 to 200 people. "Such a structure is not that radical," McGarry observed. "In 1915 when the Gear was known as the Central Gear Factory, homogeneous groups of workers had substantial authority and responsibility for their area of work. Over the years, however, we've drifted from this semi-autonomous approach. We put staff on top of staff and control on top of control."[22]

The biggest problem at the Gear was the fear and defensiveness of middle managers. As Jacques Pasquier, QWL coordinator for the Gear, said, "Their basic problem is that they simply do not trust their own people. Thus they find a QWL program based on trust a very unsettling effort. Most middle managers have come from the hourly workers' ranks. They lack education and they lack real clarification from the plant manager."[23]

Middle managers also believed that McGarry would probably be gone within two years, like the five previous plant managers, so it was pointless to cooperate with him. They also fell back on their traditional animosity towards the unions: "You can't work with those union bastards anyway." Nonetheless, McGarry proceeded to hold meetings, a "familiarization program," for all 750 salaried employees, who spent two days apiece at a conference center far from the plant's ringing telephones. In groups of 20, they attended classes in communication, participative management, and how to get out of "win-lose" situations. Most of the techniques were simple, but seemed new to most of the managers. Reaction to the seminars fell into two categories: enthusiasm, and the feeling that it was one more new program which would "never pay off."

McGarry then approached the shop committee of UAW Local 235. After the committee chairman had received assurances from UAW headquarters that QWL was not a trick, he agreed to the meeting. Members of the shop committee and a comparable group of middle managers met at the St. Regis Hotel in downtown Detroit at General Motors' expense to discuss QWL. Unfortunately, the effort coincided with the second oil shortage and a flood of Japanese imports which caused major layoffs, over 3,000 at the Gear in a six-month period.

A year later, in March, 1980, four union representatives and four managers sat down for the first joint QWL meeting. Labor had chosen the four representatives from middle management and management had chosen four from labor, showing that a substantial degree of trust had developed since the previous meetings. Through their interaction with union members and the training, the supervisors eventually lost much of their reluctance to endorse McGarry's vision.

Alfred Warren, Vice-President of Industrial Relations at GM, summarized his view of the middle management problem. "The only time we get into trouble is when the top of an organization gets all enamored with QWL and embraces the union and embraces the hourly people, and then thinks belatedly about the first- and second-level supervisors. If you're doing it right, you give that first-level supervisor and middle manager some security. They need to be a part of it too.

"Remember for years we've taught human relations. God, we've poured money into human relations—but the first-level supervisor has never had time to do any of that because he was always worrying about where he's going to get parts, some guy breaking a rule, or poor quality. Now he can start to think about the guy's family, hold meetings with his group, give them information. . . . He can finally begin to do what we taught him he ought to be doing a long time ago. Before, he was responding to the needs of the job. Now he's able to respond to the needs of the employees."[24]

Inland Steel Corporation decided to train all its 1,600 first-line supervisors at its huge Indiana Harbor works in one fell swoop. They were given six days of off-site training in the changing workforce, the worker participation movement, and communications skills.

Robert J. Darnall, then general manager of the 23,000-employee plant, said the sessions were designed by four line managers with help from the personnel department.[25] The purpose of the training was to convince them that they did not have to be hard-nosed to get the job done and that participation would not mean loss of influence or of support from their superiors. The intensive sessions also allowed the foremen to vent their spleen about the conflicting pressures and messages they felt they were getting from their superiors. Most of them were former steelworkers, and even though they had crossed over into management, they still felt emotional ties to their former fellow workers.

Darnall and his colleagues took pains to tell the foremen that they were not being singled out as special sinners. A poll at the end of the sessions revealed that one-third of the foremen were still skeptical about the benefits of changing their behavior. Darnall was not surprised. He said that any participation program would take years to really show results.

Democratization of the workplace threatens first-level supervisors and middle managers more than any other group. For years they have been taught to keep their noses clean and get the production out. Their rewards were promotions, money, prestige, and perhaps a chance to "kick ass and take names." Their job was no cakewalk, to be sure; they had to tread a fine line between the frustrations of both those above and those below them.

Increased employee participation strikes at the heart of middle management: professional identity. It questions their competence, authority—indeed their very jobs. Theoretically, their subordinates' increased responsibility frees them to be planners and coordinators. But these new roles can remain ephemeral rather than practical. The harsh fact is that redistribution of shop-floor power comes at the foremen's and supervisors' expense. For increased participation to gain his support, the foreman will need a new mission, a new power base, and a secure identity. The only people who can assure him of those things are his superiors.

Unless the organizations to which they belong take the time to understand, and work to ameliorate, the problems of middle managers, whose already difficult jobs are rendered even more rocky by the implementation of participatory methods, these disappointed "in-between" employees may well say, with the Prodigal Son's elder brother:

"... Lo, these many years do I serve thee, neither transgressed I at any time thy commandment: and yet thou never gavest me a kid, that I might make merry with my friends. But as soon as this thy son was come, which hath devoured thy living with harlots, thou hast killed for him the fatted calf."[26]

[14]

Union Reluctance
and Cooperation

With good reason, organized labor is ambivalent about the current work reform movement and employee ownership. Unions have fought hard for their present levels of dignity, decent working conditions, and adequate pay. They won them through tough and occasionally bloody proceedings at the factory gate, in the courts, and at the bargaining table. Samuel Gompers's injunction to fight always for better pay and benefits appealed to three generations of workers. The traditional division in the workplace was that managers would control the methods of production, while workers would follow orders and so get their fair share of the ever-expanding economic pie. In the relatively few cases where workers made unsolicited suggestions to improve the organization of work, "they were given the proverbial pat on the head and a buck to go to the movies."[1]

Union ambivalence about work reform appears to have several overlapping and interacting causes. The first concern is that reform is aimed primarily at boosting productivity at the workers' expense. So strongly do many unionists fear that "reform" is a euphemism for "speedup" that the Quality of Work Life agreement between the United Auto Workers and Ford Motor Company does not even use the word "productivity." A second, related fear is that increased productivity leads to worker redundancy, if not for those directly involved, then for other employees.

Third, union leaders worry that autonomous work teams, quality circles, or labor-management committees will become independent and competing representational structures, making their own jobs expendable.

William Roehl, assistant director of organizing for the AFL-CIO, remarked that such programs as quality circles "will give the workers the impression that all their problems will be solved . . . which implies that there is no need for unions."[2]

At the end of the 1960s, a number of developments threatened unions' continued strength. As Robert Schrank has pointed out, the problems facing the unions were how to adjust to the coalescing impact of the end of the industrial era, the rise of the "human" manager, and technological developments that allow for greater production with fewer and fewer workers.[3]

Many unionists dismiss work reform as insignificant compared to organized labor's other problems. For them, cooperation with management on anything—instead of hard bargaining—is a pipe dream. Adversarial relations got them to the high levels of compensation they now enjoy; why should they change to a cooperative stance, especially when the president of the National Association of Manufacturers recommends the use of QWL projects as a useful tactic for keeping a "union-free environment."[4] Offers of management cooperation seem like the offer of a boutonnière for a man's own funeral. This suspicion of any dealings with management was graphically summed up by Robert Rodman, of the International Association of Machinists and Aerospace Workers: "When labor gets in bed with management, there will be two people screwing the worker, not one."[5]

In the last twenty-five years, organized labor's representation of the American workforce has fallen by almost 50 percent and was at barely one in five employees in 1982. More and more manufacturing companies have moved out of the heavily unionized Northeast to the South, or overseas. As the economy has shifted toward an ever-larger service sector, unions have not been able to organize those workers. Unions were able to win only 50 percent of the organizational representational elections initiated in the 1970s.

For all their fabled worker-manager harmony, Japanese companies in the U.S. aren't immune to unionization. In 1981, two major Japanese facilities, Sanyo in San Diego, California, and Sharp in Memphis, Tennessee, were organized by the Communications Workers of America and the International Brotherhood of Electrical Workers, respectively.

Latter-day Japanophiles playing to management audiences have praised the slow, deliberate Japanese process of making decisions by consensus through the ranks. But when workers at the Sharp plant waited seemingly in vain for decisions on their pension and health plans, and the right to buy company products at a discount, they were ripe for the union's pitch. They were also convinced that production standards had become excessively high.

At the Sanyo plant, the CWA was able to focus attention on management blunders, such as inadequately trained supervisors and a general misunderstanding of workers' desires. In a revealing comment, a CWA organizer observed that the Japanese couldn't understand why the workers wanted six paid sick days whether they were sick or not. "The Japanese worker is very dedicated and loyal. In our society, it's 'gimme, gimme, gimme.' "[6]

The biggest trial of strength between a Japanese firm and an American union will involve the United Auto Workers, when Nissan opens a 3,100-employee light-truck factory in rural Tennessee. The factory's American manager, Marvin Runyon, a 37-year veteran of Ford Motor Company, has told everyone that he is trying to make his managerial style more participative. At the same time, he has apparently tried to avoid unionization at all costs. The UAW, for its part, has vowed "to organize the plant or compel the Japanese to raise wages to American levels."[7]

The workforce itself has greatly changed over the last decade. Young people entering the ranks in 1975 had an average of four years more education than their parents. The biggest public trauma in their lives had been the Vietnam War. On every hand, they were urged to express themselves as individuals, not to come together for some collective purpose. Some employers saw an opportunity to wean these individualistic workers away from unions. The Right-to-Work Committee and other anti-union organizations flexed their muscles. Consulting firms specializing in fighting unions sprouted like weeds.

Edward Cohen-Rosenthal, former associate director of the American Center for QWL, and now a labor consultant on QWL, has produced (Table 3) a systematic tabulation of the possible risks and benefits for unions in a QWL project:[8]

Table 3
Union Risks and Benefits

Possible Risks

Union role definition	Job classification changes
Cooptation	Violation of the contract
Weakening of union power	Exporting good ideas to non-union
Membership perception of selling	shops
out	Tackling too much
Union-busting	Speedup
Liability for decisions	Membership being lulled by
Loss of jobs	examples of management
Loss of comparability	cooperation

Possible Benefits

Access to information	Increased support for union
Prenotification of changes	leadership
Avoidance of management	Strengthened industry economic
mistakes	position
Higher visibility	Saving or increasing jobs
Better public relations	Increased employee
More money to bargain over	satisfaction
Increased membership	Improved health and safety
representation	Better worker education
Reduced costs of grievance	Reduced stress
administration	Less unnecessary supervision
Improved grievance	Improved interpersonal
handling	relations
Increased attendance at	
meetings	

Some union advocates have warned of the dangers of dismissing the current reforms. Peter diCicco, New England vice-president of the International Union of Electrical and Radio Workers, has argued for more union involvement in QWL. "The AFL-CIO has buried its head in the sand. It has failed to take into account the new workers. We keep fighting for things that already exist in most plants. Labor needs a new agenda which will promise the workers something they need. Management knows QWL is good stuff and [is] going ahead with it. The unions ignore its implications at their peril."[9]

DiCicco speaks out of a minor but honorable tradition of labor-management cooperation that has ebbed and flowed since the World War I shop committees and the movement for "industrial democracy" in the first part of the century. After a decade of the slow development of QWL in non-union firms as well as in union shops, a union position on QWL is gradually being defined. This chapter describes the evolution of that position.

Curiously, one of the first major experiments in labor-management cooperation in the 1970s involved a major railroad, harking back to the labor-management committees on the Baltimore & Ohio Railroad in the 1920s.

In 1971, Secretary of Transportation John Volpe called together leaders of the nation's railroads and railroad unions to discuss ways to arrest the deterioration of track conditions and terminal operations. Volpe urged the leaders of both sides to find inexpensive, cooperative ways to improve these operations. At first, such a request for cooperation struck some unionists as laughable.

"For twenty-five years after World War II, we had a kind of state of siege between labor and management in the railroad industry," said Dan Collins, assistant secretary of the United Transportation Union. "It was practically open warfare and things were not getting any better."[10]

After two years of talks, the representatives from both sides agreed to experiment with the St. Louis Terminal operations of the Missouri Pacific Lines. Over four million railroad cars passed through or terminated at St. Louis annually, and both parties thought they might be able to reduce the transit time of cars through the MoPac yards from an eighteen-hour average.

The St. Louis Terminal Project, as established in 1973, had four goals: improve service reliability, reduce car detention time, increase equipment utilization, and enhance job security and safety.

One abiding condition of the experiment was that no worker lose his job as a result of any improvements in the operation. A second requirement was that all experiments have a specific time limit. They would be entirely voluntary, but individual groups would be encouraged to make beneficial changes permanent after the six- or nine-month time limits had expired. Neither the unions nor management wanted to "subsidize" change. They sought "to find ways to make people more self-reliant, where they themselves [could] begin to look at these kinds of things and do what [was] necessary to change them."[11]

Labor and management representatives started by asking everyone in the yards for suggestions—clerks, car-masters, switch-engine foremen, and brakemen. The result was a long list of specific problems. In fact, the representatives made "absolutely everything in the terminal operations fair game for their study." Both sides, however, agreed not to tamper with issues that were already part of the collective bargaining process.

"This was important for us, because for six hundred years labor has in effect said that we look upon management with a jaundiced eye and therefore we'll keep you at arm's length. . . . The collective bargaining process is, after all, a horse-trading proposition. If I give, I have to get. And once you get involved in that kind of process, you have immediately set up an artificial barrier to change."[12]

Some of the improvements were amazingly effective. For example, railroad car traffic between the Ivory and L'Esperance yards was handled exclusively by Ivory crews, despite the historical preponderance of traffic in the other direction. Dispatching crews from Ivory to L'Esperance to pick up cars often delayed the shipments by twelve hours or more. The union agreed to a temporary experiment assigning the nearest and most available crew, and, once it was clear that no job loss would result, agreed to make the change permanent.

Clyde Anderson, project analyst and statistician, said the entire project saved about $1.5 million and reduced the transit time 25 percent, from 18 to 14 hours per car. He added that the "biggest value of the labor participation was their ability to go in and tell management to clean up its act. It's just amazing how a high-ranking labor representative seems to open management's ears. It shows that labor is vitally interested in trying to bring about innovation."[13]

As Dan Collins said, "What we are really talking about is the right of people to share in that so-called democracy in the workplace. We spent a long time in this country developing the right to participate in the political process. We haven't been half as concerned with trying to enhance our roles in the economic arena. The collective bargaining process provided us with some of these opportunities, but in my own view, [labor-management cooperation] is an untapped field, one that offers us great opportunity."[14]

In his enthusiasm, Collins was not quite right to call labor-management cooperation an "untapped field." As we have seen, in his own railroad industry, unions have cooperated with management on shopfloor production problems off and on for over fifty years. Almost all these programs, however, were sponsored by management alone, and labor had no choice in the matter. The novel element of the Terminal Project was the assembling of labor and management leaders through the sympathetic prodding of a governmental third party.

The St. Louis Terminal Project employed no outside organizational development consultants. Labor and management defined their own problems and worked them through alone. The model they developed was subsequently used in MoPac yards in several other cities, and eventually expanded to all the railroad lines using the St. Louis Terminal. But the first project was the most successful: the others were complicated by too many carriers, too many unions, and conflicting personalities. The initial project did provide a model for the very successful "labor-management action group" on the Milwaukee Road.[15]

The Terminal Project, like all union-management cooperative committees before it, left the collective bargaining agreement inviolate. All committee work specifically avoided any encroachment upon this legal document.

At Buffalo, New York, the leader of an area labor-management committee saw no conflict between maintaining the purity of the contract and allowing vigorous expansion of labor-management cooperation even on contractual matters.

In the early 1970s, Buffalo was faced with economic stagnation, possible plant shutdowns, capital flight, and bitter labor strife. A delegation of union and business leaders visited Jamestown, fifty miles away, and returned to set up its own Buffalo-Erie County Labor-Management Council. With a regional labor leader and a major industrialist as co-chairmen, the council grew in five years to include over 50 in-plant labor-management committees, with 17 in the National Fuel Gas Company. Over 15,000 workers were involved in operations as diverse as milling, tire-making, and running the public bus company.

The executive director of the council, Robert Ahern, is a former company personnel chief who became a passionate and articulate believer in organic links between the collective bargaining process and the recently developed field of organizational development. Ahern believes that the separation of collective bargaining and cooperative labor-management efforts is "not just naïve, but stupid."

Ahern backs up his position with an opinion from Supreme Court Justice William O. Douglas, who wrote in the landmark Warrior & Gulf Navigation case that a collective bargaining agreement is "more than a contract; it is a generalized code to govern a myriad of cases which the draftsmen cannot wholly anticipate. The collective bargaining agreement covers the whole employment relationship. It calls into being a new common law—the common law of a particular industry or of a particular plant. A collective bargaining agreement is an effort to erect a system of industrial self-government."[16]

To Ahern, the collective bargaining process is the sum of all the contracts between the parties, with negotiation the means for changing the agreement. "Mandatory subjects for collective bargaining in this country are wages, terms, and conditions of employment. . . . Tell me what matters of substance on which parties seek to cooperate do not impact on those things? Productivity? Health? Management rights? Job design? Upward mobility? Dignity on the job? . . . The collective bargaining agreement is the original QWL document. . . . You can't divorce negotiations from the process of getting people to talk about common problems in the workplace. It is a seamless web."[17]

In essence, Ahern views QWL agreements as a means of keeping a company going during the other 34 months of a 36-month collective bargaining cycle. Conflict is central to the workplace, but it need not—indeed should not—be a bloodletting. "The most paradoxical reality we face is that cooperation makes sense because it is rooted in an adversarial process."[18]

Labor-management committees provide a continuing forum for problem definition and (in most cases) resolution. If the resolution requires contractual change, the parties can either defer the matter until negotiations or set up a joint study committee.

This broadened definition of collective bargaining in no way threatens management or its prerogatives. Ahern says that "unions are still under the illusion that management knows what it's doing and they want to continue that way. The unions don't want to manage. They want tools that work. They want dignity. They want to be treated fairly, and they don't want to be co-opted."[19]

Ahern's three-person staff works closely with nascent labor-management committees. To managers, it stresses how the process will affect the structure of their organization by broadening the base of those making decisions. To union leaders, it points out that the process must offer substantive results, and how it is likely to reach down into their ranks to build strong leadership. The council staff emphasizes the need for patience and lasting commitment from both sides.

One major difference between the Buffalo Council and the Jamestown Area Labor-Management Committee is the role of their respective staff members: in Buffalo, they don't spend nearly as much time on in-plant committees. In part, this is a matter of economics—with over fifty committees and only three staff members, they don't have the time to "baby-sit" everyone. In addition, the Buffalo Council is conscious of the mediation tradition that provides for a sympathetic listener but doesn't rely on a "change agent" to alter the way the parties interact. In Jamestown there is a much broader use of outside consultants.

One of the longest-running and most firmly established QWL experiments in a unionized setting involved 500 employees of the

Minneapolis *Tribune* and *Star* newspapers. According to John Carmichael, executive secretary of the Twin Cities Newspaper Guild, its QWL program grew out of a trend toward "reporter power" in the late 1960s and early 1970s.

Few groups of workers or professionals (journalists often wear both hats) spend more time than journalists on postmortems of their work and that of their bosses. Reporters can talk until dawn about how stories should have been written, how those that were covered could have been improved, and how insensitive their editors sometimes are.

Formal worker participation at the newspapers began as a result of a fracas over the selection of two assistant city editors in 1971. As Carmichael recalled, "We became aware of the fact that over on the Minneapolis *Tribune* they were about to appoint two assistant city editors. Assistant city editors on the *Tribune* are important people. If they don't do their job right, it can screw up the whole newsroom. We had had some unfortunate appointments in those jobs in the past.

"Most people involved in quality of work programs have indicated that by and large they stay away from involvement in the appointment of supervisors. We didn't know that and we went to management and made a proposal to give us 'advise and consent' authority over the appointment of these two assistant city editors."[20]

Management flatly refused to give the Guild veto power, but the executive editor said he would be willing to consult on the appointments, as well as on other supervisors in the future. As it turned out, management and the Guild picked the same two people for the position. This happy ending emboldened the union to request and win the inclusion of a formal system of worker participation in the 1972 contract. The Guild and the *Tribune* agreed to form a labor-management committee "to discuss matters affecting relations between employees and employer . . . in an effort to encourage discussions of subjects not covered by the normal bargaining and grievance machinery." All matters discussed, the contract continued, "will be on a consultative basis, and in any case, the Publisher retains the right to make final decisions."[21]

Initially, the committee discussed matters such as the number of typewriters and improved lighting, but then they moved on to more substantive issues, such as consultation on the hiring of a new editor, and departmental budgets. The largest single project was a paper-wide analysis of the very identity and purpose of the *Tribune*. With the work participation committee as overseer, a score of smaller committees studied a range of issues and practices over a six-month period and came up with 200 pages of proposed changes. These led to the *Tribune*'s becoming a state-wide paper, instead of a regional one, with consequent changes in format, style, and emphasis.

According to Carmichael, the Guild did several things to help avoid serious intra-union suspicion and squabbles:

1. "We took the issue to the membership before we started out, and obtained its approval.
2. "We then went to the table and bargained on the issue.
3. "When we achieved it, we wrote it into the contract.
4. "We elected our part of the committee."[22]

One common fear among union leaders is that labor-management committees can provide a base for serious challenge to existing leadership. The committee in Minneapolis was aware of this danger, and sought to avoid it by appointing at least one member of the bargaining team to the participation committee, but electing the other. Carmichael pointed out that the two functions of negotiation and cooperation require different temperaments: aggressive in the first instance, accommodating in the second. The committee offered a way for members less given to confrontation to participate in union affairs, which resulted in a notable and beneficial increase in member participation.

At the same time, Carmichael emphasized the importance of formalizing participation through the collective bargaining process, since for many members the contract had both practical and symbolic importance. Putting QWL into the contract was "the acquisition of power—not the whole loaf by any means, but a slice. Power is what the rank and file understands."[23]

However, the committee could not resolve all differences. In

September, 1980, the *Tribune* became the scene of one of the first strikes in the country over a QWL issue. The Guild was concerned about the effects of new electronic equipment that could cut jobs in the circulation department, a quarter of whose workers were union members. The Guild also feared that a new electronics division could be staffed by non-journalist—thus non-Guild—members.

After twenty-seven days on strike, the Guild returned to work when the company agreed to set up a worker-management committee to assess the potential effects of the electronic gear on the labor force. It did not, however, win a job-security clause.[24]

Carmichael remains optimistic about the future of worker participation, but has realized the union can not relax, even with contractual validation of QWL.

At American Telephone & Telegraph, members of the Communications Workers of America complained increasingly through the 1970s about equipment and supervisory attitudes that turned people into robots and measured their work in classically Tayloristic ways. AT&T had tried a range of motivation programs and techniques over decades; it had sponsored the Hawthorne experiments at one of its subsidiaries in the 1920s. However, operators felt increasingly frustrated as phone centers became more and more like assembly lines. One quite typical complaint was that of an operator who said she was not able to do her job properly because of the high pressure. "If someone misses a call, or a drunk calls and fumbles with a number and the operator runs over the alloted time, the supervisor is soon on her back asking why she had trouble."[25]

The pressures on the job built to a crescendo as the CWA organized Job Pressure Day in 1979. There were demonstrations at phone company offices across the country. Someone brought an old car to one office, put the names of the managers on it, and charged fifty cents a whack to pound the car with a sledgehammer.

In 1980, the leadership of the CWA was able to convince AT&T

that job pressures were responsible for many of its problems of low motivation, absenteeism, and resentment. The problem was so severe for the membership that remedies had to be included in the contract. There had been various company-sponsored attempts to reduce employee discontent, but most of them had not been in cooperation with the unions, and had failed. The few successful efforts had been based on local commitment, involvement, and mutual trust.[26]

At the 1980 bargaining sessions, the union asked for a sign that the company was serious about wanting to improve employee morale. AT&T agreed to give up the remote monitoring of operators during training, and to provide the union with six months' advance notice of the introduction of any new technology. Both sides agreed to the establishment of a Joint Working Conditions and Service Quality Improvement Committee to work with committees in member companies and districts across the country. The agreement read, in part:

"Recognizing the desirability of mutual efforts to improve the work life of employees and enhance the effectiveness of the organization, the Company and the Union express their mutual belief that activities and experiments initiated and sponsored jointly by management and the Union can prove beneficial to all employees and the Company, and that by encouraging greater employee participation, work can be made more satisfying and organizational performance and service quality can be improved. . . .

"The parties agree that organizational and technological innovations are necessary and desirable; that every individual has the ability to contribute to the objectives of the organization; and that work should satisfy personal needs for self-respect and fulfillment as well as service and financial objectives."[27]

Glenn Watts, president of CWA, said the mutual recognition of the need to improve working conditions was a "radical" change. "You couldn't believe how warmly the contract [August, 1980] was received by the members of my union. I, for one, know that it's not the best contract we ever negotiated. But you can't convince the membership that it's not."[28]

Watts said that since top AT&T management was committed

to the concept of joint efforts, there would soon be beneficial results from programs in individual Bell companies. In the Birmingham, Michigan, installation and repair district of Michigan Bell, the new contract did provide an umbrella under which to bring in a consultant to straighten out the tangled labor-management relations there. Union and management leaders were trained together to try to reduce long-standing mistrust, and they set up a steering committee and problem-solving teams to consider such matters as "flex-time" and job titles. A major improvement at Birmingham has been a reduction in grievances, which between January 1979 and July 1979 fell from 40 to 12, and have remained more or less at that level ever since.

The 1980 Basic Agreement between the United Steelworkers of America (USWA) and the major steel producers contained some of the most significant language endorsing QWL ever printed in a labor contract, even though it was an experimental program limited to the length of the agreement and dependent upon local agreements between plants and unions.

The QWL endorsement implied that the existing contractual language and grievance procedure were not perfect instruments for speedy resolution of many problems that arise in the workplace. Since both sides were dependent upon the competitiveness of the company for survival, the parties agreed to experiment with Employee Participation Teams at the local plant level. These teams and an overseeing Participation Committee would be free to "discuss, consider and decide upon proposed means to improve department or unit performance, employee morale and dignity, and conditions of the work site."[29]

The list of "appropriate subjects" for a team to consider was long: use of production facilities; quality of products and the work environment; safety and environmental health; scheduling and reporting arrangements; absenteeism and overtime; incentives coverage and yield; job alignments; contracting out; energy conservation; and transportation pools. The agreement also provided for the teams to consider a range of responses to performance improvement, including bonus payments. The agreement specifically excluded the grievance process from the teams' purview.

According to Sam Camens, assistant to the president, United Steelworkers, the Employee Participation Teams were the "beginning of trying to reorient our relationship on the plant floor to a kind of participative, problem-solving [arrangement], with constant communications between employee and management to really try to get our people involved for the first time in solving problems that were up to this date totally management functions. . . . It's a very tough thing to change the collective bargaining relationship but still make sure it exists. That's what we're experimenting with."[30]

In 1981, it was too early to tell how the experiments would evolve. Both sides were cautiously optimistic that they could change the long-term adversarial relationship, but they knew it would not come easily or quickly. The key question in practice and in theory will be how to reconcile the new language endorsing QWL and the management rights clause, which in the agreement between the U.S. Steel Corporation and the USWA reads, in part: ". . . The Company retains the exclusive rights to manage the business and plants and to direct the working forces."[31]

Taken together, the agreements between the United Auto Workers, the Communications Workers of America, and the United Steelworkers of America and their respective industries indicate that a coherent union approach to QWL is emerging. According to Charles Heckscher, a research economist with CWA, the new approach includes the following elements:

- QWL is a fully *joint* activity, from planning through implementation: the union participates at an equal level in training and in the guidance of the programs. The "jointness" is manifested in the fact that these efforts are grounded in contract provisions.

- The goal of QWL is not productivity increase, though this may be an outcome. Unlike quality control circles, QWL sessions can legitimately discuss issues which are of concern to workers but not to management. Human values are at least as important as production values, and that statement is explicitly accepted by both parties.

- QWL is founded on explicit protection of worker rights: in particular, contract provisions may not be violated, and no one may be laid off as a result of ideas which come out of the process.

- The QWL process is separate and distinct from collective bargaining. The bargaining and grievance procedures continue unchanged (though they may be affected by the improved level of trust which is a by-product of QWL).

- QWL is voluntary for all participants—management, the union, and each individual worker.[32]

While some managers have recently looked to Japan for models of how to build a happy corporate community—preferably without unions—several unions have looked to Europe's strong labor tradition for advice and counsel, sending delegations to study wage-earner funds in Sweden and co-determination in Germany.

The German experience with co-determination has drawn attention to the inclusion of worker representatives on industrial boards of directors. Co-determination is a system of labor representation on company boards and plant-wide works councils. Interest in this model became practical with the election of Douglas Fraser of the UAW to the board of the Chrysler Corporation.

In May 1980, faced with a staggering $1.1 billion in losses, and in desperate need of $1.5 billion in federal loan guarantees, stockholders of Chrysler made corporate history by voting to place Fraser on its board. Fraser had once called the board a group of "well-meaning, honorable, but incompetent men."

Never before had a union member sat on the board of directors of a major American corporation. A few observers hailed it as the dawn of a new era in American labor-management relations. Most thought Fraser would find himself beset by conflicts of interest.

Arthur Burns, former chairman of the Federal Reserve Board,

favored giving Fraser the seat, saying, "We want to educate some of those labor leaders. I work on the theory that by sitting in a board meeting and studying the company's affairs, they will learn something about the company's needs and problems, and especially its need for profits."[33]

Of course, Chrysler did not court Fraser for altruistic reasons; his election came because the 120,000 UAW members at Chrysler conceded $403 million in wages and benefits to help the company stay solvent. One *quid pro quo* for the union members was that they were issued enough stock under an ESOP to give them 16 percent of the total outstanding common stock within three years.

Fraser told the *New York Times,* "I want Chrysler to really conduct experiments that make the workers part of the decision-making process on the organization of work and on the quality of the product. We're being brutalized on the quality issue by the public in general. Some of the criticism is unfair, but there is enough warrant for criticism to make a joint problem. If Chrysler makes a poor product, they don't have sales and we don't have jobs."[34]

In his first year on the board, Fraser won high marks from union members and his fellow board members for his balance and his ability to represent all interests. Robert B. Semple, the chairman of BASF Wyandotte Corporation and a Chrysler board member, praised Fraser for acting "just like a normal board member [and not] being just a labor advocate."[35] His union colleagues were pleased that he helped them obtain access to financial data and a more equitable layoff ratio between hourly and salaried employees.

Fraser thought his most important accomplishment was the establishment of a committee to study the human and social implications of plant closings. Martha W. Griffiths, former Michigan congresswoman and another board member, said that when Fraser described the closings in terms of flesh and blood, "you could feel the shock go through the board room."[36] "I've talked to a lot of board members since then," Fraser said, "and they said they had just never thought of it. I thought to myself, That tells the whole story."[37]

For a further $622 million in wage concessions in early 1981, the UAW gained perhaps an even greater alteration in corporate governance. Chrysler agreed to allow them access to their most prized possession, the management rights clause in the national contract, which gives the company "the exclusive right to manage its plants and offices and direct its affairs and working forces." Modification of that clause required management to consult and possibly negotiate with the UAW local committees on decisions that might "adversely affect" job security and plant closings. "Management has made so damn many mistakes—and so many thousands of workers are affected—that we want a voice in work-force decisions," said Marc Stepp, director of the UAW Chrysler Department.[38]

Fraser talks boldly about the unions obtaining seats similar to his on the boards of Ford and General Motors, but a constituency for increased UAW board membership does not seem likely unless the other auto makers suffer similar financial throes. Few companies will reach out on their own for employee directors. Union or worker seats on boards will probably continue to occur at companies *in extremis,* where management has little choice but to bring labor in. Of course, workers may also join boards of employee-owned firms—in which case they would be representing themselves as owners, not necessarily as union members. Unlike the European system of union board representation, worker board membership in this country will probably grow on a case-by-case basis, not spring into full existence through legislation.

Fraser admitted that his seat on Chrysler's board was not the best way to make the case for co-determination, because so much of the board's time was spent talking about "the very survival of the corporation." As the sole union representative, he saw his position as bordering on "tokenism." On the other hand, he said, "particularly with the shifting economy that we have, I just don't think that you can adequately represent your members unless you have a voice through representation on the board. The role the labor movement now plays is just inadequate to present and protect the workers' interests and jobs."

Fraser is opposed to legislating board membership until the

Chrysler board experience has been repeated several times. In any case, he doesn't believe that under the Reagan administration the idea has any chance of congressional approval. "They think this would *really* be the end of the capitalist system."[39]

Dr. Alfred Thimm, an economist knowledgeable about co-determination, has argued persuasively that worker representation on boards of directors in the U.S. should grow out of widespread stock ownership by both wage and salary employees. Given the in-breeding and myopia of many American corporate boards, Thimm suggested a scheme for employee board members that is a "natural organic consequence of widespread employee stock ownership. . . . I could conceive of no better crew to challenge the 'clubbiness' of the boards than a group of employee directors, consisting of skilled craftsmen, professionals, and middle managers. . . . The political, economic, and social sophistication of a board consisting, say, of two-thirds stockholder representatives and one-third employee representatives ought to be equal to the best contemporary boards."[40]

Such smooth transition assumes amenable unions, and that is by no means certain. Indeed, even though a union position on QWL is now on paper, a companion position on employee ownership does not exist at all. In the 1980 Basic Steel Agreement, the union was authorized to experiment with employee stock ownership on a voluntary basis, but there was no rush to do so. The USWA position was summed up in a speech by James W. Smith, assistant to United Steelworkers president Lloyd McBride, in February, 1981.

"We know what a struggle we've had to wring a living wage from the pockets of organized business. We simply don't expect our adversaries to gracefully give up the whole store anytime soon."[41]

Smith went on to launch a vitriolic attack on the management of South Bend Lathe Company and ESOP promoters for trying to destroy the United Steelworkers local there. He was upset because the terms of the ESOP as a subject of mandatory collective bargaining remained in limbo into the fall of 1981. Second, he was angry that workers were sold the ESOP as an alternative to pensions, making the workers instant, unwilling, and often ignorant investors, without any kind of training for the investor role. Further, he argued that the claims of higher profitability for ESOP companies were overstated, because those profits were often made by not funding pension obligations. Worker-owners, whatever kind of stock they held, would continue to have separate interests as workers and as owners. "Business managers, even if the worker helps select them through stock voting processes, cannot effectively represent workers' interests *as workers.*"

Smith therefore said that the union position on ESOPs would be:

- ESOPs would only occur in addition to a fully funded pension plan.

- Full pass-through of voting rights to every employee must occur.

- The stock should have a public market or be appraised by persons jointly chosen by workers and managers.

The Rath Packing Company, a majority of whose stock is owned by members of Local 46 of the United Foods and Commercial Workers, may not survive for a variety of reasons, high interest rates among them. But the union leaders were determined not to make the mistake of accepting ownership without control, as workers at South Bend Lathe had done five years earlier.

A second generation of employee-owned, unionized firms was born in 1979 in a huge, red brick building in Waterloo, Iowa. In that out-of-date relic, two leaders of Local 46 served as midwives to the union's purchase of a controlling interest in the century-old Rath Packing Company.

One of the few meat-packing companies to remain independent in the 1970s, Rath had suffered from capital shortage, mismanagement, and five straight years of losses totaling $23 million. Consultants hired by the company estimated it needed $4.5 million in immediate capital improvements to remain in the highly competitive pork products market. Conventional financing was out of the question, given the company's perilous financial condition. Rath management began to look for a buyer. Several investor groups trooped in, but all of them demanded massive wage and benefits concessions from the union. Having made substantial concessions already, the union members balked.

Instead, union president Lyle Taylor and chief steward Charles Mueller proposed that the union purchase 1.8 million shares, or 60 percent, of the authorized but unissued stock through some form of wage checkoff. Such a purchase would satisfy the Department of Housing and Urban Development's request for new equity investment to accompany its $4.5 million loan.

Taylor and Mueller sought out researchers at Cornell University who had studied other employee buy-outs. William Foote Whyte, Robert Stern, and Tove Hammer pointed to Vermont Asbestos Group and South Bend Lathe as places where the management approach to the company failed to shift despite the change to employee ownership.

Taylor and Mueller concluded that "it didn't make sense to own the company if you didn't control it," and directed their union lawyers to make sure that their 60 percent of the stock would translate into 60 percent of the seats on the board of directors.

After a year of complicated legal maneuvering through the thickets of ESOP legislation, Department of Labor regulations, and HUD financing requirements, Rath Packing Company became employee-owned in June, 1980. The six-member board was expanded to include ten new members chosen by the union, including Professor Tove Hammer, of Cornell; former Iowa Senator Dick Clark; and Lyle Taylor. Hammer subsequently chaired a subcommittee which hired a new president, Howard Epstein, former chairman of the Armada Corporation.

At the suggestion and urging of the Cornell researchers and Professor Warner Woodworth of Brigham Young University, union leaders pressed for changes in the way the company was run at the shopfloor level. They did not believe that it was sufficient to influence the overall direction of the company if the day-to-day operations were left untouched.

Mueller recalled that the researchers kept asking, "What have you done about communications between management and the employees?" "At first," he said, "we didn't even know what they were talking about. Then they began telling us about the Jamestown Area Labor-Management Committee's communications cells. It began to soak in. We had been thinking along the same lines, but didn't know what to call it. We knew the guys in the shop had a lot of good ideas to transfer to the company to make money. They know the best way to run their individual jobs. But Rath wasn't too good at listening to the monkeys in the zoo, so the ideas were not transmitted to management."[42]

With the help of consultants Woodworth and Christopher Meek, funded by a grant from the county development agency, management and the union established a multi-tiered system of labor-management cooperation. At the top was a Strategic Planning Group, composed of top managers and union officers. Its job was to discuss and assess finances, marketing, and overall production issues. It began by negotiating a charter to keep its functions distinct from the union contract. The second-level Steering Committee served to coordinate all plant labor-management cooperative efforts, and respond to suggestions for new areas of cooperation. Below that committee and feeding into it were Action Research Teams in departments such as Hog Kill, Sliced Bacon, and Ham Canning. The teams' mission was to tap the experience and intelligence of those who were closest to shopfloor problems to improve productivity. The most successful early effort was in Sliced Bacon, where machine down-time was reduced by two-thirds.[43] According to Meek, one of the most fascinating and encouraging manifestations of employee involvement at Rath has been the amount of voluntary work done by dozens of employees on their own time to tackle problems from accounting to meat-processing techniques.

A host of questions remain for the Rath employee-owners. Foremost is the difficult financial situation. They have also yet to face the possibility of conflict of interest if the union ever decides to strike. Theoretically, the union members on the board represent the employees as employees, not as unionists, but they are elected to their local posts as union members. Can union leaders represent their members as employees in one forum and as union members in another?

It seems likely that without union commitment, energy, and money, Rath Packing Company would have closed. The union was fortunate in having persistent leaders who could draw upon "reserves of trust from the membership while they saw [the purchase] through its inevitable delays, rumors and challenges from both inside and out."[44]

As Earl Murray, a shipping clerk for twenty-six years at Rath, said, "Management and employees have to be bound in what I call a spirit of togetherness. It just won't work if they're always fighting back and forth. All of a sudden we're married, and we've got to make sure that marriage lasts."[45]

While there are questions about the role of a union in an employee-owned firm, the idea of a union in a democratically structured cooperative may seem totally contradictory. However, David Ellerman of the Industrial Cooperative Association says there are three major reasons for the presence of a union in a cooperative. He makes a direct analogy between political and workplace democracy: there will always be a need to counterbalance a majority position, because true democracy cannot exist without protection of dissenters.

- "There is a need for institutionalized, constructive criticism of the way the cooperative is being run.

- "The union is the logical choice to handle member grievances.

- "The members may need some forum through which to balance the short-term interests of workers and the long-term interests of the company. Even in a cooperative, [these] are not co-terminous."[46]

One union in a co-op sounded feasible, but what happens when there are four? Such was the case at Denver Yellow Cab.

Yellow Cab had a history of acrimonious relations between its owner and its four unions. The drivers' union, the Independent Drivers Association, had set up a strike fund of $1 per shift following a 1977 lockout of the three "inside" unions with the cabbies honoring the picket line. In April 1979, boosted by a $200,000 loan from the strike fund, the drivers formed the Yellow Cab Cooperative Association and bought out their former employer for $2 million. The YCCA thus became owner of Denver Yellow Cab, Airport Limousine Company, Boulder Yellow Cab, and the Checker franchise for Colorado, and, with 950 members, one of the largest producer cooperatives in the United States.

Steve Johnson, former president of IDA and originator of the cooperative idea, told how the union purchase came about. He was sitting in a restaurant one Saturday morning ". . . cooling my heels and listening to these three women talk about their husbands' investments . . . wondering what to do next with our strike fund money, which had reached a hundred thousand dollars. We couldn't invest in another Certificate of Deposit because it would mature before the contract ran out. I had to do something else, and I felt like an investor looking for a company to buy.

"And then it hit me. *The company's for sale!* I got this incredible rush, goose pimples and all that. I said to myself, 'We've got a hundred thousand dollars in the strike fund. Maybe we have enough for a down-payment.' I had this buzz all weekend and finally called our lawyer and said, 'Is this crazy?' And he said, 'No!' "[47]

Johnson broached the idea to the union executive board, which authorized its lawyer to approach the owner, who proved receptive. Johnson described various methods of purchase to the members. He told them they could not legally form an ESOP, as at South Bend Lathe, because although they were considered employees for organizing purposes, they were also independent contractors for tax purposes, and ESOPs did not cover independent contractors. He also pointed out that if they bought the company shares in the conventional manner, a split would likely develop between the original purchasers and any drivers who joined later on.

A key mechanism for the discussion of alternatives was the Independent Drivers Association *News,* of which Johnson (as IDA president) was editor. Through its columns, question-and-answer sheets, and public meetings, Johnson presented a logical plan to establish a co-op. The plan called for all drivers to make a non-refundable $40 membership contribution as well as a $1.50-per-shift co-op payment for five years. This was in addition to the rental on the cab, but drivers would be free to drive as much or as little as they wished. The drivers approved the purchase plan 85 percent to 15 percent, and in May, 1979, bought their own jobs.

Co-op membership was mandatory for the drivers but voluntary for members of the other three unions. The 100-odd "inside" workers belonged to the Teamsters (doing body work), the Machinists (repairing the engines), and the Office Workers (running the vital switchboard and doing clerical work). Only about a fourth of these inside workers joined the co-op. Despite the drivers' sympathy strike in 1977, tensions between the drivers and the inside unions remained high. As one driver said, "Lots of us say, 'Hell, the phone operators don't answer the phone. The dispatchers don't hear me when I call for an order. The mechanics don't fix the cab when I shop it. Why should I do anything for them?' "[48]

Leaders of the Independent Drivers Association offered several strong reasons for retaining a union in a cooperative structure: First, the former owner was still the principal creditor and would take over if even a single payment was missed.[49] Given the creditor's known anti-union sentiments, it was important to have the security the union would provide for individual drivers if that happened. Second, it seemed practical to continue the union's sponsorship of the pension plan. Third, the union could still handle the grievances of individual drivers against the co-op management. As Johnson said, "The co-op board has a different job, which is to look after the welfare of the business as a business. In a way, we are back to the dual identity of independent contractors and employees. A dual identity is part and parcel of being a member of a co-op. As an individual worker you have one set of interests, and as a member of the ownership group you have another. These are not necessarily identical. As an individual worker, I want to maximize my welfare day by day, which may lead me into violating the rules. As a member of the ownership group, I think violations of the rules tend to screw things up and I want to deal harshly with violators. I think this duality is peculiar to this being a cab company, bought by a maverick independent union, but I also think it's a structural reality of any co-op."[50]

In 1980, the "inside" workers almost struck the co-op over wages. Paradoxically, the drivers unanimously vowed they would break such a strike rather than let the company revert to the former owner. Johnson said such internal confrontation "would have been very sad and the ill will would endure for many years."

Formal cooperation between labor and management on management affairs is still the exception rather than the rule, but it seems certain that management will continue to explore the possibilities of increased employee participation in ownership and management. Without doubt, some companies are using some forms of participation as an anti-union device. That is to be expected, but, as Irving Bluestone says, "Unionists just have to be smarter."

Bluestone, a fervent labor supporter of union involvement in QWL, dismisses the notion that workers are unable to distinguish between genuine and counterfeit participation. He has also spoken out against those who say any form of participation cannot go far enough. "For those who want to wait for the ultimate in industrial democracy to bear fruit in the United States, they had better leave a message for their great-grandchildren, because it's not going to come that quickly or easily," he said. "They say you have to go from here to there in one fell swoop. I never believed that. Unions don't operate that way.

"The efforts that are being undertaken through QWL, where there is union co-equality in the development and implementation of the program, are a step in the right direction, away from what historically has made the worker an adjunct to the tool, rather than the master of the tool. If we are, as a democratic society, interested in the worth of the individual, let's get that worth into the workplace."[51]

Robert Zager, of the Work in America Institute, writing in the *New York Times* about the Quality of Work Life Agreements involving the CWA, USWA, and UAW, spoke optimistically of a "new unionism" among unions with almost middle-class incomes. These unions have muted the old we-they split, believing "they stand to gain more from helping employers prosper than they do from destroying them." He suggested that this "new unionism" may strike a responsive chord in managerial and professional employees—foremen, junior managers, and accountants—who "consider themselves exploited but dislike the class implications of old-style unionism."[52] New unions may not even be called unions. If they call them professional associations but fight for and win the same things, it doesn't make any difference.

Until 1978, Thomas Donahue, secretary-treasurer of the AFL-CIO, repeatedly took the position that labor didn't want to be a "junior partner in success and a senior partner in failure" in participation schemes. But in November, 1980, he called for a "limited partnership—a marriage of convenience—in the search for solutions to economic problems, management problems, and political problems that, in sum, have created this productivity problem and the quality of work life problem for all of us.

"We insist, however, that this marriage of convenience ought to be one of the so-called 'new marriages,' in which neither partner is the exclusive head of the household.

"We are ready for that kind of relationship. We hope we will not be left waiting at the altar."[53]

[15]

Making a Difference

"This is a new day for American industry," proclaimed the editors of *Fortune* magazine in a series of articles called "Working Smarter" which appeared in the summer of 1981.

To attend a conference on Employee Stock Ownership Plans, quality circles, or Quality of Work Life that year was like going to a revival meeting. Proponents of a philosophy of increased employee participation in ownership or management decisions provided born-again testimonials to its human and economic benefits.

In late 1981 and 1982, Motorola Corporation ran a series of advertisements in national newspapers about Japan's "challenge to American industry." Under its logo, the company promised Americans "Quality and Productivity Through Employee Participation in Management."

The leadership of American labor unions, long committed to workshop warfare, is radically changing its position. Victor Gotbaum, executive director of the New York City Council of the American Federation of State, County and Municipal Employees, described this new attitude in the *New York Times*: "Unions that traditionally chose to stay out of management's prerogatives now realize that the quality of management is labor's business, too." Both management and the unions are "learning the necessity of working together."

In September 1981, Pope John Paul II, in his encyclical on work, called for employee participation as the basis for a new social contract among workers, managers, and owners. "Each person is fully entitled to consider himself a part owner of the great workbench at which he is working with everyone else." He should be a "sharer in the responsibility and creativity . . . and working for himself."[1]

By early 1982, over six thousand firms and agencies had substantially increased employee participation in ownership or management.

Despite the flurry of attention, one could rightly ask if participation deserved the label "new industrial relations," as *Business Week* asserted. After all, managers had been trying to reinterest their workers in their jobs since Frederick Winslow Taylor's time. Labor and management achieved extensive cooperation during World Wars I and II, management analysts such as Peter Drucker had written about "plant community" in the 1940s, and Douglas McGregor's Theory X and Y had become part of most managers' lexicon in the 1960s. Like bread, jobs had been "enriched" and redesigned, but whenever times were prosperous, the old hierarchy and dichotomy between thinkers and doers had reasserted themselves.

Three factors, however, make the present situation different. First, beginning in the 1970s, American companies, especially those competing in the international market, faced a multitude of interlocking problems which had not existed before. Productivity increases dropped significantly. The workforce increasingly resisted traditional authority and incentives. Volatile energy costs, high interest rates, and severe foreign competition became the norm. The common reaction, according to Reginald H. Jones, former president of General Electric, was to concentrate on short-term profits rather than on building for the future.[2]

Second, while these clouds were building, the decade also saw the evolution of organizational development theory and practice which could provide the means for significant organizational change. The human relations movement, which had sprung up in reaction to Taylorism, had urged managers to treat workers decently, on the assumption that happy workers were productive workers. The problem was that sometimes they were and sometimes they weren't. In McGregor's Theory Y, managers found what might be called a philosophy of participation, but they lacked techniques for implementing it. Quality of Work Life programs and, to a lesser extent, quality circles gave them those tools.

The third element in the economic equation of the 1970s was a burgeoning interest in employee ownership. In just a few years, employee ownership has developed a broad constituency. As Joseph R. Blasi of Harvard University wrote: "The idea combines the conservative Republican values of small business, private vs. state or public ownership, voluntary citizen cooperation and less government, local control, and broadened vs. concentrated ownership with the Democrats' valuing of economic democracy, community action, expanded role for unions in American society, improvement in the conditions of workers, and an experimental approach to economic and social problems in the tradition of Roosevelt."[3] To be sure, employee ownership as producer cooperatives had a history going back to the eighteenth century, but it had never affected more than a tiny number in the United States, most of which were in industrial clusters such as cooperage and plywood production.

Employee ownership developed in two directions. The first was to the Employee Stock Ownership Plan (ESOP) movement, with its mixed appeal of spreading both wealth and tax benefits. "Populism without Robin Hood" was the way its chief Congressional proponent, Senator Russell Long, described it. The largest constituency for ESOPs was formed by closely held corporations, whose owners sought the tax benefits of sharing stock but who were rarely interested in sharing control. Few of these companies were in difficult financial straits.

The second impetus toward employee ownership came from the last-ditch efforts to stave off plant closings in, and capital flight from, the industrial Northeast. In some cases, the plants were not actually losing money; they were just not making enough for their absentee conglomerate owners. These buy-outs were often hasty, disorganized attempts to save jobs and the economic bases of surrounding communities. As the decade progressed, approaches developed that provided a body of information and skills to assess the problems and possibilities of employee ownership on a sounder basis. Rath Packing, Denver Cab, and Hyatt Roller Bearing were the first of such "second generation" employee buy-outs to make use of this knowledge.

Between 1974 and 1981, Congress passed fifteen pieces of legislation relating to employee ownership. One bill, called the Small Business Employee Ownership Act, became Title V of the Small Business Development Act of 1980. It declared that employee ownership of firms provides a means to preserve jobs and business activity, to keep a small business small when it might otherwise be sold to a conglomerate, and to create new small businesses from the sale of a subsidiary by a large enterprise.

Participation efforts occur along two paths: increased worker involvement in management and increased employee ownership. Some organizations are beginning to combine the two, like a QWL program and a stock ownership plan. (See Figure 5, page 186.) The result is that each organization develops a unique form of employee participation.

The firms that have the longest commitment to a philosophy of participation, and the best programs, provide for significant participation by their employees in both ownership and management. While General Motors started by involving employees in decision-making in 1972, it soon saw the importance of stock ownership and in 1979 added a TRASOP,* a form of ESOP. At Hewlett-Packard, the employees own the majority of the common stock. Although the Mondragón cooperatives started with equal ownership among their employees in 1956, they first began to introduce autonomous decision-making groups in 1976.

The combining of participation in ownership and in management was not part of an initial grand plan for these firms, but rather evolved as the result of trying to find "a better way" of working together. The conflicting interests of employee and owner seemed to be resolved more quickly and at lower cost through effective participation. For the employees, the results were often improvement in income, job security, and working

*Tax Reduction Act Stock Ownership Plan.

conditions. For owners and management, the result was a better organization and higher profits. The combining of participation in management and ownership was an unexpected fortunate result.

Genuine participation in the workplace depends upon a radical change in management philosophy. Although some managers are reluctant to talk about it, participation represents a shift in the power and control that have long been theirs. It means blurring the distinction between managers and the managed. But, contrary to the fears of traditionalists, it does not mean holding a board meeting every time the company buys a new forklift. At a conference on Quality of Work Life, an insurance executive from Texas, after listening to a panel discussion about employee participation, remarked, "I like participation, but why do you have to share control with the workers if you don't want to?"

Part of this power shift is also an effort to deal with the new breed of educated workers and the alienation they feel because of boredom or reduced responsibility at work. The research of Daniel Yankelovich shows that alienation is the same as powerlessness. "Quality of Work Life programs and employee ownership," he adds, "are important efforts to deal with powerlessness at work."[4]

The problems for the managers have been stated concisely by George C. Lodge, of the Harvard Business School: "Whether we make the transition from contract to consensus comfortably may well depend on whether the good of the corporation and the community as a whole will outweigh the needs and desires of existing managers for power and prestige. The change that confronts them will be as difficult as the change that confronted the traditional Roman administrators forced to accept Christianity."[5]

Before discussing the results that this shift in management and ownership philosophy is achieving, it is important to distinguish between democracy in politics and democracy in the workplace.

When many people first hear about democracy in the workplace, they think immediately about political democracy and how inefficient it is. The two forms are similar in their effort to share fairly the privileges and burdens of responsibility for decisions across an organization or the national electorate. But the similarity ends there.

With the exception of some town meetings in New England, where each adult taxpayer is eligible to participate in decisions, political democracy is indirect or representational. People elect their representatives every several years, and generally think little about politics betweentimes. In sharp contrast, democracy in the workplace usually means direct involvement in daily decisions through problem-solving groups and consensus decision-making. It also can mean choosing fellow employees to sit on committees or the board of directors, or selecting one's own manager. Finally, with workplace participation, people see the results of their efforts, while they often do not in political democracy.

If the attempts to change the philosophy of ownership and management are successful—and many of them fail—there are significant benefits, both economic and human, for the individual, the organization, and the community. Productivity increases of 10 percent and more are not unusual, and continue for several years. Early in programs, productivity per employee may jump 100 percent, or the costs of scrap may be cut by 75 percent. Grievances have fallen from 3,000 to 15, and stayed at that level. Absenteeism and turnover can be cut in half. Through profit-sharing and stock ownership plans, blue-collar employees have received yearly bonuses of up to 50 percent of their salaries, and some have retired on pensions of more than $660,000. Flexibility in the use of employees improves: Delta Airline pilots handle passenger baggage if their flights are canceled; Toyota has six job descriptions for blue-collar employees versus 200 at Chrysler. Martin Marietta reduced its accidents by 57 percent. These are the economic benefits that directly affect the individual and the organization, and may indirectly affect consumers and citizens through lower costs and better products.

In a 1981 study, 1,400 companies with ESOPs were interviewed. The survey revealed the companies had experienced improved productivity between 1975 and 1979, compared to a decline for the average non-ESOP company in the same period and industry. The survey also found that one-third of the companies with ESOPs over three years old reported a reduction in employee turnover and an improvement in the quality of work. More than half reported an improvement in employee morale and employee interest in company progress. A study of 98 firms by the U.S. Senate found that profits of ESOPs averaged 50 percent higher than those of firms without ESOPs in the same type of business. This study also found that the more equity the employees owned, the greater the company profits.[6]

For some people who have led the way in introducing participation, the more important benefit has been human development. The material benefits are secondary. People feel better about themselves. They like to go to work. They have more self-esteem and self-confidence. They have gained control over their lives, if only a little, and lost some of their sense of powerlessness.

The benefits of participation to the community are less well established. It appears that people who have worked cooperatively often take a more active role in church and community affairs than they did previously. Labor unions report higher attendance at regular meetings. Alcoholism declines, bringing lower health costs and fewer deaths from drunken driving. The insurance premiums for workmen's compensation fall. If product quality and design improve, and the retail price decreases, this can also be seen as a benefit of participation to consumers.

Despite the episodic but growing evidence of financial and human benefits from participation, its acceptance and spread are still not assured. Significant impediments remain. The first is resistance to a shift in power: having spent their careers slowly amassing it, managers are usually unwilling to share it. Second, participation involves consensus, compromise, and flexibility. While some managers may use these words, they are often unwilling to put them into practice. Third, even when people are convinced that participation is important, they often do not know *how* to cooperate with their peers, superiors, and subordinates. Unless they are like the unusual leaders discussed in this book, they are not ready to "stick their necks out" and propose that management change its philosophy. Fourth, the success of participation is not guaranteed, and people do not like to be associated with failure. Finally, the idea of getting people involved is deceptively simple; its execution is not.

Once enough men and women in an organization think that participatory management or ownership ought to be tried, six basic problem areas need to be dealt with in planning and implementing the philosophy. These six areas are: conflicting objectives among the parties; getting participation efforts started; establishing new ways of making decisions; determining the appropriate leadership; redesigning the responsibilities of middle managers; and building a new relationship with unions.

One of the reasons there is little trust in many organizations is that managers and other employees seem to have conflicting objectives for the organization. Managers want to speed up production, while employees desire work that does not leave them exhausted at night, and that will be there next week. Managers with company stock would like to see less paid in wages and more in dividends, while non-stockholder employees would prefer the reverse. If managers and owners avoid discussing such conflicting objectives, they will not be able to construct a workable philosophy of participation. It is only by dealing directly with these problems that both parties grow to see they share objectives that often transcend the conflict: unless a company makes superior products or supplies services at competitive prices, neither chief executive nor janitor will have a job for long.

The specific objectives for a philosophy of participation are usually the same for most companies: reducing workers' fear of losing their jobs; greater equity in hiring and promoting, as well as in sharing the gains from increases in productivity; and as much accommodation of individual needs as possible.

Launching a philosophy of participation is easy to describe and hard to accomplish. People who have been successful managers by telling others what to do find it hard to ask for advice, and harder to take it. Many managers also fear being seen as failures if they use participatory management. Similarly, workers who have been accustomed to taking orders find it difficult to make suggestions, let alone to "talk back to the boss," as Dana Corporation employees are encouraged to do.

In starting successful participation programs, the level of trust between management and other employees has to be raised, if it isn't high already. Participation must be voluntary; while senior executives may place pressure on managers to change their approach, other employees should not be manipulated or coerced into participating. Learning new skills of listening, problem-solving, and how to run meetings is important for everyone, from the shopfloor people to the president. Finally, as the explorers in the American West had to have a trusted Indian guide to show them the best route over the mountains, so people who wish to develop a philosophy of participatory management or ownership in their organization need a consultant—usually an outsider—to help them distinguish the false trails from the right ones.

The distinction between decision-making and problem-solving is at the heart of the new philosophy. Anyone can make decisions, but not everyone can solve problems. Participation works as well as it does because people who are closest to the problems are encouraged and trained to solve them; they make decisions, instead of people distanced from the problems by levels of hierarchy.

A participatory approach to decision-making usually means that people spend more time in meetings, especially at the beginning of a program. Not everyone, however, wants to get involved in every decision. In the plywood and the Mondragón cooperatives, employees must have great confidence in their management to make the right decisions: after all, the employees were either directly or indirectly—through their representative on the board —involved in selecting them. As employees in firms that are not employee-owned grow to trust their colleagues and understand the nature of the problems they face, they can give their managers strong support to do their jobs.

A paradox of participation is that it often begins at the top of the organization, with owners or chief executive officers like John

Donnelly, Sidney Harman, or Rene McPherson taking a personal interest. Despite the rhetoric about participation bubbling up from the bottom, support for a program from both top management and union leaders is essential. Participation flattens the hierarchy, sometimes removing whole layers of it. People at any level of an organization may propose changes of such magnitude as participation, but only the person at the top can insure that the right climate is set to encourage their acceptance.

The leader sets the tone and direction of change. He or she must often take the first leap of faith and then stand ready to lend a hand when subordinates hesitate. Above all, the leader must believe that power can be shared. In an essay entitled "Power, Politics and a Sense of History," Yale University president A. Bartlett Giamatti wrote: "Far better to be one who knows that if you reserve the power not to use all your power, you will lead others far more successfully and well, for to restrain power is in effect to share it. . . . Whoever knows how to restrain and effectively release power finds, if he is skillful and good, that power flows back to him."[7]

None of the leaders we studied set out to democratize the management of their organizations; their objective was to find a better way of working together. As people shared more equitably in problem-solving, the organization's performance improved.

The new leaders see themselves more as "resource people" than as decision-makers. They have made the shift, as David Easlick, the president of Michigan Bell, says, from "warlord to colleague." They have the vision to identify the critical problems for the future of the organization, and the humility to be one voice among equals in resolving them.

The leaders of successful programs in participatory management appear to possess a set of values that go beyond profits. They care a great deal about the people in their organization, and are able to translate that caring into developing new organizational structures and processes that improve the lives of thousands of employees. They believe that most employees are not being used to their full potential, and that people want to do a better job but have been held back by the defects of organizations. In sharing power and decision-making, these leaders have found that their employees welcome trust and responsibility. Their purpose is to realize different values. Money, privilege, specialization, and career become less important than the satisfaction of a job well done, fair treatment across the community, helping others to achieve their goals, reduction in the division of labor, and the demystification of expertise.[8]

One of the basic problems in introducing participation is the pressure it puts on middle managers. As workers accept more responsibility for the functions middle managers used to perform, such as discipline and coordination, these managers fear for their jobs. When firms like General Motors and American Telephone & Telegraph have abolished—almost overnight—entire levels of their management pyramids, managers everywhere have good reason to be fearful. (They also need to know that, at least at these two companies, the changes were made by attrition, not dismissals.) There is a role for first-line supervisors in new organizations, but it is not "kicking ass and taking names." They are involved in planning future activities and in being a resource to the work teams.

Unions have been both skeptical and supportive of participation. It was Irving Bluestone of the United Auto Workers who helped convince General Motors that the cooperative approach was a useful one. The United Steelworkers and the Communication Workers agreed. William Winpinsinger, president of the machinists, however, is still opposed to the idea, even though a growing number of his locals disagree with him. Some union officials believe that participation might transfer worker loyalty from the union to the firm. But an understanding is growing among them that they have more to gain from helping organizations prosper than they do from weakening them through promoting adversarial relations.

The road to successful participation is strewn with potholes and washed-out bridges, and some travelers have not made it. While those who know most about the failures are reluctant to say much about them, several common features emerge. First, management did not have a good idea of what it was doing, and would not learn from others' experience. Second, the quality of the leadership at these firms was poor. Managers and union officials lacked both concern for their people and basic management skills. They did not want to share control over "their" organization. Third, management thought it could install a participation "experiment" in one plant, or a corner of the plant, and avoid dealing with the implications that such a change in philosophy had for itself and for the entire organization.[9]

Sometimes there is too little trust between management and other employees before management tries to establish cooperation. Premature publicity, at least about the early projects (which the media saw as oddities), has created friction among insiders. Giving or selling employees stock without sharing voting rights has caused basic problems. Greedy and selfish leadership, which voted raises to itself but not its employee-owners, has contributed to the failure of participation.

The absence of gains-sharing is a problem that may become more critical as people in the offices and on the shopfloor see productivity benefits going to outside shareholders and to managers with stock options. Participation will be viewed as "speedup" and "a rip-off." In the best programs, such as the Scanlon Plans and the cooperatives, gains-sharing is an essential feature. It is included in some QWL programs, and if the unions have their way, will be in more soon. Programs that contain quality circles tend not to have gains-sharing; it was central at the Harman Industries and to the UAW approach at Bolivar, but not at General Motors. (So far, GM workers have been satisfied just to keep their jobs, but their attitude may change if dividends and managerial salaries start to rise again and wages do not.)

Employees are becoming truly empowered in only a few—mostly grievously wounded—firms. In a survey of approximately 100 firms with over 51 percent employee ownership, Joseph R. Blasi and William Foote Whyte found little sign of worker participation in decisions that affect their work.[10] Enfranchisement is the watershed of participation when control over policy-making—i.e.

sovereignty—is shared or changes hands. There are in this country probably no more than a couple of dozen firms of over fifty employees that have fully democratic structures, where control over work belongs to those who work, not to those who own property, in the form of stock.

To use the analogy of our political heritage, political enfranchisement once derived from ownership of property. Over the last two hundred years that link has been severed. It seems highly unlikely that such a severing will occur soon in the economic realm.

Small, owner-operated firms have played an important role in implementing the philosophy of participation. These range from Harman Industries and Hewlett-Packard, now grown to multinational scale, to Lincoln Electric, Fastener Industries, and Donnelly Mirrors. They were the innovators that firms like General Motors copied. Why did the smaller firms come to these ideas early? Owner-operators like Sidney Harman and William Hewlett worked side by side with the employees. The owners trusted their employees, and gave them freedom to take responsibility and challenge management's authority. They saw every day how participation in decision-making and ownership enhanced employee commitment to the customers, the products, and the organization. They understood the energy and loyalty that grew out of establishing equitable, caring relationships among employees at work.

One happy result of the shift in power from the executive suite to the shopfloor and the back office has been the demystification of management. Workers are learning they can manage, and it may be just in time. Malcolm Baldridge, Secretary of Commerce, has blamed American management for being "too fat, dumb, and happy in the past ten years."[11] He said that he did not "think it's labor productivity that's a problem. It's management, and I speak as a former manager." The effort to reunify the worker's hand and brain has played a major role in the demystification of management. Furthermore, the distinction between those who work and those who manage has been blurred as workers have taken on management functions in autonomous groups and quality circles.

It is interesting to note that the Japanese have never developed a high priesthood of professional management with an M.B.A.-like initiation rite; rather, everyone starts at the bottom, and works in all principal parts of the organization to earn the chance at a desk in the executive suite.

What are the limits of participation? Vivian Creviston, a first-line supervisor at the General Foods Topeka plant, which has an advanced program, was asked if she should be involved in choosing the next plant manager. "No," she said, "that is not my role."[12] At employee-owned Fastener Industries in Berea, Ohio, the reverse is true. There the employees elect the board of directors, and help pick (through their representatives) managers and all company officers. Before the employees achieve a majority ownership of a company, management sets the limits of participation. Until that point is reached, participation can go only so far in reducing the fundamental differences in power, status, and income between workers and owners.

Even after ten years of well-publicized illustrations of participation, most American employees are still not demanding it. Those who have requested it, however, are enthusiastic supporters. Gary Bryner, assistant to the president of the United Auto Workers, states: "The thing I believe so sincerely is that once you get workers involved in a system of participation, you can't turn them off. You can't suddenly say, 'Look, we don't want your ideas anymore; it won't work that way.'"

Lyle Taylor, president of the United Food and Commercial Workers local, which bought 60 percent of the Rath Packing Company, went even further: "One of the things we want to do is make corporate executives out of everyone in the company."[13]

It would be naïve to think that QWL programs, ESOPs, or cooperatives can cope with the sometimes insuperable difficulties of antiquated technology, eroding markets, prolonged mismanagement, and inadequate financing. Simply working together in a spirit of cooperation does not guarantee success.

. . .

The application of the philosophy of participation raises four issues for the remainder of the 1980s. How will firms that have embraced shopfloor and back-office participation deal with requests for participation on the board of directors? Will the system of formal education support the reversal of Taylorism, or simply reinforce the old way of separation of thinkers and doers? Will the holders of financial power, such as pension fund trustees and other institutional investors, support participation, or use their power to contain it? Is there a role for government?

Inviting employee representation on a board of directors is a powerful indication of owners' and management's trust in employees' ability to contribute to the organization. Chrysler board members were horrified when UAW president Douglas Fraser was first considered for election. However, after a year, they praised him for "acting just like a normal board member, [and not] being just a labor advocate."[14]

Employees at Eastern Airlines were twice refused when they asked the company to nominate Charles E. Bryan, president of the machinists local in Miami, as a candidate for the board of directors, although he was permitted to solicit proxies from the shareholders. Forty percent of Eastern's annual costs are wages, salaries, and benefits for employees. Employee board representation, Bryan argues, could build trust and loyalty which would pay off in better performance and a sounder economic footing for Eastern.

In a letter to Eastern's president, Frank Borman, Bryan asked why he ignored the lessons of history that "the British learned regarding 'taxation without representation.' " He said that Eastern had continued to ask the employees to sacrifice, but had not let them "get involved at the top."[15] Borman replied that "a board of directors is concerned with the overall welfare of the corporation—not the special interests of any particular group. . . . We therefore do not look for persons [as board candidates] to represent particular interests."[16]

Several companies, such as Donnelly Mirrors, have developed a compromise on the board problem. Employees and management elect representatives to the Donnelly Committee, which makes company policy on all personnel matters. It has more influence than that of a typical top-level QWL joint committee. At Supreme Aluminum, Ltd., in Scarborough, Ontario, where four hundred employees manufacture pots and pans, management has given responsibility for most operating policies to a committee with elected employee representatives. Still, the Donnelly and Supreme solutions are not board representation.

European executives and board members who have had up to thirty years' experience with employee representatives on boards find the hostile attitude of their American colleagues puzzling. Two hundred members of Norwegian corporate boards were interviewed three years after a law was passed requiring that a third of the board seats be given to employee representatives in firms of more than fifty employees. Eighty percent were fully satisfied with the effects of the law. There was little difference between the results from employee and shareholder representatives, but they had different reasons for approving the system. Shareholder representatives liked the improved communication from boards to employees, especially about company objectives. Employee representatives said they had better insight into company problems, and improved chances of influencing the outcome. Twenty percent of the members had experienced some problem with inadequate secrecy about board information, but they did not consider this a major difficulty.[17]

Per Grobstok is chairman of the board of a group of twenty-five firms in advertising, public relations, and publishing in Norway, none of which has the required fifty employees. Yet employees are on the boards. He said, "It is correct to have employees on the board. Nothing is hidden. Employees need to be fully involved in what the organization is doing from the planning and management standpoint. . . . Employees need to know that management is listening."[18]

Employee board representation will more likely come from union bargaining on a case-by-case basis or from employees' becoming shareholders. At Pan American World Airways, the five-union Labor Council made concessions of over $150 million to help keep the company afloat. In return, it received 15 percent of the stock and two seats on the board of directors. Pan Am union members will use a one-share, one-vote principle, with the majority determining how the block of votes will be cast on company decisions. In concert with the distribution of the stock, the Labor Council and company management will develop a wide-ranging program of communication.

Most American board members, however, have not enjoyed the experience of their colleagues at Chrysler or in Europe. They cannot perceive representation as an effective way to understand employees' viewpoints and to reconcile conflicts before they disrupt the business. Given the success of participation outside the boardroom in North America, and the success of representation inside it in Germany and Scandinavia, American employees may be expected to become more insistent in the 1980s.

A second issue for the 1980s is the role of both formal schooling and on-the-job training in supporting an organization's shift to participation. While leaders have to learn new roles, followers, according to consultant Lee Ozley, "have to learn to stop being the silent majority." On-the-job training, which teaches specific skills such as how to run meetings, has been essential to the success of participation programs. But training is costly. AT&T spent $1.2 billion on it in 1980. Small firms often believe that they cannot afford the investment.

Are skills learned in schools relevant to the new philosophy? The short answer is that many of them are not. In fact, the competitive attitudes and behavior that students are often taught have to be unlearned if they are to participate effectively. The amount of schooling most people acquire has also contributed to the problems in the Taylorized workplace. While the level of education of the average worker has increased, the average job now requires less skill. This growing mismatch between education and work has been a major cause of management's interest in job reform designed to make better use of employee abilities.

Schools have played an essential role in the preparation of children for the workplace. Schooling was not needed until the end of the eighteenth century, because most work was done at home. In 1780, 80 percent of the workforce (excluding slaves) were independent producers. By 1880, 80 percent were wage and salary workers. Schools expanded most rapidly in those areas of the country where the factory system was expanding.[19] Factory managers needed people who could take orders, work long hours at boring, repetitive work, and respond to the extrinsic rewards of payment and promotion.[20]

Schools molded the sons and daughters of independent farmers and business people to become willing workers in factories and offices. Students first learned to compete for grades and in sports against each other for advancement to higher levels of education, then later as workers progressing in their careers. They were not taught to take a role in planning their curriculum or selecting their teachers. They were motivated by grades and promotion, not internal satisfaction with a job well done. As workers lost control over the process and product of their work when they went into the factories and offices, so students learned that it was not their role to be involved. Teachers, principals, advisers, and superintendents—the specialists—had the authority and knowledge to make the right decisions. It is only recently that we find even 14 percent of American institutions of higher learning with student representatives on their boards of trustees. Only one-quarter of the boards have faculty representatives and only 58 percent of the student members can vote.[21]

As long as schools do not generate attitudes and behavior that are consistent with the philosophy of workplace democracy, organizations will have to maintain their training and consulting budgets and hope that the schools will catch up. Lack of participation in the schools is not attributable to a poverty of ideas, but rather to a lack of movement in business to embrace participation. John Dewey, the progressive educator, thought schools should have the full participation of students and parents. This would help develop good citizens who enjoyed the rights and freedoms of political life. This contrasted with the restrictions of life at work. The history of education and efforts to reform it indicate that the world of work shaped the education system, not the other way around.[22]

Another educational problem is the importance of financial

and administrative knowledge among employees who become owners. While in the traditional corporate model most shareholders understand the financial and administrative rationale of the firm, new employee owners often do not even understand the nature of a balance sheet or an "income producing asset." It isn't that they can't learn, but the process takes time and often gets short shrift when the company is fighting for its very survival.[23]

As the produce manager of a twenty-employee cooperative grocery in Minneapolis said, "The biggest problem in our cooperative is thinking and working on a long-term basis. It's relatively easy just to keep the store going day to day, but to make decisions, to have the vision about two, three, twenty years hence, is very hard. It is difficult to discuss this kind of thing in a group in the first place, and second, when you're under the pressure of running the business, the future is the last thing you have energy for."

Who then will train managers and workers to think in more cooperative ways? In the short run, it will probably be the consultants. There are companies that have started successful programs of participation in management or ownership without outside help, but most have used consultants. The best consultants walk a thin line between reminding managers and workers that participation is not a quick fix and yet trying to work themselves out of the job of consulting. They are more than mediators. At their best, they are agents of change, organizational guerrillas wearing down ossified battlements of hierarchy and bureaucracy. At their worst, they play solely to the prejudices of their paymasters.

The third issue for the future is the problem of financing employee participation in ownership. There are currently three main sources: individual employees, who use their savings to buy stock; the company treasury, which pays part of the share price; and pre-tax corporate profits, which, through ESOPs, help employees buy stock in their companies at little cost to themselves or to the firms. (Normally most of this income would be paid as taxes to the government.) Most banks have been hesitant to lend money to employee-owned firms, despite their record of high performance compared to non-employee-owned companies. Other potential sources of funds such as the following have inspired little discussion: the establishment of new banks that would lend only to employee-owned enterprises in their geographic area; venture capital and mutual funds; and pension funds.

Two banks of the new type already exist. The Agricultural Cooperative Bank, established by Congress in 1934, lends mainly to agricultural marketing cooperatives like Land O' Lakes and Agway. The National Consumer Cooperative Bank, owned by its borrowers, was established by Congress in 1979 to lend to consumer cooperatives producing food, housing, and energy. Only 10 percent of its portfolio can be in "producer cooperatives," employee-owned firms; by the end of its second year of operation, the bank had five times more requests for assistance from employee-owned firms than it had been set up to handle. There is no equivalent in the United States of the Caja Laboral in Mondragón, which channels the savings of 300,000 small depositors to employee-owned enterprises. The establishment of such banks in American towns and cities could promote the expansion of feasible employee ownership.

Venture capital and mutual funds could assist the private investor in locating profitable investments in employee-owned enterprises. Because of the relatively high rate of return from existing employee-owned enterprises compared to other firms in the same industry, such funds should be attractive to both individual and institutional investors.

Pension funds are another financial source for employee-owned enterprises. The funds are owned by the participants and beneficiaries and are legally considered to be deferred wages, but they are controlled by trustees who normally turn the assets over to professional investment managers such as banks, insurance companies, and brokerage firms. In 1981 they totaled about $800 billion.[24] Union-negotiated pension funds in the private sector alone totaled an estimated $300 billion, of which $60 billion was jointly controlled by the union and management-appointed trustees. Most private-sector pension plans are solely controlled by the sponsoring corporation even when the plan is subject to collective bargaining.

Pension funds are often invested in American corporations

that are involved in activities to which the owners of the funds are opposed. Thus, these funds have helped open plants abroad or in the South, taking jobs away from the pension fund owners in the North. Unions have found their funds invested in anti-union firms such as du Pont, Kodak, and IBM. Sixteen of the top 25 companies where union pension funds are invested have been classified by the Union Label Department of the AFL-CIO as having predominantly non-union shops or anti-union policies.[25]

State and local governments control about $240 billion in pension funds, half of which come from the sixteen Northeastern states. The trustees of these funds are also investing in the South and abroad rather than in their own states. The owners of the funds, the employees, who are often, but not always, represented on the board of trustees, are now starting to ask their trustees to invest the funds to promote jobs in their communities and states. Increasingly, state and local government public employee funds are investing in local housing and even in small business and venture capital. The Ohio legislature recently passed legislation that permits public employee pension funds to invest up to 25 percent of their assets in limited partnerships and venture capital firms that have significant activity in the state. California's Public Employees Retirement System decided to seek seats on the boards of directors of companies in which it has substantial investments.

The fourth issue for the 1980s is the role of government. Should federal and state governments use their power to encourage firms to start quality circles, elect employees to the board of directors, sell common stock to their workers? In six European countries, shopfloor and board participation are legislated for medium-sized and larger organizations. And in Sweden sharing stock ownership is a major issue in the 1982 election. By the spring of 1982, however, American legislators and members of executive branches of state and federal governments had shown little interest in this philosophy. As one member of the (democratically elected!) U.S. House of Representatives said, "Call it employee participation, not workplace democracy."

Matthew McHugh, a member of the U.S. House of Representatives from Binghamton and Ithaca, New York, who chaired a congressional task force on employee participation, is one of the exceptions. The task force recommended that legislation be drafted to provide greater financial and tax advantages to employee-owned firms; to alert employees and their communities to plant closings well before the lights are turned off for the last time, to give them an opportunity to consider buying the plant; and to provide funds for organizations to start programs in participatory management. These recommendations, however, are far short of the European mandate requiring board membership for employees. The congressmen emphasized that they preferred the voluntary nature of the American approach. They feel that it is more consistent with the philosophy of participation than the European; if you don't want to join a circle or buy stock, you should not be forced to.

The task force also concluded that the major effort should be for them personally to encourage organizations in their districts to explore the advantages and disadvantages of participation. Senator Bill Bradley of New Jersey, for example, held a day-long seminar in the state for business and labor leaders.

How long this attitude favoring voluntary participation will prevail among legislators is uncertain. If more American managers and owners become supporters of participation, if the competitive gap with Japan and Europe widens for American products, and if union leadership at the local level becomes convinced that the benefits outweigh the risks, more people may ask for laws requiring participation. Employees in firms without it may feel that the future of their jobs is less secure, that they suffer an unfair disadvantage compared to other workers.

A small but increasing number of Americans have become aware through their experience at work that Frederick Winslow Taylor was wrong: there is no single best system to organize work. The rebuttal to Taylor's theory of division of the hand and the head— at least for this new minority of owners, managers, and workers— is to get people involved in management and ownership. When men and women take more responsibility for their work, they do a better job. Their involvement can affect alienation, mismanagement, and productivity. People will feel better about themselves and their work, and organizations will perform better.

The American economy is beset by aggressive special interests that are unwilling to take a holistic view of the social fabric; instead, they pull on single threads and thus weaken the whole cloth. The level of U.S. labor grievances per 100,000 workers is 17 times that of West Germany, and mostly wasted effort. In cooperating with management, German labor has not given up its traditional objectives of higher pay, better working conditions, and job security. Nor has management surrendered its objectives of better products and return on equity. As managers and workers are learning, they share some common goals, including the reduction of adversarial relations.

Managers and workers are changing their ways of working not because it is "good" but because it is good business. They are coming to realize that they must change in order to compete or hold on to their jobs. Necessity thus becomes the mother of cooperation as well as invention. It is difficult, however, to develop a common purpose if "the bottom line" and "company loyalty" are the major motivating factors. "When we overvalue organization as an end, not a means," a Volvo manager said, "it becomes an idol. The company is only worth supporting if it serves society."[26]

People are beginning to recognize the psychological and economic importance of self-esteem and dignity for the individual. These values are as rooted in the American tradition as those of the Pilgrims fleeing religious persecution and the colonists decrying taxation without representation. The frustration and alienation that our organizations provoke are weakening the economic heart of the nation.

The rising feeling of powerlessness is one result of the systems of decision-making and ownership that have been relentlessly, and often unwittingly, developed during this century to take responsibility away from people. Participation can re-engage people in their lives at work and renew their organizations. They learn that by working together they can make a difference.

Participation and Productivity

The purpose of these data is to illustrate changes in productivity under different types of employee participation. They were chosen because of the sustained nature of their improvement.

Project	Type of Change	No. of Employees	Productivity Results
JOB ENRICHMENT:			
Harwood Manufacturing Co., garment plant	Job enrichment (some participatory management)	1,000	Productivity rose 25% in two years, compared to 10% in other Harwood plants.
Monsanto Corp., agricultural division plant, Muscatine, Iowa	Job enrichment (and group goal-setting)	150 machine operators and maintenance personnel	Started 1967. In four months experienced 75% increase in productivity. Sustained at least through 1971.
Monsanto Corp., textile plant, Pensacola, Florida	Job enrichment	50 chemical operators	Started 1968. Productivity rose 50%. Cut number of supervisory personnel in half.
PPG Corp., fiberglass plant, North Carolina	Job enrichment	120 twist-frame operators	Started 1969. In two years, productivity rose 12%.

Project	Type of Change	No. of Employees	Productivity Results
SCANLON PLANS: Study of 9 representative companies	Scanlon		Published 1958. In first two years of plan, productivity rose in all firms. Plants averaged 23.1% higher productivity than before plan.[1]
Study of 44 firms	Scanlon		Published in 1975. Review of 22 studies found 30 successes and 14 failures.[2]
Adamson Co., steel storage tanks	Scanlon		Started 1945. Profits rose 150% in first year, 41% bonus to workers. Profits rose 100% in second year, 54% bonus to workers.
DeSoto Corp., paint manufacturing	Scanlon		Started 1971. Productivity rose 41% in first three years. Corp. then introduced plan in 3 other plants.
Donnelly Mirrors, automobile parts	Scanlon	460	Started 1953. In first 20 years, productivity doubled, return on investment tripled. Since 1968, absenteeism down from 5% to 1.5%.
Parker Pen Corp., Janesville, Wisconsin	Participation, including Scanlon	700	Started 1954. Average bonus 13%. Productivity rose 100% between 1966 and 1976.
TRW Corp., aircraft engine manufacturing, Harrisburg, Pennsylvania	Scanlon	1,072	Started 1975. Bonus of $750,000 first year. April, 1976, 95% of workers voted to continue plan.

Project	Type of Change	No. of Employees	Productivity Results
PARTICIPATORY MANAGEMENT:			
57 field studies	Quality of Work Life		Positive results found in 80% of field studies.[3]
Review of 103 experiments	Most of which included participatory management		Over 80% reported positive impact on productivity.[4]
Corning Glass Corp., electronic instrument manufacturing plant, Medford Massachusetts	Autonomous teams	58 Hot plate department	Started 1966. In first 6 months, productivity rose 84%, rejects fell from 23% to 1%, absenteeism fell from 8% to 1%.
		Glass shop	Productivity rose 20%.
		Instrument division	Productivity rose 17%, quality rose 50%.
Texas Instruments, Dallas, Texas	Autonomous teams	120 cleaning and janitorial employees	Started 1977. Needed 49 fewer employees. Cleanliness rating rose from 65% to 85%. Quarterly turnover fell from 100% to 9.8%.
LABOR-MANAGEMENT COMMITTEES:			
Study of shipbuilding during World War II by U.S. Maritime Commission	L-M committees		From 1942 to 1944, worker suggestions saved industry $45 million and 31 million person-hours.[5]
Jamestown New York	Area L-M Committee plus QWL 14 firms		1,300 jobs saved and 2,000 new jobs started.
Youngstown Sheet & Tube Co., metal fabricating, Youngstown, Ohio	L-M committee	150	Started 1974. Over 3-year period, productivity rose 5.5%, average delays fell from 10% to 3%, absenteeism from 15% to 7%.

Project	Type of Change	No. of Employees	Productivity Results

PROFIT-SHARING PLANS:

Project	Type of Change	No. of Employees	Productivity Results
Six major profit-sharing retailers compared to six major non-profit-sharing retailers	Profit-sharing		Profit-sharing firms had 85% higher median return on sales. Median return on equity was 11% in profit-sharing firms compared to 91% in non-profit-sharing firms.[6]
Fortune 500 largest retailers and 1 other company; 10 of these had profit-sharing	Profit-sharing		Average net income to net worth in profit-sharing companies rose from 10.41% in 1952 to 12.78% in 1969. This compared to rise from 7.78% to 8.0% in non-profit-sharing companies. Company earnings per employee were 50.3% higher in profit-sharing companies in 1958, 80.1% higher in 1969, than in non-profit-sharing companies.[7]

EMPLOYEE OWNERSHIP:

Project	Type of Change	No. of Employees	Productivity Results
Plywood cooperatives, Northwestern U.S.	100% employee-owned		In 1950s, study found that firms averaged 20–30% higher productivity than their competitors. In 1960s, firms averaged 30% higher productivity than their competitors.[8] Internal Revenue Service case in 1960s found firms 25–60%

Project	Type of Change	No. of Employees	Productivity Results
Plywood cooperatives (cont'd)			more productive than competitors.[9]
98 worker-owned companies	100% employee-owned		All managers interviewed said that worker ownership had a positive impact on profits and productivity.[10]
30 worker-owned companies	100% employee-owned		Found these firms averaged 1.5 times as much profit as non-worker-owned firms.[11]
75 ESOP companies	Employee Stock Ownership Plans (average 20% employee-owned)		In average 3-year period after introduction of plan, 25% increase in sales per employee, 37% increase in number of employees, 157% increase in profits.[12]
Chicago & Northwestern Railroad, Chicago, Illinois	75% employee-owned	14,800	After buy-out in 1972, had positive profits 5 out of 6 years, compared to 5 years of losses before buy-out.
E Systems, electronics and aerospace equipment, Arlington, Virginia	25% employee-owned	9,000	Conversion 1972. First four years, labor turnover fell 50%, employee suggestions were up 140%.
Saratoga Knitting Mill, Saratoga, New York	70% employee-owned	140	Takeover 1975. In first two years, value of common stock rose 200%.
South Bend Lathe, South Bend, Indiana	100% employee-owned	450	Productivity rose 25% in first year. Sales averaged 25% higher during first three years following buy-out.

Sources: Except where noted, all cases from Karl Frieden, *Workplace Democracy and Productivity* (Washington, D.C.: National Center for Economic Alternatives, 1980).

1. Frederick Lesieur, ed., *The Scanlon Plan: A Frontier of Labor-Management Cooperation* (Cambridge: MIT Press, 1958), chap. 10.

2. National Center for Productivity and the Quality of Work Life, *A Plant-Wide Productivity Plan in Action. Three Years Experience with the Scanlon Plan* (Washington, D.C., May 1975), pp. 37–43.

3. Suresh Srivastva et al., *Job Satisfaction and Productivity* (Cleveland: Case Western Reserve University Press, 1975), p. xvii.

4. Raymond Katzell et al., *A Guide to Worker Productivity Experiments in the United States* (New York: New York University Press, 1977), pp. 39–40.

5. Frederick Lane, *Ships for Victory* (Baltimore: Johns Hopkins University Press, 1951), p. 455.

6. Bert Metzger and Jerome A. Colletti, *Does Profit Sharing Pay?* (Evanston, Ill.: Profit Sharing Research Foundation, 1971), pp. 7, 72.

7. Bert Metzger, *Profit Sharing in 38 Large Companies* (Evanston, Ill.: Profit Sharing Research Foundation, 1975), p. 4.

8. Katrina V. Berman, *Worker-Owned Plywood Companies: An Economic Analysis* (Pullman: Washington State University Press, 1964), p. 189.

9. Paul Bernstein, "Worker-Owned Plywood Companies," *Working Papers for a New Society* (Summer 1974), p. 28.

10. Institute for Social Research, *Employee Ownership, Report to the Economic Development Administration* (Washington, D.C.: U.S. Department of Commerce, 1977), p. 36.

11. Michael Conte and Arnold S. Tannenbaum, "Employee-Owned Companies: Is the Difference Measurable?" *Monthly Labor Review,* July 1978, p. 25.

12. From 1979 U.S. Senate Finance Committee Report. Cited in Frieden, *op. cit.,* p. 10.

Examples of Employee Ownership
In the United States

The purpose of this list is to illustrate the wide range of firms which have broad employee ownership. It is not comprehensive.

Firm	Product	Location (Headquarters)
FIRMS WITH MORE THAN 1% AND LESS THAN 50% OF COMMON STOCK OWNED BY EMPLOYEES:		
American Telephone & Telegraph	Communications	Basking Ridge, New Jersey
Chrysler Corp.	Automobiles	Detroit, Michigan
Dana Corp.	Transportation	Toledo, Ohio
E Systems	Electronics and aerospace equipment	Arlington, Virginia
Eastern Airlines	Air travel	Miami, Florida
Eastman Kodak Corp.	Photographic equipment and processing	Rochester, New York
General Motors Corp.	Automobiles	Detroit, Michigan
Mohawk Valley Community Corp.	Library furniture	Herkimer, New York
J. C. Penney Co.	Retail sales	New York, N.Y.
Procter & Gamble	Non-durable consumer goods	Cincinnati, Ohio

Firm	Product	Location (Headquarters)
Sears, Roebuck & Co.	Retail sales	Chicago, Illinois
Valley Health Plan	Health insurance and care	Amherst, Massachusetts

FIRMS WITH MORE THAN 50% EMPLOYEE OWNERSHIP:

Firm	Product	Location (Headquarters)
American Cast Iron Pipe Co.	Valves, tubes, and pipes	Birmingham, Alabama
Associated Freight Lines	Trucking	Oakland, California
Bates Fabric	Textiles	Lewiston, Maine
Chicago & Northwestern Transportation Co.	Railroad	Chicago, Illinois
Consumers United Group	Insurance	Washington, D.C.
Denver Yellow Cab	Transportation	Denver, Colorado
Fairbanks *Daily News-Miner*	Newspaper	Fairbanks, Alaska
Fastener Industries	Industrial fasteners for metal fabrication	Berea, Ohio
Fort Vancouver Plywood	Plywood	Vancouver, Washington
Good Things Collective	Clothing	Northampton, Mass.
Hyatt Roller Bearing	Auto bearings	Clark, New Jersey
Jamestown Metal Products	Metal cabinets	Jamestown, New York
Jones & Presnell Studios	Photographs	Charlotte, North Carolina
Law Collective	Lawyers	Boston, Massachusetts
Linnton Plywood Association	Plywood	Portland, Oregon
Milwaukee *Journal*	Newspaper	Milwaukee, Wisconsin
Moose Creek	Construction	Burlington, Vermont
Mulach Steel	Steel fabrication	Bridgeville, Pennsylvania
Oakland Scavenger Co.	Refuse collection	Oakland, California
Okonite Co.	Wire and cable	Ramsey, New Jersey
Pacific Paperboard Products	Cardboard boxes	San Francisco, California

Firm	Product	Location (Headquarters)
Puget Sound Plywood	Plywood	Tacoma, Washington
Rath Packing	Processed meats	Waterloo, Iowa
Rich-Seapak	Processed seafood	Brunswick, Georgia
Saratoga Knitting Mill	Garments	Saratoga Springs, New York
Simmons Construction Company	Construction	Decatur, Illinois
South Bend Lathe	Machine tools	South Bend, Indiana
Sunset Scavenger	Refuse collection	San Francisco, California

Suggested Readings

Introduction to Workplace Problems

Balzer, Richard. *Clockwork: Life In and Outside an American Factory* (New York: Doubleday, 1976).

Braverman, Harry. *Labor and Monopoly Capital* (New York: Monthly Review Press, 1974).

Carnoy, Martin, and Derek Shearer. *Economic Democracy: The Challenge of the 1980's* (White Plains, New York: M. E. Sharpe, 1980).

Cole, Robert E. *Work, Mobility and Participation* (Berkeley: University of California Press, 1979).

Edwards, Richard C. *Contested Terrain: The Transformation of the Workplace* (New York: Basic Books, 1979).

Frieden, Carl. *Workplace Democracy and Productivity* (Washington, D.C.: National Center for Economic Alternatives, 1980).

Maccoby, Michael. *The Gamesman* (New York: Simon & Schuster, 1976).

Schrank, Robert. *Ten Thousand Working Days* (Cambridge: M.I.T. Press, 1978).

Terkel, Studs. *Working* (New York: Pantheon Books, 1974).

United States Department of Health, Education and Welfare. *Work in America* (Cambridge: M.I.T. Press, 1973).

Participation in Ownership

Bernstein, Paul. *Workplace Democratization: Its Internal Dynamics* (New Brunswick, N.J.: Transaction Books, 1980).

Brandow, Karen, James McDonald, and Vocations for Social Change. *No Bosses Here! A Manual on Working Collectively and Cooperatively* (Boston: Alyson Publications, 1981).

Kelso, Louis, and Patricia Hetter. *How to Turn Eighty Million Workers into Capitalists on Borrowed Money* (New York: Random House, 1967).

Oakeshott, Robert. *The Case for Workers' Co-ops* (London: Routledge & Kegan Paul, 1978).

Perry, Stewart. *San Francisco Scavengers* (Berkeley: U. of California Press, 1978).

Rifkin, Jeremy. *Own Your Own Job* (New York: Bantam Books, 1977).

Rosen, Corey. *Employee Ownership: Issues, Resources, and Legislation* (Arlington, Virginia: National Center for Employee Ownership, 1981).

Thomas, Henk, and Chris Logan. *Mondragón: An Economic Analysis* (London: George Allen & Unwin, 1982).

Participation in Management

Anthony, William P. *Participatory Management* (Reading, Mass.: Addison-Wesley, 1978).

Cole, Robert. *Work, Mobility and Participation* (Berkeley: U. of California Press, 1979).

Davis, Louis E., and Albert B. Cherns, eds. *The Quality of Working Life* (2 vols., New York: Free Press, 1975).

Emery, Fred, and Einar Thorsrud. *Democracy at Work: The Report of the Norwegian Industrial Democracy Program* (Leiden: Martinius Nijhoff, 1976).

Hackman, J. Richard, and Lloyd J. Suttle. *Improving Life at Work: Behavioral Science Approaches to Organizational Change* (Santa Monica, California: Goodyear Publishing Company, 1977).

Hersey, Paul, and Kenneth H. Blanchard. *Management of Organizational Behavior: Utilizing Human Resources* (3rd ed., Englewood Cliffs, N.J.: Prentice-Hall, 1977).

Maccoby, Michael. *The Leader* (New York: Simon & Schuster, 1981).

O'Toole, James. *Making America Work* (New York: Continuum Publishing Co., 1981).

Ouchi, William. *Theory Z: How American Business Can Meet the Japanese Challenge* (Reading, Mass.: Addison-Wesley, 1981).

Pascale, Richard T., and Anthony Athos. *The Art of Japanese Management* (New York: Simon & Schuster, 1981).

Sproul, R. C. *Stronger Than Steel: The Wayne T. Alderson Story* (New York: Harper and Row, 1980).

Witte, John. *Democracy, Authority and Alienation in Work* (Chicago: University of Chicago Press, 1980).

Regular Publication

Workplace Democracy. A quarterly magazine about organizational efforts to increase participation in management and ownership. Association for Workplace Democracy, 1747 Connecticut Avenue NW, Washington, D.C. 20009.

Notes

Chapter 1

1. New York Times/CBS News Poll, *New York Times,* December 9, 1981.

2. Edward Denison, "The Puzzling Setback to Productivity Growth," *Challenge,* November/December, 1980. Denison measured output by national income per person employed in constant (1972) prices for non-residential business, reflecting 75 percent of the economy.

3. Lester Thurow, *Newsweek,* August 24, 1981, p. 63. Employment increased 89 percent between 1950 and 1979. Seventy-two percent of the increase was among women. The change in occupations and sector is shown by the following data.

Table 4
Change in American Occupations
(Percent)

	1950	1979
White collar	38	51
Blue collar	39	33
Service	11	13
Farm	13	3

Table 5
Employment by Sector (Excluding Farms)
(Percent)

	1950	1979
Goods Producing	41	30
Mining	2	1
Construction	5	5
Manufacturing	34	23

Table 5 (continued)

	1950	*1979*
Service Producing	59	71
Transportation & public utilities	9	6
Trade (retail & wholesale)	21	23
Finance insurance	4	6
Real estate service	12	19
Government	13	17

Note: Occupations and sectors overlap substantially (i.e., service occupations include work in finance, insurance, and real estate, but not salespersons, who are considered white-collar employees).

Sources: *Manpower Report of the President* (Washington, D.C.: U.S. Government Printing Office, 1950 & 1960), pp. 143 and 225; and the *Employment and Training Report to the President* (Washington, D.C.: U.S. Government Printing Office, 1980), p. 6.

4. Profitability figures calculated by deflating corporate profits (with inventory valuation and capital consumption adjustments) by the Consumer Price Index for all commodities. This is the same index used to deflate gross weekly earnings. When profit is indexed at 1960 = 100, levels for 1970 = 114; 1978 = 169; and 1981 = 129. Source: *Economic Report of the President 1982*, pp. 327 and 294.

5. Houston *Chronicle,* September 29, 1980.

6. Daniel Yankelovich, speech to National Conference on Human Resource Systems, Dallas, Texas, October 1978.

7. Robert P. Quinn and Graham L. Staines, *The 1977 Quality Employment Survey* (Ann Arbor: Survey Research Center, University of Michigan), p. 210.

8. Ibid., p. 241.

9. Michael Maccoby and Katherine Terzi, "What Happened to the Work Ethic?," report submitted to the Joint Economic Committee, U.S. Congress, Washington, D.C., 1979.

10. Daniel Yankelovich, Sidney Harman, and Pehr Gyllenhammar, "Jobs in the 1980s" (Aspen, Colorado: Aspen Institute, 1981), p. 17.

11. George Strauss, "Workers: Attitudes and Adjustments," in Jerome Rosow, ed., *The Worker and the Job* (New York: Prentice-Hall, 1974), and Quinn and Staines, p. 202.

12. Robert Schrank, Seminar for Five College Project on Work and Democracy, Amherst, Massachusetts, May, 1981.

13. *New York Times,* August 20, 1980.

14. Interview, December 26, 1980.

15. Robert B. Reich, "The Profession of Management," *New Republic,* June 27, 1981, p. 27.

16. Thomas F. Fitzgerald, "Why Motivation Theory Doesn't Work," *Harvard Business Review*, July/August 1971, pp. 42–43.

17. U.S. Chamber of Commerce poll, 1979, and Jeremy Rifkin, *Own Your Own Job* (New York: Bantam Books, 1977), p. 52.

Chapter 2

1. Frederick Winslow Taylor, "Workmen and the Management" (Cambridge: Harvard University School of Business Administration, mimeographed, 1911).

2. Ibid.

3. Frank Copley, *Frederick Taylor*, Volume 1 (New York: Harper & Row, 1923), p. 52.

4. Daniel Nelson, *Managers and Workers* (Madison: University of Wisconsin Press, 1975), chap. 3.

5. Frederick Winslow Taylor, *Principles of Scientific Management* (New York: Harper & Row, 1947), pp. 41–47.

6. Ibid.

7. Ibid.

8. Ibid.

9. Nelson, *Managers and Workers*, p. 77.

10. Robert F. Hoxie, *Scientific Management and Labor* (New York: A. M. Kelly; reprint, 1966), pp. 137–138.

11. Ibid., pp. 131–132.

12. Ibid.

13. Taylor, *Scientific Management*, p. 7.

14. Ibid., p. 36.

15. William R. Spriegel and Clark E. Myers, eds., *The Writing of the Gilbreths* (Homewood, Ill.: R. D. Irwin, 1953), p. 10.

16. Studs Terkel, *Working: People Talk About What They Do All Day and How They Feel About What They Do* (New York: Avon Books, 1975), p. 260.

17. Charles Walker and Robert Guest, *Man on the Assembly Line* (Cambridge: Harvard University Press, 1925), p. 155.

18. Midge Whitcomb, Interview, September 1980.

19. Studs Terkel, *Working*, p. 524.

20. Peter Drucker, *The Practice of Management* (New York: Harper & Row, 1954), p. 280.

21. V. I. Lenin, *The Immediate Tasks of the Soviet Government* (Moscow: Collected Works, Progress Publishers, Vol. 27, 1965), p. 259.

22. William M. Batten, "Productivity and the Working Environment," address at The Wharton School, University of Pennsylvania, 1979.

Chapter 3

1. Daniel Rogers, *The Work Ethic in Industrial America, 1850–1920* (Chicago: University of Chicago Press, 1978), p. 61.

2. Glen Frank, *Century*, No. 101 (1921), p. 411.

3. Elton Mayo, *The Human Problems of an Industrial Civilization* (Cambridge: Harvard University School of Business Administration, 1933), p. 71.

4. Ibid., p. 72.

5. Ibid., p. 71.

6. In Richard Franke and James Kaul's statistical study of the "Bank Wiring Room" part of the Hawthorne experiments, they found that the human relations approach had little to do with the productivity increases. Rather, they look to changes in the quality of raw materials and authoritarian practices. However, as they readily admit, the statistical proof for their assertions is very weak. See "The Hawthorne Experiments: First Statistical Interpretation," *American Sociological Review*, vol. 43, October, 1978.

7. Drucker, *Practice of Management*, p. 305.

8. Interview, April 1981.

9. Samuel Gompers, *Labor and the Employer* (New York: E. P. Dutton, 1920), p. 286.

10. Robert E. Cole, *Work, Mobility & Participation* (Berkeley: University of California Press, 1979), pp. 104–105.

11. Ibid., p. 104.

12. Milton Derber, *The Idea of Industrial Democracy, 1865–1965* (Urbana: University of Illinois Press, 1970), p. 528.

13. Charles Heckscher, *Democracy at Work: In Whose Interests?* (Cambridge: Ph.D. diss., Harvard University, 1981), chap. 3.

14. Louis A. Wood, *Union Management Cooperation on the Railroads* (New Haven: Yale University Press, 1934), p. 118.

15. Sumner Slichter, *Union Policies and Industrial Management* (Washington, D.C.: Brookings Institution, 1941), p. 443.

16. Ibid., p. 503.

17. "Labor Management Production Committee Studies," United States War Production Board, pamphlet no. 3, 1943, p. 4.

18. Stuart Chase, *Men at Work* (New York: Harcourt & Brace, 1944), p. 37.

19. Ibid., p. 39.

20. Derber, *Industrial Democracy*, pp. 469–470.

21. Bureau of Labor Statistics, United States Department of Labor, bulletin no. 1425–5, "Management Rights and Union-Management Cooperation" (Washington, D.C.: U.S. Government Printing Office, 1966), pp. 12–13.

22. Douglas McGregor, *The Human Side of Enterprise* (New York: McGraw-Hill, 1960), p. 113.

23. Ibid., pp. 33–34.

24. Ibid., pp. 47–48.

25. Frederick Herzberg, *Work and the Nature of Man* (New York: Mentor Books, 1973), p. 59.

26. David Jenkins, *Job Power* (London: Penguin Books, 1973), p. 258.

27. Fred Emery and Einar Thorsrud, *Democracy at Work: The Report of the Norwegian Industrial Democracy Program* (Leiden: Martinius Nijhoff, 1976), p. 159.

28. Harold J. Leavitt, *Managerial Psychology* (Chicago: University of Chicago Press, 1978), p. 326.

29. Interview, Howard Carlson, June, 1981.

30. Jenkins, *Job Power*, p. 199.

31. *Automotive News*, October 4, 1971.

32. *Time*, November 8, 1970.

33. Jenkins, *Job Power*, p. 204.

34. *Work in America* (Cambridge: MIT Press, 1973), p. 13.

35. Emma Rothschild, *Paradise Lost—The Decline of the Auto-Industrial Age* (New York: Vintage Books, 1974), p. 119.

Chapter 4

1. Interview, April 1981.

2. J. Patrick Wright, *On a Clear Day You Can See General Motors: John Z. DeLorean's Look Inside the Automotive Giant* (New York: Avon Books, 1979), p. 126.

3. Ibid., p. 128.

4. Ibid., pp. 128–130.

5. Ibid., p. 121.

6. Ibid., p. 125.

7. Ibid., p. 124.

8. Ibid., p. 137.

9. Alfred P. Sloan, Jr., *My Years with General Motors* (Garden City, N.Y.: Doubleday, 1972), p. 502.

10. Ibid., p. 59.

11. Ibid., p. 512.

12. Ibid., p. 507.

13. Interview, April, 1981.

14. Wright, *On a Clear Day*, p. 226.

15. Ibid., p. 46.

16. Ibid., p. 47.

17. Ibid., p. 228.

18. Interview, November, 1980.
19. Interview, April, 1981.
20. Interview, April, 1981.
21. Interview, November, 1980.
22. Interview, November, 1980.
23. Robert H. Guest, "Quality of Worklife—Learning from Tarrytown," *Harvard Business Review*, July/August, 1979, p. 78.
24. Ibid., p. 77.
25. Ibid., p. 79.
26. Ibid., p. 85.
27. Speech, Five College Project on Work and Democracy, Hampshire College, Amherst, Massachusetts, October 12, 1981.
28. Interview, November, 1980.
29. Interview, November, 1980.
30. Interview, November, 1980.
31. Interview, November, 1980.
32. Interview, November, 1980.
33. Interview, November, 1980.
34. "GM's Quality of Worklife Efforts," an interview with Howard Carlson, *Personnel*, July/August, 1978.
35. Interview, November, 1980.
36. Interview, November, 1980.
37. Interview, November, 1980.
38. Interview, November, 1980.
39. Interview, November, 1980.
40. *New York Times.*, July 1, 1981.
41. Interview, November, 1980.

Chapter 5

1. Interview, May, 1980.
2. Interview, May, 1980.
3. "Commitment at Work," Five-Year Report of JALMC, 1977, p. 5.
4. Interview with Christopher Meek, May, 1980.
5. Interview with Christopher Meek, May, 1980.
6. Interview with William Foote Whyte, April, 1980.
7. Five-Year Report of JALMC, pp. 10–11.
8. William F. Whyte and Christopher Meek, "The Jamestown Model of Cooperative Problem Solving," mimeographed, 1980.
9. Ibid.
10. Robert Franco, talk at Jamestown, May, 1980.
11. JALMC movie on Corry-Jamestown.
12. Talk at Jamestown, May, 1980.

13. Ibid.
14. Ibid.
15. Interview, May, 1980.
16. Interview, May, 1980
17. Interview with Christopher Meek, May, 1980.

Chapter 6

1. Taylor, *Scientific Management*, p. 140.
2. *International Herald Tribune*, September 25, 1980.
3. William Ouchi, *Theory Z: How American Business Can Meet the Japanese Challenge* (Reading, Massachusetts: Addison-Wesley Press, 1981); Richard T. Pascale and Anthony G. Athos, *The Art of Japanese Management* (New York: Simon & Schuster, 1981).
4. *New York Times*, March 21, 1982.
5. Ibid.
6. Ezra Vogel, *Japan As Number One* (Cambridge: Harvard University Press, 1980), p. 27.
7. W. Edwards Deming, "The Statistical Control of Quality," *Quality*, February, 1980.
8. W. Edwards Deming, "What Happened in Japan?" *Industrial Quality Control*, vol. 24, no. 2 (August, 1967), p. 91.
9. Cole, *Work, Mobility*, p. 136.
10. Houston *Chronicle*, April 24, 1980.
11. Cole, *Work, Mobility*, p. 136.
12. Interview, October, 1980.
13. Deming, "Statistical Control."
14. Interview, December, 1980.
15. Ibid.
16. *Business Week*, March 2, 1981, p. 56.
17. Interview, May, 1981.
18. Interview, July, 1980.
19. Ibid.
20. Kawasaki Corporate Philosophy, n.d.
21. Interview, July, 1980.
22. Interview, October, 1980.
23. Interview, October, 1980.
24. Interview, May, 1981.
25. Robert E. Cole, "Made in Japan: A Spur to U.S. Productivity," *ASIA*, May/June, 1979, p. 22.
26. Ibid.
27. Interview, March, 1982.
28. Interview, April, 1981.

29. Cole, *Work, Mobility*, p. 121.

30. Richard J. Samuels, "Looking Behind Japan Inc.," *Technology Review*, MIT, July, 1981, p. 45.

31. Interview, July, 1981.

32. Ibid.

33. Interview with Richard Danjin, January, 1981.

Chapter 7

1. Interview, April, 1980.

2. Sam Hemingway, "Old GAF Mine Officially Gets New Lease on Life," Burlington *Free Press*, March 15, 1975, p. 17.

3. Interview, April, 1980.

4. "A Lack of Common Goals," Draft Master's Thesis of Janette Johannesen, New System of Work and Participation Program at Cornell University School of Industrial and Labor Relations, p. 29.

5. Burlington *Free Press*, August 3, 1977, p. D7.

6. Interview, October, 1981.

7. Burlington *Free Press*, September 27, 1977, p. 1.

8. Interview, April, 1980.

9. Burlington *Free Press*, October 6, 1977.

10. Interview, April, 1980.

11. Janette Johannesen, "Vermont Asbestos: Pragmatic Worker Ownership," Burlington *Free Press*, April 15, 1979, p. 11A.

12. Interviews, April, 1980, and October, 1981.

13. Stacy Jolna, "Horatio Alger in the Pits: Workers Buy, Run, Sell Mine," Washington *Post*, April 15, 1978, p. A3.

"We're talking about unsophisticated people who didn't know what being a stockholder means. Not more than a dozen of them ever owned a share of stock in their lives"—Stanley Parsons, company controller and, with 100 shares, the largest shareholder in the company.

14. Johannesen, "Vermont Asbestos."

15. Interview, June, 1981.

16. Louis O. Kelso and Patricia Hetter, *How to Turn Eighty Million Workers into Capitalists on Borrowed Money* (New York: Random House, 1967).

17. "Assessing ESOP's" (New York: Research Institute of America, 1979), p. 4.

18. Interview with Corey Rosen of the National Center for Employee Ownership, December, 1981.

19. William Greider, "Russell Long's 'Share the Wealth' Program," Washington *Post*, August 25, 1975, p. A1.

20. "Viewpoint," with Ronald Reagan, radio program, February, 1975.

21. "Lowe's Largesse," *Newsweek,* March 31, 1975, p. 61.

22. "Employee Ownership Report to Economic Development Administration of Department of Commerce. Project #99-6-09433" (Ann Arbor: Survey Research Center, Institute for Social Research, University of Michigan, 1978), p. 41.

23. Ibid., p. 43.

24. Ibid., p. 46.

25. Ibid., p. 60.

26. "Assessing ESOP's," p. 27.

27. Interview, October, 1980.

28. Warren Brown, "Workers at Employee-Owned Firm Find the Going Rough," Washington *Post,* September 30, 1980, p. A4.

29. Interview, October, 1980.

30. Ibid.

31. Interview, November, 1980.

32. South Bend *Tribune,* October 17, 1980.

33. Interview, November, 1980.

34. Interview, November, 1980.

35. William F. Whyte, "In Support of the Voluntary Employee Ownership and Community Stabilization Act," draft, School of Industrial and Labor Relations, Cornell University, March 20, 1980.

36. Interview, November, 1980.

37. Ibid.

Chapter 8

1. Speech to the Five College Project on Work and Democracy, Hampshire College, Amherst, Massachusetts, December, 1979. See Robert Oakeshott, *The Case for Workers' Co-ops* (London: Routledge & Kegan Paul, 1978), for an overview of producer cooperatives. See Henk Logan and Chris Thomas, *Mondragón: An Economic Analysis* (London: George Allen & Unwin, 1982), for an analysis of Mondragón's performance.

2. Oakeshott, *Workers' Co-ops,* p. 175.

3. Ibid., p. 198.

4. Interview with Antonio Perez de Calleja, director of the Management Division, November, 1979.

5. Ibid.

6. Interview, April, 1980.

7. Oakeshott, *Workers' Co-ops,* p. 188.

8. Ibid., p. 187.

9. Albert Fried, *Socialism in America, from the Shakers to the Third International* (Garden City: Doubleday, 1970), p. 66.

10. Daniel T. Rogers, *Work Ethic in Industrial America, 1850–1920* (Chicago: University of Chicago Press, 1974), p. 43.

11. Terence Powderly, *Thirty Years of Labor* (New York: Augustus M. Kelley, 1899, reprinted 1967), p. 235.

12. Interview, August, 1981.

13. David Ellerman, "What Is a Worker's Cooperative?" (Sommerville, Massachusetts: Industrial Cooperation Association, 1979), p. 3.

14. Interview, May, 1980.

15. Interview, May, 1981.

16. Interview, May, 1981.

17. Interview, May, 1981.

18. Interview, May, 1981.

19. Estimate by Corey Rosen, National Center for Employee Ownership, Alexandria, Virginia, 1981.

20. Interview with Corey Rosen, "Employee Ownership," vol. 1, no. 1, (June, 1981), p. 1. Published by Center for Employee Ownership, Arlington, Virginia.

21. Interview, August, 1981.

22. Interview, August, 1981.

23. Interview, August, 1981.

24. Interview, August, 1981.

25. Interview, August, 1981.

Chapter 9

1. Wright, *On a Clear Day*, p. 43.

2. Abraham Zaleznik, "Power and Politics in Organizational Life," *Harvard Business Review,* May/June, 1970, p. 47.

3. Harold M. F. Rush, "A Non-Partisan View of Participative Management," *Conference Board Record,* vol. 10, no. 4 (April, 1973).

4. John Witte, *Democracy, Authority and Alienation in Work* (Chicago: University of Chicago Press, 1980), p. 2.

5. David McClelland and David Burnham, "Power Is the Great Motivator," *Harvard Business Review,* March/April, 1976, p. 104.

6. Detroit *News,* May 14, 1980.

7. Jim Fuller, "Workers Gaining Voice in Job Policy," Minneapolis *Tribune,* July 8, 1979, p. 1D.

8. Ron Blum, "Dana: A Tough Management Approach," *Financial Times* of Canada, March 3, 1980.

9. James F. Lincoln, *A New Approach to Industrial Economics* (New York: Devon-Adair, 1961), p. 22.

Chapter 10

1. Interview, April, 1981.
2. Dick Youngblood, "Valspar Employees Are Painting a Brighter Picture," Minneapolis *Tribune,* June 13, 1976, p. 11c.
3. Interview, September, 1980.
4. Interview, June, 1981.
5. Interview, September, 1980.
6. Speech, Kennedy School of Government, Harvard University, April 14, 1981.
7. Interview, June, 1981.
8. Daniel Zwerdling, *Democracy at Work* (Washington, D.C.: Association for Workplace Democracy, 1978), p. 42.
9. Ibid., p. 43.
10. Ibid., p. 44.
11. Ibid., p. 44.
12. Interview, May, 1981.
13. Interview, April, 1981.
14. Interview, February, 1981.
15. Interview, May, 1981.
16. Leonard Schlesinger, speech at Ecology of Work Conference, St. Louis, June, 1980.
17. Interview, May, 1981.
18. "Participatory Management at the Bank" (Washington, D.C.: Participation Advisory Committee, World Bank, July, 1979); and John Simmons, "Participatory Management at the World Bank," *Training and Development Journal,* March, 1980.
19. Interview, May, 1981.
20. Interview, June, 1981.
21. Interview, May, 1981.

Chapter 11

1. Interview, April, 1981.
2. Ibid.
3. Paul Bernstein, *Workplace Democratization: Its Internal Dynamics* (New Brunswick, N. J.: Transaction Books, 1980), p. 47.
4. "Employment and Earnings" (Washington, D.C.: Bureau of Labor Statistics, January, 1981). Survey estimated that 1.2 million people worked at jobs such as polishers, cutters, bottlers, etc. which could generally be defined as assembly line work.
5. Interview, October, 1980.
6. Interview, October, 1980.

7. Interview, October, 1980.

8. Interview, October, 1980.

9. Interview, October, 1980.

10. Interview, October, 1980.

11. Jenkins, *Job Power,* p. 226.

12. Ibid.

13. Zwerdling, *Democracy at Work,* p. 21.

14. Jenkins, *Job Power,* p. 227.

15. Richard Walton, "Work Innovation at Topeka; After Six Years," Harvard School of Business, mimeographed, December 12, 1976.

16. Ibid.

17. Zwerdling, *Democracy at Work,* p. 27.

18. Ibid., pp. 27–28.

19. Ibid., p. 28.

20. Interview, September, 1981.

21. "Participative Management at Work," an interview with John F. Donnelly, *Harvard Business Review,* January/February, 1977, p. 120.

22. Ibid., p. 126.

23. Interview with Robert Benningfield, compensation manager, Donnelly Mirrors, October, 1981.

24. "Participative Management," p. 119.

25. Ibid., p. 122.

26. Ibid., p. 127.

27. Zwerdling, *Democracy at Work,* pp. 94–95.

28. Ibid., p. 95.

29. "When Employees Run the Company," interview by the editors, *Harvard Business Review,* January/February, 1979, p. 79.

30. Edward Greenberg, "Producer Cooperatives and Democratic Theory" (Palo Alto, California: Center for Economics, 1978).

Chapter 12

1. *Bell Telephone* Magazine, Edition 4, 1980, pp. 20–21.

2. Interview, July, 1980.

3. McClelland and Burnham, "Power Is the Great Motivator," p. 101.

4. See Robert L. Tannenbaum and Warren H. Schmidt, "How to Choose a Leadership Pattern," *Harvard Business Review,* March/April, 1958, pp. 95–101, for a summary of the evidence.

5. Interview, November, 1980.

6. Ibid.

7. Interview, May, 1981.

8. "The H-P Way," mimeographed, Hewlett-Packard, p. 2.

9. Interview, May, 1981.

10. Ibid.

11. "When Employees Run the Company," p. 76.

12. Ibid., p. 79.

13. Interview, June, 1981.

14. Ibid.

15. "Steel Jacks Up Its Productivity," *Business Week*, October 12, 1981, p. 86.

16. Pehr Gyllenhammar, *People at Work* (Reading, Mass.: Addison-Wesley Press, 1977), pp. 161–162.

17. Michael Maccoby, *The Leader* (New York: Simon & Schuster, 1981), p. 223.

18. Interview, April, 1981.

19. Interview, April, 1981.

20. Interview, May, 1981.

21. Interview, November, 1980.

22. Interview, November, 1980.

23. Robert Townshend, *Up the Organization* (New York: Alfred A. Knopf, 1970), p. 80.

24. Maccoby, *The Leader*, p. 223.

25. Thomas J. Peter, "A Style for All Seasons," *Executive*, Cornell University Graduate School of Business Administration, Summer, 1980, pp. 12–17.

26. Interview, July, 1981.

Chapter 13

1. Interview, May, 1981.

2. Michael R. Cooper, Peter A. Gelford, and Patricia M. Foley, "Early Warning Signals: Growing Discontent Among Managers," *Business* Magazine, College of Business Administration, Georgia State University, Atlanta, January/February, 1980.

3. Ibid.

4. Ibid.

5. Interview, October, 1980.

6. W. Earl Sasser, Jr. and Frank S. Leonard, "Let First-Level Supervisors Do Their Job," *Harvard Business Review*, March/April, 1980, p. 116.

7. William F. Whyte and Burleigh Gardner, "Facing the Foreman's Problems," *Applied Anthropology*, Spring, 1945, p. 19.

8. Interview, May, 1981.

9. Interview, November, 1980.

10. Einar Thorsrud, "Democracy at Work," mimeographed (Oslo: Work Research Institutes, 1980).

11. Ibid.

12. Interview, September, 1980.

13. Interview, November, 1980.

14. Pehr G. Gyllenhammar, "How Volvo Adapts Work to People," *Harvard Business Review*, July/August, 1977, p. 112.

15. Ibid.

16. Ann Howard and Douglas Bray, mimeographed (Morristown, N.J.: American Telephone & Telegraph, 1980), p. 7.

17. Ibid.

18. Letter from C. L. Brown to presidents and American Telephone & Telegraph officers, March 18, 1980.

19. Robert N. Ford, "Job Enrichment Lessons from AT&T," *Harvard Business Review*, January/February, 1973, pp. 96–106.

20. *New England Topics*, New England Bell Telephone Company, Boston, January 23, 1981, p. 2.

21. Interview, Richard Christie, assistant vice-president for human relations, Michigan Bell Telephone Company, April, 1981.

22. Interview, April, 1981.

23. Interview, April, 1981.

24. Interview, November, 1980.

25. Interview, September, 1981.

26. Luke 15: 29–30. King James Version.

Chapter 14

1. Thomas Donahue, AFL-CIO, speech to American Arbitration Association, quoted in "Productivity Through Equal Partnership," *World of Work Report*, vol. 16, no. 4 (April, 1981), p. 25.

2. Robert Greenberger, "Quality Circles Grow, Stirring Union Worries," *Wall Street Journal*, September 22, 1981, p. 22.

3. Robert Schrank, "Are Unions an Anachronism?," *Harvard Business Review*, September/October, 1979, pp. 107–115.

4. Harry and Joanne Bernstein, "Industrial Democracy in Twelve Nations," *Bureau of International Labor Affairs Bulletin*, U.S. Department of Labor, Monograph no. 2, January 2, 1979.

5. Zwerdling, *Democracy at Work*, p. 165.

6. "Japan's U.S. Plants Go Union," *Business Week*, October 5, 1981, p. 75.

7. Ibid., p. 76.

8. Edward Cohen-Rosenthal, "Should Unions Participate in Quality of Working Life Activities?," *Quality of Working Life: The Canadian Scene*, vol. 3, no. 4 (1980), p. 10.

9. Interview, January, 1981.

10. Dan Collins, Speech at Ecology of Work Conference, St. Louis, Missouri, June, 1980.

11. Ibid.

12. Ibid.

13. Interview with Clyde Anderson, June, 1980.

14. Collins speech.

15. Fritz K. Plous, "Labor-Management Action Saves Jobs—and the Railroad," *World of Work Report,* vol. 6, no. 5 (May 1981), p. 33.

16. *United Steelworkers* v. *Warrior & Gulf Navigation Company,* 363 U.S. 574 (1960).

17. Robert Ahern, "The Collective Bargaining Process and Organizational Development," unpublished paper, Buffalo-Erie County Labor-Management Council, Buffalo, New York, February, 1980.

18. Ibid.

19. Ibid.

20. John Carmichael, "Worker Participation: A Newspaper Experience," an address presented at Kennedy School of Government, Harvard University, October 1979. Mimeographed.

21. Agreement between Newspaper Guild of Twin Cities and Minneapolis Star and Tribune Co. (August 1, 1980, through July 31, 1983).

22. John Carmichael, "Worker Participation."

23. Ibid.

24. James Boyd, "The Electronic Newspaper," *Nieman Reports,* Winter, 1980, p. 9.

25. Interview, November, 1980.

26. Michael Maccoby, Richard Balzer, Charles Heckscher, and Cheryl Pierce, "Participation: Summary Report to the Communications Workers of America," mimeographed, Washington, D.C., 1980.

27. Contract between Communications Workers of America and American Telephone & Telegraph, 1980, p. 53.

28. Glenn Watts, speech at Kennedy School of Government, Harvard University, May, 1981.

29. Basic Agreement between the United Steelworkers of America and the U.S. Steel Corporation, August 1, 1980, sec. 3.1, p. 17.

30. Interview, January, 1981.

31. Steel Industry "Basic Agreement," Appendix I, "Memorandum of Understanding on Labor-Management Participation Teams," sec. 4, p. 210.

32. Charles Heckscher, letter to the authors, August, 1981.

33. A. H. Raskin, "The Labor Leader as Company Director," *New York Times,* April 27, 1980.

34. Ibid., p. F15.

35. Robert L. Simison, "Chrysler Lauds Strong Performance of UAW's Fraser as Board Member," *Wall Street Journal,* March 3, 1981.

36. Ibid.

37. Interview, July, 1981.

38. John Hoerr, "Auto Workers Inch Toward Driver's Seat," *Business Week*, February 9, 1981, p. 30.

39. Interview, July, 1981.

40. Alfred L. Thimm, "How Far Should German Co-Determination Go?" *Challenge*, July/August, 1981, p. 22.

41. James W. Smith, "The Labor Movement and Worker Ownership," speech at Yale School of Organization and Management, February 25, 1981.

42. Interview, May, 1980.

43. William F. Whyte, "Restructuring Work at Rath Packing," *Employee Ownership*, vol. 1, no. 2 (September, 1981), p. 5.

44. Christopher Gunn, "The Fruits of Rath: A New Model of Self-Management," *Working Papers*, March/April, 1981, p. 17.

45. Interview, March, 1981.

46. David Ellerman, "The Union as the Legitimate Opposition in an Industrial Democracy," mimeographed (Somerville, Mass.: Industrial Cooperative Association, 1979), p. 23.

47. Interview, June, 1980.

48. Ibid.

49. The former owner's note has now been assumed by a bank.

50. Interview, June, 1980.

51. Interview, April, 1981.

52. Robert Zager, "A Working Model," *New York Times*, September 7, 1981.

53. Thomas Donahue, speech to American Arbitration Association, *World of Work*, p. 28. See also his speech "Labor Looks at QWL Programs, January 7, 1982, Labor Relations and Research Center, University of Massachusetts, Amherst.

Chapter 15

1. Charles G. Burck, "Working Smarter," *Fortune*, June 15, 1981; *New York Times*, April 22, 1982; *National Catholic Reporter*, September 25, 1981.

2. Peter Behr, "Easy Profits Deflect Business from Long-Range Goals," Houston *Chronicle*, February 8, 1982.

3. "Employee Ownership and Self-Management in Legislation and Social Policy." Paper presented to the American Sociological Association Conference, August 24, 1981, Toronto, Canada.

4. Interview, July, 1981.

5. George C. Lodge, *The New American Ideology* (New York: Alfred A. Knopf, 1978), p. 176.

6. Thomas R. Marsh and Dale E. McAllister, "ESOP's Tables: A Survey of Companies with Employee Stock Ownership Plans," *Journal of Corpo-*

ration Law, Spring, 1981, pp. 619–620; and Select Committee on Small Business, "The Role of the Federal Government and Employee Ownership of Business" (Washington, D.C.: U.S. Government Printing Office, 1979).

7. A. Bartlett Giamatti, *The University and the Public Interest* (New York: Atheneum, 1981), p. 169.

8. Joyce Rothschild-Whitt, "The Collectivist Organization: An Alternative to Rational-Bureaucratic Models," *American Sociological Review,* vol. 44 (August, 1979), pp. 519, 524.

9. For additional perspective on failure, see P. H. Mervis and D. N. Berg, eds., *Failure in Organizational Development and Change* (New York: John Wiley, 1977).

10. Joseph Blasi and William Foote Whyte, "From Research to Legislation on Employee Ownership."

11. Boston *Globe,* October 1, 1981.

12. Conference on QWL and the 80's, Toronto, Canada, August 31, 1981.

13. Blasi and Whyte, interviews, June, 1981, and November, 1980.

14. *Wall Street Journal,* March 3, 1981.

15. Letter from Bryan to Borman, April 21, 1981.

16. Letter from Borman to Bryan, May 5, 1981.

17. Bjorn Gustavsen and Gerry Hunnius, *Industrial Democracy in Norway* (Oslo: Work Research Institute, 1980), pp. 120–124.

18. Interview, September, 1980.

19. Henry Levin, "Education and Organizational Democracy," in Frank A. Heller and Colin Crouch, eds., *International Yearbook of Organizational Democracy* (New York: John Wiley, 1982).

20. Jules Henry, *Culture Against Man* (New York: Vintage Books, 1975); Rossabeth Moss Kanter, "The Organization Child: Experience Management in a Nursery School," *Sociology of Education,* vol. 45; and Samuel Bowles and Herbert Gintis, *Schooling in Capitalist America* (New York: Basic Books, 1975).

21. Asa Knowles, ed., *Encyclopedia for Higher Education,* p. 3163.

22. John Simmons et al., *Lessons from Educational Reform* (New York: Praeger, 1983).

23. Interview with Professors E. Lauck Parke and Michael Gurdon, University of Vermont, March, 1982.

24. Interview with Randy Barber, April, 1982. See also Jeremy Rifkin and Randy Barber, *The North Shall Rise Again: Pensions, Power and Politics* (Boston: Beacon Press, 1978), p. 234.

25. Ibid., p. 149.

26. Michael Maccoby, *The Leader* (New York: Simon & Schuster, 1981), p. 234.

Index

A NOTE ABOUT THE AUTHORS

John Simmons is a professor of Labor/Management Relations at the University of Massachusetts at Amherst. He is president of Participation Associates, a firm that assists organizations interested in improving organizational effectiveness, and he also serves as national coordinator of the Association for Workplace Democracy, a coalition of individuals from both labor and management who seek to foster participatory management and ownership. In addition, he publishes the Association's journal, *Workplace Democracy*. A graduate of both Harvard and Oxford, Mr. Simmons, who was raised in Illinois, helped found a participatory management program while working at the World Bank. He is the author of more than forty articles and books on management and economic development.

William Mares was raised in Texas and educated at Harvard and the Fletcher School of Law and Diplomacy. A writer and journalist for most of his working life, he has worked as a reporter and editor for the *Chicago Sun-Times*, the Grand Rapids *Press*, and the Burlington (Vermont) *Free Press*, and has written for the *Christian Science Monitor* and *The Economist*. He is the author of *The Marine Machine* (Doubleday, 1971) and co-author of *Passing Brave* (Knopf, 1973) and *The Golden Ode* (University of Chicago Press, 1974). Mr. Mares lives in Burlington, Vermont.

A NOTE ON THE TYPE

The text of this book was set, via computer-driven cathode-ray-tube, in a film version of Caledonia, a typeface designed by W(illiam) A(ddison) Dwiggins for the Mergenthaler Linotype Company in 1939. Dwiggins chose to call his new face Caledonia, the Roman name for Scotland, because it was inspired by the Scotch types cast about 1833 by Alexander Wilson & Son, Glasgow type founders. However, there is a calligraphic quality about Caledonia that is totally lacking in the Wilson types. Dwiggins referred to an even earlier typeface for this "liveliness of action"— one cut around 1790 by William Martin for the printer William Bulmer. Caledonia has more weight than the Martin letters, and the bottom finishing strokes (serifs) of the letters are cut straight across, without brackets, to make sharp angles with upright stems, thus giving a "modern face" appearance.

Composed by The Haddon Craftsmen, Inc.,
Scranton, Pennsylvania
Printed and bound by R. R. Donnelly & Sons,
Harrisonburg, Virginia
Designed by Joe Marc Freedman